*brief spring*

A
JOURNEY
THROUGH
EASTERN
EUROPE

*In memory of*
*Stefan Cordescu*

# brief spring

## A JOURNEY THROUGH EASTERN EUROPE

*Iris Gioia & Clifford Thurlow*

ALAN SUTTON

First published in the United Kingdom in 1992 by
Alan Sutton Publishing Ltd · Phoenix Mill · Far Thrupp · Stroud
Gloucestershire

First published in the United States of America in 1992 by
Alan Sutton Publishing Inc. · Wolfeboro Falls · NH 03896–0848

British Library Cataloguing in Publication Data

Gioia, Iris, *1941–*
Brief Spring: a journey through Eastern Europe.
I. Title II. Thurlow, Clifford
914.7

ISBN 0–7509–0014–8

Library of Congress Cataloging in Publication Data applied for

Typeset in Bembo 10/13.
Typesetting and origination by
Alan Sutton Publishing Limited.
Printed in Great Britain by
The Bath Press, Avon.

# Contents

# Acknowledgements

The publishing of a book is like a contest between rival teams and all those who become involved must pull with all their strength to get the manuscript across the great divide from the typewriter to the library shelves.

There are many people in Eastern Europe who joined our team, took us into their confidence and who made our journey an intricate blend of the enthralling and informative. As all travellers soon learn, while the stories you hear in the cafés and on the street may be apocryphal, they are invariably founded on fact and are frequently more reliable than official sources and newspaper columns. The mills of gossip and anecdote grind with peculiar efficiency and we were extremely privileged to be on the receiving end of so much advice, information, generosity and good humour. The ambitious waiters, unimpressed country folk and shady black market dealers we remember as the spice in a soup that owes a great debt of gratitude to the solid ingredients supplied by: Professor Andrew Kawczak in Warsaw; Otkar and Sylvie Mach in Prague; Miklos Voros and Donna Smith in Budapest; Emilia Konstantinova in Sofia; and Sonia Cordescu and her late, courageous husband, Stefan, in Bucharest.

On the home front, we would also like to pay tribute to Jacintha Alexander, for her special support and encouragement; Steven M.L. Aronson; Ariane and Michael Batterberry, who believe that when important jobs need doing it is best to do them yourself; Nova Chomel; Katia Fieve; Tudor Gates, who subscribes to Kipling's maxim that prose should be written as if one is sending a telegram and every word must be paid for; Susanna Giordano; Stephan Groueff; Shirley Lord Rosenthal; Catherine Skira; and the French explorer Michel Peissel and his wife Missy, in whose house in Cadaqués the manuscript was written and where the library of books relating his own adventures was both inspiring and awesome.

At Alan Sutton Publishing, we would like to thank Peter Clifford and Jaqueline Mitchell. And, finally, we appreciated the assistance given us by the staff at Stanfords, the map shop in Long Acre.

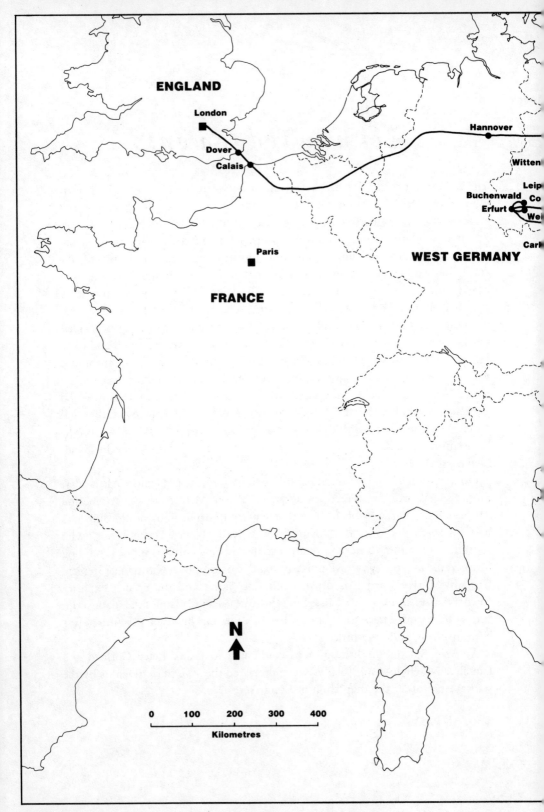

**Map of the journey through Eastern Europe**

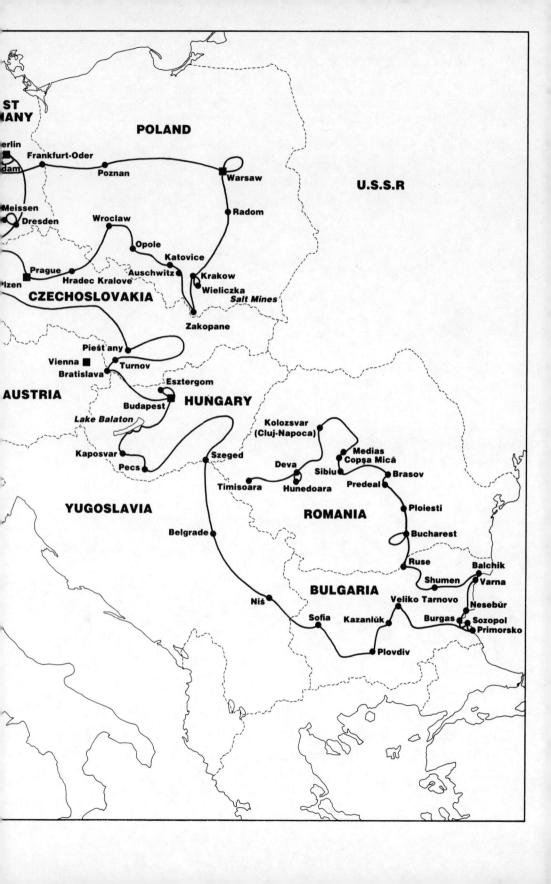

# Introduction

I arrived in London with five suitcases to see me through the time we would be away. Clifford, standing in the middle of my hotel suite at Claridge's, looked around with dismay. He had brought a small duffle-bag and told me confidently that everything I needed would easily fit inside.

'You must be joking,' I protested.

But he was not giving in. 'We're going to Eastern Europe. You're going to have to rough it. There may be nights when we have to sleep in the car. And remember, there won't be porters. We're going to have to carry it all ourselves.'

Later, as I tearfully discarded most of my belongings, I reflected on how I had agreed to this journey in the first place.

We had met at a cocktail party in New York. My friend, Jackie, was celebrating her divorce from her husband of eleven years and had invited all the people who had stood by her through the ordeal.

Clifford was standing in a corner, a drink in one hand, a half-eaten shrimp in the other, surveying the room with quiet amusement. He was the only person I did not know. When I asked Jackie who he was, she said he was English and someone had brought him. He was wearing little round steel-rimmed glasses, the kind John Lennon always wore. I decided to talk to him.

'Hello. How are you enjoying New York?' Not brilliant, but a start.

Soon, our talk quickened, sparked by the flicker of shared laughter. Later we went off to dinner nearby, and he told me his plans, his face lighting up with excitement.

'I am going to drive to Berlin at Easter,' he said, 'then I'm going to explore all the countries in Eastern Europe as far as the Black Sea. I want to see what is happening firsthand.'

I caught his enthusiasm. 'I wish I could go with you,' I said. His clear grey eyes focused on mine. 'Why don't you?'

# East Germany

## Clifford

It was the Thursday before Easter, a few months after the Berlin Wall had opened, and we were on the road to Berlin. A traffic jam stretched endlessly in both directions but the drivers were oddly patient, even festive. A pair of yellow-haired children were making faces at us from the vehicle in front and then a man with a wide grin leaned out from the car at our side and presented Iris with two shiny green apples.

'*Vielen dank,*' she said and the man's grin became even bigger.

Iris had a map unfolded on her knees and was busy punching words into an electronic translator that answered in four languages, all with a Japanese accent.

We had left London on 10 April and, after getting lost briefly searching for the Hoverport in Dover, there we were like voyeurs at a very private celebration. The two Germanys were joining as one and families from the divided country were being reunited that long weekend, the majority for the first time since the Wall had been completed twenty-eight years before.

The car was weighed down with more than I had wanted to carry, although we were empty compared to most of the other vehicles with their great piles of suitcases and provisions, dogs howling from windows, grandmas in spare corners with neat grey curls and expressions that contained a mixture of relief and uncertainty. Like an army convoy the cars all wore German insignia, the D for Deutschland, West Germany; and the DDR in discs on the rear of the East German Trabants and Wartburgs, the first D and the R frequently and symbolically struck out.

We inched along practising German. The children in front had stopped pulling faces and were waving. Fields rolled gently to the horizon. There were no farmhouses and few buildings within sight of the *autobahn*, the 'corridor' through East Germany linking Hanover with West Berlin. What we could see were fences trimmed with barbed wire and look-out towers that loomed like giant locusts over the spring crops. The different ways in which the two Germanys had developed were emphasized in the stream of cars, Mercedes, Audis, BMWs, the very essence of perfection beside the midget two-stroke Trabants that were pouring out great gasps of black smoke as they rattled along like exploding drum kits. They were strewn along the hard shoulder in clouds of steam and some were being towed by West German cars as if in parody of the new relationship.

Service stations were scarce and, further east, among the few stations, fewer still had regular supplies of petrol. Not that this was a particular area of concern. I was driving a Sherwood green Range Rover with an extra large fuel tank and carried a 5-gallon jerry can I intended filling in West Berlin. It was a rugged vehicle built for bad roads, the military lines and polished paintwork giving us an 'official' appearance I hoped would serve two purposes: the walls were coming down but Communism's bureaucratic labyrinth was still in place and I had heard tales of people being delayed for days at frontiers while border guards strip-searched everything, including hapless travellers.

The second, more important reason for wanting to appear vaguely important was to deter potential car thieves. Luci, a Polish friend in New York, had told me there were people so desperate in Warsaw they would jack up the car and steal your wheels while you waited at traffic lights.

I had one other small doubt: mechanically, I had not been blessed. I had some tools and a box of spares – plugs, fan belts, light bulbs – but anything more serious was going to be a problem.

We did, however, have a good set of maps, our visas, a hidden cache of dollar bills in ones and fives and a sense of entering the unkown. History was being made. We were strangers in a changing world with feelings of elation and just a little bewilderment.

## Iris

As we approached West Berlin, only two days from London, I knew the difference between a tourist and a traveller, and that I had always been the former. I had been to exotic places, but always with everything organized in advance. I had never had to think of practicalities, only enjoy what I was seeing.

Now, it was an unexpected strain being the pilot on the trip and having to manoeuvre us through the maze of French, Belgian, Dutch and German roads with turn-offs through places with names like Opglabbeerk and Nieuwerkerken. We were constantly getting lost. The scenario was always the same. We would be on the correct road, the name of the next town imprinted on my brain and I would relax for a moment. Without warning the road would split in three directions, with groups of place names atop each arrow, none of which I recognized. It was like picking a direction out of a hat, and we usually picked the wrong one.

Clifford was always surprisingly agreeable about this. He said he loved getting lost, that it made the journey more interesting. It was an attitude totally foreign to my New York-honed instincts.

Then there were the roads themselves. I did not know which was worse: the two lane variety, filled with enormous trucks and buses, or the autobahns, where there did not seem to be any speed limit. I also discovered that Clifford did not believe in making hotel reservations. 'We want to be free,' he said. 'We don't want to be held to any schedule, do we? Let's decide every morning what we want to do that day – stay where we are or move on. Don't worry, we'll always find a room somewhere.'

Before we were allowed to enter East Germany, however, to comply with the existing law, we had to arrange where we were going to stay and pay in advance, which put a severe dent in our spontaneity. After that, we were in the hands of fate.

Before we had left London I had also made a booking in West Berlin for the two nights we were going to be there. It had occurred to me that, being Easter, many people would be visiting the city; I had only been able to think of the Intercontinental Hotel chain, and had called their London office. The world class traffic jam coming into the city convinced me that I had been right.

Clifford snorted as we pulled up in front of their hotel on Budapester Strasse and a uniformed doorman and bellhops rushed out to take our luggage and whisk the car away. 'I hope this isn't your idea of roughing it,' he said.

'Let's just enjoy it. Later on we'll do it your way.'

It was very late. We had dinner in the hotel dining room and went to bed. I was exhausted.

The next day was Good Friday. We were both agreed on what to see first: the Wall. We took a taxi to the Brandenburg Gate.

'When did the Wall go up?' I asked the driver.

'13 August, 1961,' he replied without hesitation. 'It was so fast, you wouldn't believe. Some people who had left their house early in the morning couldn't get back in the evening. At first, there were just boards, but quickly came the stone and brick.'

'You must be very happy to see it going.'

'Yes, at first it was very exciting. I remember taking two tourists to see the Wall on 8 November, and telling them that I did not believe it would be removed in my lifetime. The next day they began taking it down.' He laughed. 'But now the problems start. The East Germans are like little children trying to get everything they can out of an older brother.'

I could not remember when it had not been a symbol of East–West tension, and yet, the real impact did not hit me until I actually saw it. Even though it was no longer a threat, it was still a chilling sight. Twenty feet high and made of reinforced concrete, it cut through neighbourhoods, streets, houses and families with the impersonal destruction of an earthquake.

It was sunny and warm and thousands of people were strolling on the streets. There was a feeling of joy and liberation in the air. Almost everyone had a camera and the favourite subjects were the East German border guards, poking their heads through the holes in the Wall and grinning at the people on the other side. Some looked to be no more than seventeen or eighteen years old. They seemed a little dazed and embarrassed, as if they did not know what to make of the sudden changes.

Street vendors were out in force, many selling pieces of the Wall in various sizes, the most prized chunks showing traces of the graffiti that had built up over the years. Other potential entrepreneurs were banging away with hammers, trying to put together enough stock to set themselves up in business. Some of the more talented vendors had glued bits of stone on cards and sketched pictures around them. The most enterprizing were doing a brisk trade in military headgear, helmets and service hats that bore the insignia of the East German and Russian armies. Some were quite elaborate, with velvet brims and gold braid trim.

Because the barricade was so massive, there were still only a few places where East Berliners could enter West Berlin and a steady stream poured through. Hardly anyone was going in the other direction. The next day I was to understand why.

## Clifford

The Wall curved away in both directions like a knife scar, not one wall, but two, a no man's land of barbed wire and booby traps between them. I had seen it before, twenty years earlier, and it remained a compelling sight, horrifying and grotesque, yet ludicrous and illogical.

The flags of the United States, Great Britain and France slapped in unison over the frontier post at Checkpoint Charlie. Three soldiers with different uniforms were chatting together and waving the East Germans through without a moment's pause to glance at their papers. Beyond them, across twenty yards of bare cement, there was a red and white border gate and, above, the solitary flag of the USSR. Tall towers, empty now, were outlined against the sky like the scaffolding for a vanished building. The Communists had put so much effort into trying to keep the people in, many became obsessed with trying to get out.

There is a museum dedicated to their escapes next to the checkpoint. They built tunnels and wire runways; like birds they flew away on hang gliders, a hot air balloon, a one-man aeroplane; ingeniously, a girl crossed hidden in the fuel tank of a car and a group of five burst through in a van plated in steel. There is one photograph that shows a young Vopo shedding his helmet and gun as he sprints for the western gate, his face filled with all the hope and determination I had witnessed on his countrymen ever since we had arrived in Germany. The Vopos, the people's police, had always patrolled in groups of three, one eye on the Wall and the other on their companions. If one of them tried to make a sudden dash for freedom, his comrades did their duty and shot him. It was difficult to imagine.

Outside the museum, we climbed the observation deck and scanned the horizon like sailors on the bridge of a ship. People were tapping away with hammers and the makeshift stands were loaded down with chunks of stone. There were experts from the West teaching East Europeans how to start a small business and they were clearly doing a fine job: we paid $2 (£1.20) for our souvenir pieces of the Wall.

We passed through the frontier with a disappointing absence of harassment. The immigration officer took one look at our cameras and coats, endorsed our visas and hurried us on with the bored, disdainful air of a ticket collector at a railway station. '*Ja, ja, ja,*' he said and I drove through the Iron Curtain into East Berlin.

My first impression was that we were on an unfinished film set for West Berlin. It was deserted. The streets were empty of cars. The shops were closed and the shop windows were empty except for modest displays of bottled beetroot and canned fish. The pavements were empty, but for the occasional family of West Berliners all wandering aimlessly along eating ice-cream and wondering what to do next. Everyone who lived in East Berlin had crossed the border the other way and was shopping on the Kurfurstendamm.

As West Berlin had become a showpiece of Western consumerism and achievement, East Berlin was Socialism's window to the East, its wide boulevards named for Communist heroes, its buildings stark and lifeless. There was no litter, no graffiti, no advertizing signs and, although this combined to give the city an unfinished effect, in the weeks ahead it was something I would begin to appreciate more and more.

The museums and art galleries were open, and also empty. We paid one Ostmark, about twenty cents (12p), to see a major exhibition of contemporary work and drifted through a maze of high-ceilinged halls filled with the bold strokes of Socialist Realism: muscular men wearing grins as they stoked fiery boilers and slender pretty girls, blonde and blue-eyed, singing as they drove tractors and laboured on the factory production lines; gleaming machines, bright skies, a phoney Utopia. They were from the early years of East German Communism. The more recent pieces were both more subtle and depressing. They were cries of pain, for help, for freedom; twisted forms in dull, dirty colours that drew their inspiration from Munch's *The Cry* and Picasso's *Guernica*. The figures were thin, haunted, blank-faced and bore absolutely no resemblance to the people of West Germany.

The cloakroom attendant, an elderly woman, frail in a faded blue dress, gave me our coats and replaced the numbered brass discs on the two vacant hooks as if she were adding the final pieces to a complex puzzle. She turned with an apologetic smile.

'*Danke,*' I said.

'*Bitte, bitte,*' she replied, and I had a sudden urge to pick her up and give her a hug.

Outside, I hugged Iris instead.

We carried our coats and walked slowly through silent streets. Among the new apartment blocks were bomb sites like missing teeth and the restored buildings on the Unter den Linden, the main avenue leading to the Brandenburg Gate, had the lifeless quality of an architect's model. The old synagogue on Oranienburger Strasse was one of the derelicts that had not been rebuilt. It had been fire-bombed in November 1938 during Kristallnacht, the forty-eight hours of Nazi terror that destroyed Jewish homes, businesses and places of worship all across the Third Reich. A rusting padlock sealed the synagogue doors as if to lock away the past.

At the Dorotheenstadt Cemetery in East Berlin, the graves of the playwright Bertolt Brecht, a non-Jew, and his Jewish wife, were mutilated and desecrated with swastikas shortly after our pilgrimage to the graveyard and the writer's house nearby on Chaussee Strasse. When I read the story, I remembered that day when we had hunted for the famous names among the long aisles of crumbling tombs and realized that for all the optimism German reunification inspires, the divisive evils of Nazism continue to haunt the new Germany.

It is impossible to get lost in East Berlin. The 365 metre-high television tower stands at one side of Alexander Platz, the main square, and can be seen from anywhere in the city. We made our way towards it through the old quarter reconstructed around the thirteenth century church of St Nicholas. The church was open, and visiting West Germans shuffled around the medieval interior studying the carved stonework.

Alexander Platz is as large as an airfield. There is a row of fountains around the steps leading to the television tower which, from the opposite side, look no bigger than bouquets of flowers. At the centre of the square stands the larger than life-sized statue of Karl Marx and Friedrich Engels, the two bearded gentlemen staring into space with expressions that are kindly and faintly amused. The statue, Marx sitting, Engels standing behind him, a hand paternalistically on his shoulder, is dark with verdigris and shiny at knees, bootcaps and noses. They seemed very alone in all that open space, like men in the court room of history, and the arrival of a party of American college girls filled the vacuum with the welcome sound of noise and laughter.

We left Marx and Engels staring benignly into a greying sky preparing for rain, and went to find somewhere to have a drink. The city was empty but, as exceptions make the rule, the few bars were full and we were lucky to find seats in the self-service restaurant below the television tower. It was a large, dismal place full of teenagers trying to look stylish and appearing sadly anachronistic in bits of fashions like signposts marking the decades since the war. A woman at the next table was wearing lace-up ankle boots and a coat held together with safety pins. She was sipping a vodka from a brandy glass and was slipping slowly from her chair like a wrecked ship about to sink beneath the waves. A lot of people were getting drunk.

When I ordered coffee and mineral water, the man serving at the long wooden counter shook his head in silence and then spoke to one of his companions. They both laughed and sent me away with coffee in a cracked cup and an imitation Fanta. I returned to find two Dutchmen had joined us. Their names were Pieter and Jan and they clearly approved of our being English and American.

'It is *gut, ya*, we mix everything up,' said Jan. He hoisted his bottle of beer into the air in a toast.

I asked them if they approved of the idea of German reunification and their brows furrowed as they thought about the question.

'You know, twice the Germans march into Holland,' Pieter finally replied. 'But now, maybe it is good for us. We are all one family.'

'I like,' Jan added. 'A strong Germany makes a strong Europe.'

'It is a pity you have your Mrs Thatcher. She is not a European,' said Pieter.

He laughed but the comment was serious. Britain was dragging its feet on greater political and monetary union. I had noticed on the drive through Europe to Berlin that in every small town there was a Community flag, the twelve stars in a circle on a blue background, and could not recall ever having seen the flag in England.

## Iris

The rain promised all day came as we walked to the Schauspielhaus on Platz der Akademie to hear the East Berlin Symphony Orchestra. The building had been completely destroyed during the war and rebuilt down to the last detail. Inside, the main hall was a long rectangle, brightly lit, with huge crystal chandeliers and ornate panelling. The orchestra sat on a stage at one end. Three narrow tiers rose to the ceiling on all four sides. We managed to get two last minute seats in the first tier, directly over the musicians.

The music, pieces by Brahms and Haydn, was superb. Concerts and other theatrical performances were state-subsidized and our tickets were ridiculously cheap: about $1.60 (95p) each. My glass of champagne during the intermission was a paltry 60c (36p).

The women attending the concert constituted my first exposure to Eastern European style. They had taken great care to dress as well as they could, but their clothes, especially their shoes, were badly made and old-fashioned. One of the main complaints about Communism was its inability to produce consumer goods. Still, they probably found me an oddity, in my corduroy trousers and running shoes.

Clifford and I had been getting along very well. I knew that if we survived the first few days together, we could make it to the end. We had constant philosophical discussions while driving and over dinner.

My views on life had been shaped on New York's Upper East Side, surrounded by people dedicated to the pursuit and enjoyment of money. Clifford's life had taken a different course. A trip to India during his early twenties had changed his thinking.

'Before then, I had been just as ambitious and greedy as the next person. I worked fourteen hours a day as a reporter. I wanted to be the best and advance faster than anyone else. But India knocked all that out of me. And when I was in Malaysia I saw so much injustice and suffering among the Cambodian refugees that getting ahead didn't seem so important after all. I decided to leave journalism and become a writer.'

We must have picked the busiest day in the history of Potsdam to visit the Sans Souci Park and the glorious baroque palaces that were to Germany what Versailles was to France. Only twenty miles south of Berlin, it had been out of bounds to West Germans for three decades. On that Easter Sunday, the first since the Wall was opened, thousands of West Germans had made it their destination. The car-parks overflowed and more cars lined both sides of the roads that wound around the palaces and landscaped gardens.

If the West Germans were expecting a national treasure, they must have been appalled by its condition. Once the home of the Hohenzollern family who had ruled Prussia for hundreds of years, it had been public property since 1918 when the monarchy had been abolished. While some time and money had been spent on maintenance, the condition of the numerous buildings, fountains and gardens fell far short of the high standards in West Germany.

It had started to drizzle. We joined the throngs shuffling through the Orangery and the Sans Souci Palace, a fine example of German rococo architecture. We admired the paintings by Rubens, Caravaggio and Van Dyck in the Picture Gallery.

In countries that have overthrown their monarchies, notably France, Russia and China, I have seen how the people gape with dismay at the splendour of the palaces, the treasures they contain and the way of life that was enjoyed by the monarchy. Their faces reflect their thoughts: this was wrong; one family should not have had so much. I saw the same expressions again on the faces of

Germans at Sans Souci Park. Whatever one's political beliefs, it is difficult to reconcile that kind of tax free, dynastic, glorified existence with the world of today.

The Cecilienhof Palace on the outskirts of the park was the scene of the conference of the victorious Allies in the summer of 1945. There the famous Potsdam Agreement was signed by President Truman, Sir Winston Churchill and Premier Stalin, sealing the fate of the defeated Germany for the next forty-five years. Large photographs of the three of them, taken when the conference was over, are displayed inside: Truman, looking serious and new at the job; Churchill, appearing tired now that the long war was over; Stalin, his eyes glinting with satisfaction.

Cecilienhof, finished in 1916, was built in the style of an English country manor and was the last palatial building commissioned in Potsdam by the Hohenzollern monarchs. Crown Prince Wilhelm used it as his residence and it remained in the possession of the family until 1945. Part of the building has been turned into a luxury hotel and we were able to fortify ourselves with coffee and apple strudel.

The rest of Potsdam was surprisingly bleak. It was cold, and a nasty little wind cut through our clothing. People were walking aimlessly along the main pedestrian thoroughfare. Everything was closed. The streets and buildings looked forlorn and depressing. We were hungry and started searching for somewhere to have lunch. We noticed a crowded doorway and went to investigate. The dark, smoky room inside had the appearance of a refugee station. People stood around the walls or huddled on benches at the few tables. Two men, wearing what looked like hospital gowns, were passing out food from behind a counter. We got in line and were handed bowls of soup with *würstchen* floating on top, thick chunks of bread and spoons. We managed to find a space on one of the low benches and sat down to eat. It was the best bowl of soup I have ever had in my life.

## Clifford

More bombs were dropped on Dresden than on any city, anywhere. The raid by British and American planes lasted through the hours of one long day and night in February 1945, three months before the fall of Berlin, and was designed to break the German spirit and bring hostilities to a close. Dresden had been undefended, an open city where, apart from manufacturing cigarettes and fine porcelain, they housed prisoners of war.

I walked among the smoke-darkened ruins; black spires and towers rose above the buildings that were being restored and relics of charred stone from shattered statues had been gathered in wire compounds, the heads, torsos, arms and pairs of feet in macabre piles. The old city stands on a looping bend on the River Elbe and, across an ornate bridge, as black as everything else, featureless apartment blocks stand in careful lines.

The shops were still closed and the new entrepreneurs with their drink stands and home-made ice-cream were working towards their first BMW. We queued for twenty minutes to buy warm orange juice and met an insurance broker from Hamburg who had already decided he hated Dresden. 'It is the first time I come to East Germany and I think the last,' he told us. 'We should give it back to the Russians.'

He lit a cigarette from the butt about to burn his fingers and drew in the smoke with suicidal passion. 'They want to change one Deutschmark for one Ostmark,' he then said, shaking his head in bewilderment. 'One for one!'

We finished our drinks and joined the promenade. Dresden should have been depressing but the families wandering in groups did not seem to notice the gloom. It was easy to see who was from which half of Germany by the clothes and, more particularly, the haircuts, but the slogan *WIR SIND EIN VOLK*, We are one people, appearing ubiquitously on posters and car-stickers, made it apparent that the differences were soon going to vanish and, likewise, so would the ruins of Dresden.

The city enjoyed a golden age in the eighteenth century under Augustus the Strong and his son, Augustus III, when their baroque palaces standing on the banks of the Elbe were painted by Bernardo Bellotto, the nephew and student of Canaletto. The Venetian master had been a guest of the royal court when Dresden was the Saxon capital and his large canvases, stored safely in deep vaults during the Second World War, were now being used like architect's plans for the laborious task of reconstruction.

The Saxon kings had ruled during a period of stability and affluence and the monuments they left were flamboyantly detailed and distinctly German. The merchants had grown rich and their houses, with embellished stucco walls and decorative windows, faced each other across the narrow streets in a constant duel of elegance and grandeur.

Had Dresden been in West Germany, it would already have been rebuilt, but under the Communists money had always been in short supply, and for a number of different reasons. After the war, while the Federal Republic received billions of dollars in Marshall Plan aid, the DDR paid billions of dollars in war reparations. Whole factories were dismantled and the machinery transported to the Soviet Union. Lack of motivation within the system itself created inefficiency and, in turn, while productivity in the West was going up, in the East, it went down. Finally, corruption on a scale few Germans could conceive took enormous sums from the public purse.

One group of officials had employed workers in a private factory manufacturing machine guns, ammunition and hand grenades. Their products were sold in the Third World and the profits paid into Swiss bank accounts. All in secret.

It was stories like this that made it impossible to see East Germany in anything but a political context: the shop windows, curtained in dust and displaying only the undesirable, the sub-standard clothes thirty years behind the times, the chunky bakelite wireless sets designed in the 1950s with components that only appeared able to handle music from the same era, not military and strident, but Elvis Presley and Bing Crosby. The half-day journey from Berlin to Dresden had taken us through woodlands besieged by acid rain and grey funereal villages gasping for a drop of fresh paint. The houses in good repair were in very good repair and each time we saw one we glanced at each other and said the same word: 'Stasi'.

Fear of the Stasi, the secret police, had made the people polite, distant and law-abiding, even in the smallest of ways: the lights at pedestrian crossings were infuriatingly slow but the people wait for the red man to turn green even when the road is empty as far as the horizon. There was no litter, no graffiti, no billboards, virtually no crime. These were aspects of Communism that were enviable, which made it more the pity that they were the products of repression not privilege.

## Iris

The next morning we decided to drive to Meissen, about twenty miles north-west of Dresden; we found the roads filled with trucks, back at work after the long Easter weekend. Although they came in all shapes, sizes and states of repair, they had one thing in common: they spewed out billowing clouds of dense, black, poisonous fumes.

The porcelain factory at Meissen is where the secret of making thin, strong, hard paste porcelain, or 'white gold', was discovered in 1705. Before then, only the Chinese knew the process involved. The crossed swords of the arms of Saxony, adopted as the factory-mark, and painted in blue on the base of each article, is famous around the world. Johann Joachim Kandler was the first artistic genius who took the process to dizzy heights. In the museum upstairs there is a dazzling exhibition of his figurines, birds and fantasy ornaments. Rooms full of large glass cases display the works of all those who followed him, from dinner services made for kings, to astounding objects of modern design.

The tour itself was interesting, although we never actually went into the factory. Instead, we filed from room to room, directed by tape recordings, where each step of porcelain-making was shown to us, usually by attractive young women who looked very bored.

Then, abruptly, it was over. We were ushered through a door marked AUSFAHRT and found ourselves in the street, with the door firmly shut behind us, like drunks at closing time.

'What, no gift shop?' It was unbelievable. After seeing the museum and taking the tour, there was not one among us who would not have traded their child for a piece of the splendid porcelain – a saucer, a bowl, anything – and they let us go without realizing that basic fact of retailing.

We walked slowly back through town to the car. I was struck by how the streets and buildings of Meissen reminded me of China. I even saw men wearing the dark-blue pyjama style suits that the Chinese wore. Everything was dirty, run-down, and had that look of desolation endemic to towns and cities on the dark side of the Iron Curtain.

Neither Clifford nor I were feeling our best. I laid the blame directly on the previous evening's dinner. It had been good, excellent even, but extremely rich. I knew there were food shortages. The shops had reopened after the Easter holiday and we had already seen grocery stores with long queues outside and bare shelves inside. Yet our hotel dining room was stocked with delicacies. They always wanted to keep up the charade for outsiders.

I had identified the word 'veal' on the menu and ordered it. What I had received was roast veal, stuffed with kidneys, covered with mushrooms, swimming in a red wine sauce. I had also sampled Clifford's order – medallions of pork, topped with pineapple and quails eggs. Then there had been dessert: hot maraschino cherries over ice-cream and whipped cream, all washed down with beer. Back in our room, the chocolates on the pillow had to be consumed, as well as a packet of Easter eggs, gift of the management. We had no one but ourselves to blame.

I spied a sign that said 'DAMEN' and told Clifford to wait for me, I would only be a few minutes.

When making long journeys by car public toilets, and the condition thereof, assume a great importance in the day's schedule. As every traveller knows, you do not carelessly pass one by as you never know when the next will appear. Clifford and I rated them on a scale of one to ten. Anything that was reasonably clean, had a lock on the door, plumbing that worked, paper and a hook on the wall for a coat or a handbag got a solid five. I doubted if I would find anything higher on the trip. I gave the powder rooms at the Plaza Hotel in New York and Claridge's in London each an eight.

It is very rare to see a ten, but when you do, you know you are in the presence of greatness. I have only seen a few in my life, mostly in five-star restaurants in France. To rate a ten there must be fresh flowers; a selection of French perfumes; linen towels (I hate hot air dryers); a uniformed attendant (female); individual soap; and hand cream. The compartment that contains the toilet should be totally enclosed for privacy (no space over or under the door) and have its very own basin and bidet. Outside, with the attendant, there should be plenty of full-length mirrors, strong lighting and velvet sofas on which to recline in case one has had too much vintage wine. There should definitely *not* be a machine dispensing condoms.

In Meissen I was surprised to find a few odd twists. The attendant was an old man, stooped and wizened, dressed in a blue smock. He asked for five pfennigs, handed me a 15-inch long strip of paper, ushered me into a cubicle and proceeded to wipe the seat before he left. When I emerged, he handed me a paper towel and, like a conscientious nanny, stood by me as I washed my hands. I could hardly wait to relay these events to Clifford.

## Clifford

'Would you like a guide?'

'Not particularly,' I answered.

'I am starting my own business. I can speak English. . . .'

I noticed Iris in the background baring her teeth and shaking her head, but the young man was so earnest in his appeal I just had to employ him. We agreed on a price and Klaus walked us through the collection of old masters at Dresden's Albertinium. He was twenty-eight, tall, very thin and tightly wound with nervous energy with a tick on his neck. He had been a member of the Communist Party, a translator, and wanted to apologize for the past.

'We are all ashamed. We trusted our leaders. They were comrades and, all the time, they were stealing from us,' he said.

With Iris a few steps ahead of us, we moved slowly from room to room and, finally, we crossed the road and went to a pastry shop, one institution that had survived Communism and where the coffee was surprisingly good.

'It is the extent of the corruption that has surprised us,' said Klaus, continuing his theme. 'I think everyone is a little dishonest, it is natural, but the amounts of money that have gone . . .' He shook his head in the same way as the insurance broker we had met the previous day. 'Millions,' he added despondently, 'they stole millions.'

In fact, according to *The Sunday Times*, it was not millions but $60 billion (£35.7 billion) that had vanished without trace, a sum that did not include the money Party leaders had spent over the years maintaining their hunting lodges, chauffeurs, private planes, private hospitals and schools, even a private reservation of unadulterated privilege at Wandlitz, the woods north of Berlin, where members of the Politburo built mansions that rival the film star homes in Beverly Hills. All this had to be paid for and guarded and then the guards had to be paid enough to keep quiet about it.

'For twenty-five years they told us we must make do with water and all the while they were drinking wine,' he said, finishing his coffee. 'They kept telling us we were going to overtake West Germany and look . . .' He spread his arm around the room. It was shabby; everything was shabby, dusty, paint-peeling and so un-German.

Klaus frequently used the word 'ashamed' although he appeared more perplexed. He had believed the propaganda: that life on the other side of the 'anti-fascist defence wall' was in reality much worse for the majority, while the minority lived like royalty. The truth was the very opposite.

'It was all a lie,' said Klaus. 'Everything.'

We had read about the shortages and food queues but the repression was far more subtle and dehumanizing. There had been rationing in England during and after the Second World War yet for many, it had been their 'finest hour.' What had been inflicted on the East Germans was not hardship, but fear. I asked Klaus about the Stasi and the muscle on his neck gathered speed and his eyes seemed to dart nervously around the room.

'They could do anything,' he replied in little more than a whisper. 'A week before the government fell they took all the women in a factory and stripped them naked because they were going to go on strike. It was a punishment. They would take people's houses and keep them for themselves. They even made prisoners handle dangerous chemicals without giving them gloves. . . .'

'Then why did you wait so long before rising up against them?' Iris asked.

'We didn't know, not for certain. There were rumours but they might have been started by Fascists, by our enemies. That was what we were told and we believed it,' answered Klaus. 'East Germany is not America. You have always had freedom. We do not know what freedom is.'

'What has happened to the Stasi officers?' I asked and Klaus threw up his arms.

'Who knows? They have been disbanded but, you know, we now have a new organization, the National Office of Security, NASI.'

'Nazi?'

'No, no. NASI.'

We finished our pastries and Klaus marched off on his clumpy shoes to ply his trade outside the gallery. We followed him across the grass square and stopped to look at the statue in the centre. It was a life-sized bronze of a naked man rolled into a ball like a foetus. The figure has one hand with long, delicate fingers covering his face, while the other rests limply on his knees. It is called *Dresden Man*, and portrays perfectly the sense of utter despair the survivors must have felt after the city had been destroyed by bombs.

The road out of Dresden plunged into a broad valley lined with the battlements of slowly rising hills. The sun had gone in and the sky had turned grey above the trees that clung to the distant peaks. Villages appeared in tight clusters around Lutheran churches, the modest slate spires dwarfed by tall chimneys that were belching out streams of waste with the same robust enthusiasm as the Trabants.

The factories were back at work – producing machine tools, pharmaceutical products, cigarettes, electrical equipment, musical instruments and chemicals – and the smoke combined to give the air the odour of bad eggs. Iris began to cough. 'This is worse than New York,' she said. It was an understatement.

We had stopped to take photographs in a village where three gigantic cooling towers reared up behind the stone cottages like spaceships from another planet. Their pale blue, white and ochre gasses swirled calmly together in a pattern of arabesques that faded slowly into the overcast sky. The houses were constructed in the solid Saxon style with thick walls capped by low curving roofs, the red tiles pierced by oval windows like hooded eyes. The cobbled streets completed a scene that had remained unchanged for a century – except for the towers.

Iris continued to cough. 'I feel so sorry for the people who have to live here,' she said. We were taking the rural roads to Erfurt and that entailed diligent map-reading and frequent detours. The highway signs were of little help. Most were painted on wooden boards and the words were often weather-faded into meaningless hieroglyphics. At one point, approaching the same church for the third time, I stopped to ask directions from an old man who was scything the grass verge. His face was as lined as our Hallwag map. When he understood from my rudimentary German that we were on our way to Erfurt, he gestured firmly at a lone tree like an antenna above a distant hill and then continued his labour, slap-swish, slap-swish, with the scythe.

'Which way is it?' asked Iris and I nodded vaguely towards the same faraway hill.

The church doors were open and, now that we had stopped, we decided to take a peek inside. It was the sort of church I liked, simple and unadorned. There were wild flowers in old beetroot jars at the entrance and a plain cross on the back wall. The pews contained little cushions for kneeling more comfortably in prayer and were lined up below a vaulted ceiling criss-crossed with heavy beams. The light was rationed around high windows as narrow as archer's slits and, though it was sufficient to varnish the woodwork that spring morning, I imagined winter services to be very gloomy occasions.

As we returned to the car the old man pointed again at the horizon, but we set off none the wiser. We eventually found the right road and, driving along at the maximum speed of sixty-three miles per hour, a black-windowed limousine shot by and disappeared. 'Stasi,' we both said in unison and we were probably wrong. The driver was more likely to have been chauffeuring a former Party boss who still had confidence that the police, vigilant with their speed traps, would allow him to continue unhindered.

Little damage had been done to Erfurt during the war and, as little maintenance had been done since, it had the quality of being both preserved and forgotten, like a child's toy stored in an attic. The town, founded in 742 by St Boniface, had been a trading and university centre and the architecture revealed the town's history from medieval times to the end of the last century. Martin Luther had been a student in Erfurt and I could imagine him sweeping along with his shoulders bowed and his mind filled with all the theological anomalies that would result in the Reformation.

That evening an exhibition of paintings by contemporary American artists was opening at the Galerie Am Fischmarkt and, outside, an enormous Stars and Stripes decorated the main façade. Our cameras marked us out as usual though, for once, not as tourists. As we approached the entrance, we were mistaken for press photographers and whisked inside with a fast-flowing river of German that left me wondering about the validity of language as a prime source of communication. '*Entschuldigung, ich spreche nicht sehr gut,*' I kept saying but the organizer, a chubby man with an heroic moustache, didn't seem to care. We were Americans and very welcome.

I took some photographs, we drank a glass of white wine and left with two press passes.

'I think I rather like Erfurt. It has a nice feeling,' Iris remarked as we strolled along, our senses touched by the wine. Now that Easter was over, it was possible to see East German life in a more natural state and Erfurt was better for this than East Berlin or Dresden. It is a small town with a population of 250,000 and has none of the pretensions of the big city.

When we had first arrived, and while I was unloading the luggage, a crowd of youthful car enthusiasts had gathered around the Range Rover to admire its marvels. The Beach Boys had been singing 'California Girls' from four concealed speakers. I had shown them the alarm, the differential and then, when I had turned the key in the central locking system and all the locks snapped shut, they had stood back as if I had performed a feat of magic.

'American?' one of them had asked.

'No, English.'

He had pointed at the USA sticker on the back. 'The car is English. We're American,' I had explained, keeping it simple.

He had thought about my answer for several seconds and then translated for the others. The speaker, a tall boy with a sceptical expression and pale blue eyes, had studied me as carefully as they had scrutinized the car. 'I would like to go to college in the United States,' he had finally said.

'And me also,' another voice had added. 'I want to go to Boston.'

It was an echo that would follow us across Eastern Europe. It was the car sticker that usually inspired the conversation and, from that point of view, I was glad it was there. Iris had brought it with her – a little joke, she had claimed lightheartedly, although it was more a sort of insurance. Her family and friends had been convinced we were going to be mugged or worse and felt certain that if it were known that we were American, we would be treated with greater respect. I did not understand the logic of this but being identified as American did at least make us more of an oddity. The people outside the big cities saw few tourists and those they did see had rarely crossed the Atlantic to get there.

Street cars as long as trains zipped by with thin arms like feelers clinging to the overhead wires. Boys stood outside the music shop with open mouths and big eyes that feasted on an electric guitar shaped like an axe. Brown packaging covered the floor inside and behind the two assistants eagerly opening fresh cartons were shelves of record covers crisping at the corners and sheet music that could have been passed over by Franz Liszt when he was in Erfurt.

A crowd four deep mobbed the window at the travel agents where a set of bright posters advertised eight-day holidays in Spain from $125 (£74.50) – in Deutschmarks, not Ostmarks. For the first time in forty-five years people could apply for a passport and go anywhere they wanted, whenever they wanted.

We crossed the greasy black trickle of some dying river on the Kramer-brucke, the bridge erected in 1325 and lined on both sides with timber-framed shops. The buildings, huddled together as if for protection, had been carefully preserved although the promise of bookshops and antiques was thwarted by the early invasion of West Germans. There was something disconcerting about bookshops with no books and Iris had to be consoled when she found just a few oddments of junk trying to pass themselves off as antiques.

The Gothic Dom and the Severikirche, two fourteenth-century churches, stand side by side, as if to invite comparison, on a raised knoll above the medieval town square. Here dealers from across the border had set up displays of denim jeans, carpets, confectionery, shirts, skirts, and bananas – boxes and boxes of bananas that stood man high in the back of Mercedes trucks and had drawn the crowds with the same power as the holiday posters and the electric guitar. Old people mumbled to each other nostalgically, while children pointed and turned with doubtful expressions to ask; what are they?

Bananas! There was a revolution going on and this was its very heart and soul: bananas, a week in the sun at Lloret de Mar, and the courage to strike out the 'D' and the 'R' from DDR.

A platoon of West German punks in vivid costume and chain-saw hairstyles marched by lugging a stereo blaring out music by the Sex Pistols. Pornographic magazines were pegged like flags over one stall but the trader doing the most business was selling entertainment magazines that carried the current programme guide to West German television.

A *spieler* was demonstrating a new wonder wax for cars to people wearing grins that would have been more apt to a circus audience. 'Be nice if we had a car,' the man next to me whispered to his wife when the performance was over, and they wandered off laughing.

I had read that ninety-nine per cent of the women in East Germany had regular jobs but Easter was over and they must all have called in sick and taken an extra day. The changes were coming fast and furious and no one wanted to miss anything.

They were lining up for ice-cream, hot dogs and pizza at stands displaying the magic word 'American'. Pretty girls in red and white striped uniforms were dispensing hamburgers from a caravan sprayed with the name 'McGeorge' – a tribute, I assumed, to McDonalds and George Bush. Barbie dolls were being sold for $20 (£11.90), although the price tag attracted more amusement than interest. Even the local cinema was in tune with the mood and was showing that week Steve Martin and Chevy Chase in *The Three Amigos*.

There were long queues for everything affordable – at the coffee shop, the butcher's, the pastry shop. At the supermarket we waited fifteen minutes just to get a basket and its diminutive size spoke volumes on the quality and availability of basic essentials. The market traders had arrived from the West towing trailers filled with miracles, but the large stores run by monster bureaucracies seemed entrenched in the business of supplying voluminous tiers of shelving to show very few products and those we saw were anything but appetizing: fresh vegetables like props from a science fiction movie; bottled vegetables in jars with peeling labels; cuts of fatty meat, rice and beans in sacks stamped in blue with the hammer and sickle. Lenin and Stalin, perhaps learning from the French Revolution, had taught their Communist allies that the one item you had to give the peasants was bread – and it was there, crusty farmhouse loaves, smelling still of the oven and subsidized at that. We bought one, just to fill the basket, and then added some dubious slices of salami, a few brave tomatoes unsure whether to be green or red and, to the surprise of the other customers, we picked over a box of bruised and freckled apples until we found two that looked acceptable.

'I'm not sure why we bought this lot,' I said as we left the store.

'To help the economy,' Iris replied and we marched straight back to the market square to stock up on good West German bananas.

## Iris

The evening streets of Erfurt were flooded with heavy rain and it seemed sensible to have dinner in the hotel dining room. As we followed the waiter, I realized with annoyance that we were expected to share a table for four. The major problem with sharing, apart from lack of privacy, was that everyone smoked non-stop. They smoked on the street, they smoked in shops, they smoked while they ate.

This time we were lucky. The two West German businessmen, already half-way through their dinner, were non-smokers like ourselves. The older of the two, a lawyer from Munich called Hans, told us how moved he was to be back in Erfurt, where he had been born. Near the end of the war, when his parents had heard that the Russians were coming, they had fled to Hanover to stay with relatives. 'Otherwise,' he shrugged, 'I would have been brought up here, and my life would have been ruined.'

He was appalled by what he saw around him. It reminded him of West Germany just after the war. 'What saddens me the most,' he said, 'is the tremendous waste of lives. Hundreds of thousands of people have been denied an education and have had meaningless existences as a result.'

He told us of a writer who, a few years earlier, had published an article criticizing the government. To punish him, the authorities had forbidden his children to attend school. Eventually he had killed himself.

The younger man, Barthold, who had an American wife, said there was a lot of money to be made now in East Germany. He was going to buy a house in Dresden, on the river, as soon as he could because they were very cheap. 'As far as I'm concerned,' he said, 'East Germany is just another country where they happen to speak German. I have no feelings about the people one way or another.'

'You see,' smiled Hans sadly, 'the younger generation has no heart.'

They both said they were afraid there would still be reprisals and killings because many people would try to get revenge for past injustices.

'The funny thing is,' said Hans, 'the same people will still be in charge. After forty-five years, only Party officials have any idea how to run a business or a country. Like after the war, many Nazis served jail sentences and when they were released, they easily found important jobs, because only they had the skills needed.'

## Clifford

It was twenty miles to the concentration camp at Buchenwald. The morning was unusually cold. Grey mist with the inevitable odour of poisonous waste hung over the trees but we were cocooned in the warmth of the car, protected and separated from the world outside. There was classical music on the radio, a sombre clarinet in counterpoint to some mournful cellos. I turned it off.

Iris was staring silently at the bleak landscape. She remained lost in her own thoughts.

Russian soldiers with vacant, Asian faces clumped along the side of the road in baggy uniforms and heavy boots that gave them the unsteady gait of string puppets. They were all at least half my age but I would have challenged any one of them to a foot race – me in track shoes, they in their diver's boots. A group of them were whitewashing the low perimeter wall at the base with brooms on long handles. The fence gleamed in the hazy light. The Soviet Union had agreed to withdraw its forces from East Germany but the process needed to be slow because there were no facilities for the returning troops when they got home. The West German government was offering aid and had even suggested building new barracks for the Red Army in Russia. It seemed a peculiar state of affairs.

I slowed down to look at the camp. It was a dilapidated place with sheep grazing around the ramshackle wooden huts. I could not imagine a disco being there, or Hershey bars and Budweiser being ordered by the quartermaster. To make comparisons between the two superpowers was ludicrous.

The road climbed into dense trees and came to a sudden end at a spacious car-park containing a dozen cars and one small tour bus. Low buildings lined the path leading to the concentration camp. Modern brick houses were behind them. We passed a clinic. I saw a sign for a restaurant.

Entrance to the camp was free, which was only appropriate. The main gate was at the high side of a faint gradient and, from that point, the wire fence enclosed a declining sweep of dark gravel marked by small stone memorials which were identical and evenly spaced. There were no huts; perhaps they had been moved to the Russian army base. Mist still shrouded the sky. The wind charged up the slope and icy fingers found their way inside our coats.

Across the giant graveyard, on the far side of the site, stood the 'administrative' blocks and, in them, all the horrors of Nazi butchery. It was not worse than I had imagined; it was worse than I could imagine. Countless thousands of people had been murdered at Buchenwald, and it was one of the small camps. The gas ovens, untouched for four decades, were cube-shaped boxes with heavy doors that closed over cage bars. From the ovens, the victims were moved on large wheelbarrows to the crematoria, where the bodies were incinerated. The vicious-looking long rake used for dragging out the ashes was still there. In the centre of the doctor's laboratory stood a white tile operating table. It had inch-high ridges running along the edge and gullies leading to a drain hole. The numerous surgical instruments on the shelves had been placed symmetrically in neat lines.

The few visitors were German, according to their clothes and car registrations. They spoke in hushed, respectful tones or were silent. I saw one man openly crying.

There are people who would like to have the concentration camps removed, planted with trees and forgotten. Others want them to remain just as they are, a constant reminder of the holocaust. I understood both viewpoints and had none of my own. I felt empty and physically ill, moved and even ashamed, although of what I was unsure. I am not German and, that day, I was glad not to be.

We stopped to look at one of the stone memorials and the coincidence of stopping at that particular stone defies explanation. It was in English and read: 'In honour of the memory of the British and Canadian Forces murdered in Buchenwald Concentration Camp'. They would have been slave labourers in the underground armament factories where, ill-fed and harshly treated, they worked until they died. Some prominent German Communists, Ernst Thalmann and Rudolf Breitscheid among them, also perished at Buchenwald and, adopting them as national heroes, the regime that took power after the war attempted to minimize the holocaust by describing the victims not as Jewish, as most were, but as Communist heroes and anti-Fascists.

It has always been implied that West Germany alone was responsible for war crimes. Typically, it now transpires that while the East Germans were busy reshaping the past, the concentration camp remained in operation under Soviet authority from 1945 to 1949, and was maintained still later by the East Germans to intern political dissidents. Just how many 'anti-Communists' disappeared at Buchenwald remains unknown.

We spent a few quiet moments in a gallery hung with paintings and drawings made by the prisoners. They were horrifying. I was glad to leave. I felt tainted, somehow, more in empathy with Iris's initial reluctance to visit the camp. What had we achieved? Were we better people; better informed? If we said 'never again', who would listen? Did the western world send its armies to protect the people of Uganda when Idi Amin was in power; or to Haiti under Papa Doc Duvalier; or Romania under Nicolae Ceauşescu; or, even today, under Ion Iliescu?

We returned to our big comfortable car and left with the sun making a bold attempt to break through the gloom.

The Russian boy soldiers were still busy painting. Some of them had spots of white on their black leather boots. I noticed an officer in a fantastically large hat standing in a clearing surrounded by trees. Behind him rose an empty watchtower like a broken windmill, lofty and useless.

The petrol tank was half-full but the appearance of an Intertank on the brow of a low hill, a site suitable for a church or a castle, moved me to a feeling of relief that would have been more applicable arriving at an oasis in the Sahara. The woman attendant was as big as a discus-thrower, a stern, heavy blonde with a great puffy face like a half-deflated beach ball. She looked sixty and was probably thirty-five. She cleaned the windscreen and, when I gave her a generous two D-mark tip, she almost fell to her knees in gratitude. She would probably spend it at the Intershop on Godiva chocolate or a couple of packets of Marlboro.

It had taken me less than a week to become more than a little irritated by the state-run monopolies unimaginatively called Intertank, Intourist, Interhotel and the Intershop, which supplied a whole range of goodies denied the ordinary people – Johnnie Walker whisky, Lux soap, Kellogg's cornflakes, Maxwell House coffee, Levi's, all things Western but only in exchange for Western hard currency. The whisper 'change money?' followed us everywhere we went, a plea that was pathetic and at times bothersome. Foreign cash was as desirable as it was illegal for the people to have and those who did manage to get their hands on the stuff were the Party workers, the trusted officials, the waiters, the hotel clerks, policemen, fat ladies serving petrol. The money-changers standing on street corners with rolls of grubby Ostmarks were normally working on commission for someone higher up the Party ladder and offered as much as six times the official bank rate; or twice the tourist rate. It was all very confusing. For some reason I never managed to work out, everywhere in Eastern Europe the majority of the money-changers were Arabs.

## Iris

I had been looking forward to visiting Weimar. At the turn of the eighteenth century, it was the centre of German classical culture and humanism and the great names of German literature and philosophy lived and worked there. Johann Wolfgang von Goethe and his friend Friedrich von Schiller both had houses in Weimar that have been turned into museums. They in turn attracted other philosophers such as Herder and Wieland and many great thinkers of the day. Later, musicians such as Franz Liszt took up residence. In more recent times, it became the capital of Germany when the Weimar Republic was proclaimed in 1919, the great economic and political debacle that led to the rise of Hitler's National Socialist Party.

Weimar was a pretty town, cosier than Erfurt, filled with parks and small museums. We explored it easily on foot, walking up and down streets that had not changed for over two hundred years. It was easy to imagine that we had been transported back in time. Everywhere, statues, monuments and plaques reminded the visitor of its illustrious past. Nowhere did I see a mention of the short lived Weimar Republic.

After almost half a century of sleep, Weimar was waking up again. The main square was undergoing extensive renovation. Groups of workmen were busy laying new cobblestones and many of the beautiful old buildings, some dating back as far as the early sixteenth century, were covered by scaffolding.

Crowds of people gathered around market stalls where West German traders had parked their trucks and trailers filled with merchandise brought from the West. Sadly, most of the items arriving first were shoddy: plastic handbags, junk jewellery, nylon shirts from factories in Hong Kong. One vendor had almost sold out his stock of pornographic magazines; only a lone copy of *Playboy*, wrapped in plastic, remained.

The world that had been preserved for decades through its isolation was crumbling before our eyes. The young men seemed to be straining to grow their hair over their collars. The girls were hitching up their skirts a half-inch every day.

'Everything that was good in East Germany will go with all that was bad,' Clifford remarked. 'They had a low crime rate and virtually no drug problems. Have you noticed the refreshing lack of billboards and advertising? All that will change.'

We made our way to the Hotel Elephant on the Am Markt, a building filled with atmosphere and closely linked to the town's historical past. The bar was packed with people crowded around small tables covered with forests of beer bottles. We looked into the coffee shop and managed to outrace several others to the only two empty seats in the room. The air was hazy with smoke. Everyone drank coffee and ate rich cakes covered with whipped cream.

'Haven't these people ever heard of cholesterol?' I asked.

'Maybe,' replied Clifford, 'but life under Communism didn't leave them too many pleasures. Smoking, drinking and eating were about it.'

We sat glumly, saying very little. We were both still chilled by the morning visit to the concentration camp.

On the way back to Erfurt, we pulled off the road to listen to the BBC news more clearly on the radio. Gorbachev had imposed an oil embargo on Lithuania, allowing only enough oil to be exported to cover basic needs, but effectively shutting down its industries. I was sympathetic to the Lithuanian demands for independence, but I felt that there was something bigger at stake. For the first time since the Russian Revolution there was a leader in the Kremlin who was not an egomaniac or a paranoid murderer but a decent man who was allowing positive change to happen. I was concerned that the

Lithuanians would jeopardize all that. Gorbachev had told them they could have their freedom, but they were behaving like impatient children.

A dilapidated van had parked near us, and an East German family on holiday was preparing to have a picnic. They must have been serious campers as they even had plants in their windows. A boy, about eight years old, came over to our car and knocked on the window. He wanted to sell us some German newspapers. We said no, thank you, and gave him a chocolate bar. He was thrilled.

## Clifford

One of my earliest ambitions was to be a prisoner-of-war at Colditz Castle. Colditz was the most famous of Nazi Germany's camps and, apart from holding relatives of Churchill and various members of the royal family, it was where they put those who had absconded from other Stalags only to be recaptured. The castle was supposed to be escape proof but still they broke through the walls and fled. The great dream was to make a 'home run' but, even if a man was free for just a few days, he could cause chaos and the more guards needed to watch the prisoners, the fewer there would be on the battle fronts.

While they planned their escapades, the officers were busy learning languages, carving chess sets, forging passes, making civilian clothes for the escapees and costumes for the innumerable concert shows and productions of Shakespeare.

Finding the castle was almost as hard as getting out of it. It sits in the middle of agricultural Thuringia among villages with names that all end in 'itz', some not on the map and most locked in a maze of farm-tracks where the signs either do not exist or are perforated with rifle shot – a rural pastime that grows in popularity at about the same rate as the migrating birds steadily become extinct.

I decided to ignore what signs there were and took any road that climbed into the hills, the obvious place to site a fortress. We crossed and recrossed a river that snaked its way slowly down to the plains on bridges wide enough for only one vehicle, until we finally saw the high grey walls of a castle pinned to the horizon.

Iris folded the map away with a sigh of relief as I came to a halt in a large empty square surrounded by low, untidy buildings. A group of workmen were passing and, when I asked them if we were in Colditz they all rolled their eyes and pulled the pained expression my question appeared to deserve. 'Ja, ja, unless they changed the name,' said one in German, and he tapped the side of his nose. They wandered off, five men in blue Mao suits and distinctive black caps, high at the front and with a narrow, shiny peak that quickly loses its shine and contrives to give the wearer a look of poverty and defeat. The group vanished through a plastic strip curtain into a soup kitchen filled with the mechanical clatter of spoons digging into china bowls.

The square, treeless and sliced in two by sun and shade, was at the centre of a curving pattern of narrow streets that twisted their way down to the river bank. The castle loomed above us, a formidable, featureless piece of Gothic stonework similar to that of a Victorian prison. I am positive it cannot have been used by the film-makers when they made *The Colditz Story* based on a book by the wartime Escape Officer, Major P. R. Reid.

A high arch over wooden doors formed a gateway to the only entrance. The gates were open and, marching through with military vigour, I was suddenly accosted by a small, square woman with a moustache and a booming voice that belonged in opera. She sang out something I did not understand and held up two plump little hands to bar my way. I tried to explain that my father had been a prisoner at Colditz, which was not true, although being acquainted with Michael Alexander, the writer, who was, I felt I had some small claim to being allowed entry. Not to the singing gatekeeper. She now began waving her arms about like someone drowning and, as I took a step back, a truck came barrelling through the doors and Iris's swift tug at my jacket just saved me from serious injury. As it was, my heel was grazed and, hopping around on one foot, the woman took me by the arm, not to support me, but to lead us both away from the castle entrance to the street below, where she pointed towards the museum. It was closed for lunch.

The village did not live up to the images of my childhood and a brief, painful walk brought us quickly back to the main square.

'Hungry?' I asked.

'Always.'

I glanced at the soup kitchen. The clattering noise had died down. The breeze was fingering the strip curtain. Iris seemed doubtful for a moment and then shrugged her approval.

Inside, the workmen we had seen earlier were leaning over the counter in their black caps like a row of crows on a telephone wire. They acknowledged our entrance but vaguely and with disinterest.

We ordered soup which was served in pudding bowls from an enormous silver cauldron. A man in a grubby white smock brought them to the table and then cut off two thick slices of black bread from a round loaf. He put them down in front of us without a plate.

'Amazing,' said Iris.

'Better than Potsdam?'

She savoured the soup like a wine connoisseur. 'Different – but delicious,' she finally said.

The bill was also amazing: a paltry 20 cents (12p), a sum so small it was embarrassing. Was a tip now appropriate? And, if so, how much? It was a problem I had never mastered. In India, when you give a beggar one rupee it is only eight cents, which seems mean. But, when you know that a clerk who speaks three languages earns only four rupees a day, it then appears excessive. It is important to give to the beggars in places where the culture demands it, but each time you do you can almost guarantee getting it wrong. Our bill was one Ostmark; I left two.

## Iris

In addition to a badly bruised heel, Clifford had a cold: a sneezing, coughing, nose-blowing, hoarse-voiced cold. He felt lousy, I knew, but was carrying on in the British tradition. I expected no less.

I fed him a constant stream of Fisherman's Friend, a little dun-coloured lozenge made from an ancient English recipe, as well as two aspirin every four hours to alleviate the aches and pains. I desperately hoped I would not catch it.

On our way to Leipzig we went through a radar speed trap. Out of nowhere a policeman appeared and motioned us off the road. In America we would have been furious, but in East Germany we were delighted finally to have a confrontation with a *Volks Polizei*. A man of average size trying to look huge, he walked slowly to our car.

'Passport,' he said, peering in the window at Clifford.

We gave him not only the passport but Clifford's British driving license, international driver's license, the car registration, insurance papers, the green European insurance card, the AA membership, and, to confuse him further, I threw in the bill for a new tyre purchased before leaving London.

He studied everything carefully for a long time. At one point I saw he was holding Clifford's pink British driver's license upside-down. Finally he handed it all back and said in halting English, 'Twenty marks please.'

Twenty Ostmarks was about four dollars (£2.50), so we did not feel badly treated. Clifford mumbled that he would not speed any more, and the policeman said a polite goodbye, and told us to enjoy our weekend.

A few moments later Clifford said, 'Great! Now I can go as fast as I like. There won't be another policeman for miles.' My reaction, instead, was that now we should definitely keep within the speed limit!

Leipzig was the second most important city in the DDR after East Berlin. It is a major industrial centre and produced 90 per cent of all carbo-chemical products and 82 per cent of the ethylene in the country. In addition, it is heavily engaged in the manufacture of machinery, from cranes to printing presses. To the south of the city lignite is mined, a low-grade, brownish-black coal that is cheap but excessively 'dirty' when burned. To accommodate the workers, endless rows of plain, grey apartment blocks, all identical, stretch off in every direction into the polluted distance. Twice a year the city hosts two gigantic trade fairs, carrying on a tradition that goes back over eight hundred years.

'Do we have to go to Leipzig?' I asked. 'It sounds awful.'

'Are you kidding? We've already paid for our hotel, remember? Anyway, it will be interesting. Bach lived there.'

In fact, there was an undeniable beat in the air and the feeling of excitement that only a busy city can generate. The streets were crowded with people and, helped by the dozens of street vendors selling their wares, it had the same holiday atmosphere of West Berlin.

Clifford had a wonderful time chasing around the market stalls taking photographs of a group of Russian soldiers in their ill-fitting uniforms and for a while forgot he was sick and injured. It used to be illegal to take their pictures but the new laws are confusing. The soldiers had always been told they were there to protect East Germany from an invasion by the West. Now, they are there as guests of the West German government!

I noticed a cinema was showing *Nightmare on Elm Street Teil III – horror und fantasy mit Freddy Krueger*. I listened as women shuffled through the feather-light aluminium coins in their plastic purses and watched as their children wandered off with all the concentrated joy that surrounds eating ice-cream.

We stopped in a café in the Market Square for coffee and to admire the architecture – a Renaissance town hall and several eighteenth-century buildings – from a seated position. I was intrigued with the menu. The items offered never seemed to change, but strips of paper with newer and higher prices were pasted over each other to form several layers. In spite of the almost daily increases, everything was still remarkably cheap by Western standards. The pricing was meticulous. For example, a cup of tea with sugar was the equivalent of 6 cents (3p). A cup of tea with sugar and milk was 7 cents (4p). If I wanted, instead, sugar with lemon, the price soared to 9 cents (5p).

Our waiter was tall and handsome. He was pleased to practise his English. We asked him if he was looking forward to reunification. He appeared very agitated and could not find the words to express himself.

'Yes and no,' I suggested.

He smiled with relief. 'Yes and no,' he repeated. He said he was afraid prices would go up faster than the wages. He could not imagine a life where he could earn enough to take a trip to Paris or London. New York might as well be on another planet. 'It is a crazy city, no?' he asked.

'*Ja*,' I replied.

Lutherstadt Wittenberg has two great distinctions, one more famous than the other. It was here on 31 October 1517, that the Benedictine monk Martin Luther wrote out a list of ninety-five grievances against the Catholic Church and courageously nailed them to the church door in this remote corner of Saxony, thereby starting the Reformation. Sadly, the original wooden door was replaced in 1858, but the complaints are still there, now sculptured in bronze.

Wittenberg's second distinction is that it was the most polluted town we saw in a very polluted East Germany and ranks in my memory with Mexico City, where just breathing the air for a day is the equivalent to smoking two packs of cigarettes.

The town, with its pretty churches, statues and baroque town hall embellished with armorial decorations, is surrounded by factories. Tall chimneys continuously pump out yellow gas that dissipates in the atmosphere but leaves a pale stain on the sky like a sweat stain on a T-shirt. The houses are neat but covered with soot.

The countryside around Wittenberg looked beautiful from a distance. We took many roads that wound through thick forests, but on closer inspection, we saw that clumps of trees were withering and dying. The leaves on others were sparse and malformed because of acid rain. Close to Wittenberg we passed through an archway of dead sycamores, the branches against the lacklustre sky like old cobwebs in an abandoned house. The Green Party in West Germany, Europe's oldest and politically most successful environmental party, may have done a lot towards cleaning up their own country but now, as they take in their poor brother in the East, the task will be much tougher.

We spent our last night in East Germany in Frankfurt-Oder on the Polish border. We arrived at dusk but managed to squeeze in a brisk walk through town before it got too dark. It was a pleasant surprise. The town was clean and attractive, with the best designed apartment blocks we had seen so far.

'You know,' Clifford said reflectively, 'we are witnessing the end of an era. In a few months East Germany will cease to exist.'

'No one will miss it.'

'What did you like most about the GDR?' he asked.

'The history. The old towns and villages. The castles. The museums and concerts.'

'What did you dislike?'

'The pollution, the pollution, the pollution. In that order. And the lack of care the government had for the people: allowing them to be slowly poisoned; giving them the poorest quality goods; the corruption. The past forty-five years have been a big lie for them.'

*p a r t   t w o*

# Poland

## Clifford

You know you are arriving at the border between East Germany and Poland a long time before you get there. The fields – freshly ploughed and ready for planting – are severed by a barbed wire fence that follows the line of the horizon like a shadow, and could be a shadow but for the concrete watch-towers evenly spaced along its length. The fence grew larger in my vision as Frankfurt vanished from the rear view mirror, and drew us slowly into its embrace like fish in a trawler's net.

I came to a halt at the frontier post and it was two or three minutes before a guard appeared. He approached with movements that were jerky and awk-ward. He wore a puzzled expression and a pistol holster that was low-slung bobbed against his thigh. The door behind him slammed shut. Then there was silence. I felt a tingle of schoolboy excitement. There was an air of intrigue. I glanced around for hidden TV cameras. The guard was immaculate in dark olive green; a crossed hammer and sickle sparkled at the centre of his cap. He was very young and seemed ill at ease, although ours was the only car crossing into Poland that Sunday morning and a more innocent-looking pair of occupants I could not have imagined.

The guard studied me, shifted his gaze to Iris and then began his business with abrupt, wordless gestures. He motioned with flapping fingers and I gave him our passports. Then he indicated a place where I should park and there we waited. And waited.

'Why do they take so long?' said Iris.

'It's just the custom.'

'And customs that have lost their meaning are the hardest to break,' she added and that gave me something to think about.

Iris picked her nails; I cracked my knuckles. Concrete tank traps like strange stars were placed in a deliberate pattern between the two countries as if to demonstrate that the mundane is closer than the sublime. They were disguised behind a row of rather pointless, ornamental trees planted in wooden tubs. There were numerous trucks on both sides of the border but no drivers. It was not a good omen.

Twenty minutes elapsed before the guard reappeared. He returned our passports, swiftly nodded his head in a way that was probably meant to be friendly and cast his palm in the direction of Poland. Neither we nor the car were searched and for that I was grateful.

I drove forward towards a long, low building where a strikingly similar guard in gun metal grey took us through the same jerky, finger waving, pointing process in a way that so resembled the gestures of the German I could only conclude that these officials were taught their skills in the same drama academy.

The offices where the immigration staff worked had deep windows and, from our new position, I watched as an older man leafed his way through my passport about twenty times, studying the empty pages just as carefully as the visas that occupied the full ones. He did the same with Iris's passport, stamped them both and gave them to his young colleague to return, which he did with a quick nod and a hand indicating Customs.

We had no movie camera, no guns, no drugs and no live animals. The officer shaded his eyes, peered into the car through the rear window, and threw up his hands in a new gesture: welcome to Poland. But not quite. Bureaucracy remained cosmic in its proportions. There were forms to be filled in, and then we had to buy benzine coupons. Petrol was rationed but, just like the Intertank system in East Germany, there were special arrangements for foreign travellers.

Poland needed the cash; $1 (60p) that day was being exchanged for 9,500 zlotys. Two years before, it would have bought just 450 zlotys, less than one-twentieth that amount. While the country was struggling to find its feet as a democracy, inflation was running at a level normally associated with South American dictatorships. It made everything insanely inexpensive. Coffee in the best hotel in Poznan, the Orbis Merkury, served with a side-dish of miniature chocolate cookies set us back 7 cents (4p). The change was given in notes, not coins, the smallest being 100 zlotys, which must have cost more to make than they were currently worth. At the border, I changed $200 (£119) and walked away feeling very rich as a zloty millionaire.

The road from the border was empty, narrow, extensively patched and moved through gently undulating hills laced with silver birch like candles flaming in pale green leaf. We admired a herd of cows that lumbered in a single file across our path and vanished through a gate overhung with bushes. We stopped several times at primitive rail crossings that lacked barriers or warning lights and once, overtaking a wagon being pulled by two chestnut horses, I was waved down for speeding by a jolly, middle-aged policeman who took the ten Deutschmarks I gave him and gave me what looked like his laundry ticket in exchange.

Most of the houses had been built since the war and seemed unfinished. The churches, in contrast, were sturdy, colourful buildings with squat steeples and shiny silver domes that had a Byzantine influence far greater than I would have expected so far north. They stood at the heart of modest villages I had thought were totally deserted until we got out to stretch our legs in a tree-fringed square just as the church doors were flung open. Bells began to chime and the congregation spilled out, the men in Sunday suits, the women in full skirts, predominantly black, with aprons and bonnets. A man raised his hat to us before he put it on and some teenage girls stared for a moment before hurrying away in fits of giggles.

The priest emerged, a young man in gold and white robes, his round, boyish face as bright as an icon over the band of his clerical collar. He approached and said something incomprehensible and, like the girls, we all laughed. He then shook my hand in a way that was oddly moving and I felt a sudden joy just being in Poland. We were only one hour from the border but already I could feel an immense difference in the atmosphere. East Germany lacked something – soul, heart, substance? It was a society built on fear and compromise. It was half a country. The walls and fences were coming down but they would leave a scar that would remain for generations.

Poland had been under Communist rule for the same length of time as East Germany but it had been less accepted than accommodated. There had never been any question of Poland being officially atheist. It was officially Roman Catholic and proud to a man of their archbishop who had become Pope. Photographs of John Paul II were everywhere – the only picture not defaced by marker pens. Graffiti had arrived like a disease and few politicians peered from posters without the addition of sunglasses, moustaches, flowing locks and bubbles containing captions I was sadly unable to translate. We saw an exquisite drawing of Charlie Chaplin on a wall, with a line of writing in English – We are not American – which no one would deny.

Nationalistic sentiment in Poland knows no boundaries and it is this that has ensured the country's survival through a thousand years of wars with neighbours always stronger and more numerous. Poland began life in the tenth century under Boleslaus the Brave, the first king, who led the Polanie in battle against the various tribes of Slavs that wandered north and central Europe. His brief line was extinguished by the Mongol hordes and his subjects dispersed into scattered fiefdoms until the fourteenth century when they were reunited under Casimir the Great.

Casimir's great-niece married the Duke of Lithuania and founded the House of Jagellon, the second royal dynasty. Continuing conflict with the League of Teutonic Knights came to an end in 1410 when the Poles defeated their time-old enemy at the Battle of Grunwald, establishing Poland as a minor power on the changing tableau of European affairs.

The subsequent era of peace and prosperity drew to a close as the Turks began the long march of conquest from the east. The Polish army, with King John Sobieski in the field with his cavalry, finally overwhelmed the Turks in a decisive engagement at the gates of Vienna in 1683, the victory saving

Christian Europe from Muslim domination under Ottoman rule. But Poland had become weakened by war; its lands were steadily absorbed by the nascent empires of Russia, Prussia and Austria, and were not fully restored until the Treaty of Versailles was drawn up in 1919.

It was to be a short-lived freedom. The infamous peace pact, a marriage of convenience between Hitler and Stalin in August 1939, was consummated in the Nazi invasion on 1 September 1939, the final act of aggression that started the Second World War and divided a defeated Poland between Germany and the Soviet Union.

The 'liberation' of Poland by the Red Army in 1945 led to the establishment of a People's Republic the people may not have willingly chosen, but it did bring one important and treasured consolation: the Poles were united once more within the frontiers roughly hewn a thousand years before by Boleslaus the Brave.

Poland remained in hibernation behind the Iron Curtain until Lech Walesa led the independent trade union Solidarity out of the Gdansk shipyards and, after a ten year struggle, ultimately to power in a free election that toppled the Communist regime.

The young priest was now surrounded by a protective cordon of stern and ancient widows, all perfectly round like black pear drops, their little dark eyes as bright as sequins and missing not a thing. They had studied the car, me and, most of all, Iris in blue jeans and a safari jacket. She tried a few words from our phrase book, '*Dzien dobry, Milo me pana . . .*'.

The priest laughed. The old women did not. '*Milo me pana*', he repeated and then he said something else we did not understand.

We were pleased to meet him and he was pleased to meet us. That was the extent of our phrase-book conversation and so we laughed again and then it was time to leave. The widows watched as we climbed into the car. Iris waved and the priest nodded his head with the slow ease of a benediction.

'If someone had asked me three months ago to list the countries I would least like to visit, Poland would have been right up there,' Iris said.

'And now?'

'Now, we must wait and see . . . .'

Cherry and plum blossom were lifting into the air like handfuls of confetti. The fields were divided by low fences and primitive tools lay abandoned in observance of the day of rest. The hills had flattened into a vast and seemingly endless plain broken finally by Poznan, our destination, its renaissance towers and modern apartment blocks arranged on the skyline like a toy-town that gradually became life-sized, sprawling and gloomy under a pewter sky. We had seen little traffic except for horse-drawn wagons taking families home from church but now the cars appeared like a swarm of insects, the tiny Polskis and Skodas weaving curlicue patterns around screaming trams with blaring klaxons and drivers who had the right of way and vigorously exercised it. I followed the tram lines from the outskirts of town and they delivered us as if by magic at the main entrance of the Hotel Orbis Merkury.

Two elderly porters emerged from the shadows and shuffled up to the car. They were like stage generals in ragged blue uniforms, the braid hanging in moth-eaten threads, the epaulettes like balls of knotted string on their weary shoulders. They followed me up the steps to the reception desk, stood silently at my side as I checked in and then followed me back out again.

I opened the boot and Iris joined me. 'No problem,' I said nonchalantly and she looked relieved. The generals fought with our two bags as if they were filled with lead weights and Iris led them back into the hotel with the room key, an umbrella and our camera bag.

The street maps of Poznan were 'out of print' but, at the hotel reception, there was a well-thumbed, large-scale map that we studied with the two girls behind the desk, a blonde and a striking, olive-skinned girl with long Afro ringlets. They were both good humoured and had a casual efficiency that we would have regarded as normal in an international hotel but came as a surprise in Poznan.

'We never have any English or Americans here,' said the blonde. 'Only Russians and Germans.'

'Do you like Russians and Germans?'

'No,' she answered without a breath of hesitation.

'Only the young ones,' said her companion.

The blonde smiled. The dark girl remained straight-faced as she advised us to visit the museum of musical instruments, 'the biggest in all the world', (which was closed); and the monument to the workers killed by the police during the uprising in 1956. She pointed it out on the map and we set off in the direction of Plac Michiewicza.

The monument was a pair of crooked, modern art crosses interesting only in that it had been erected with official consent and paid tribute to those who had died while showing their opposition to the government, a paradox that could be compared to the Americans putting up a memorial to the Japanese after the bombing of Pearl Harbour.

It was a good illustration of Poland's peculiar, if more liberal, approach to Communism. The government had not slavishly followed the Kremlin's line, particularly over land, which had never been collectivized. There were shortages of most things but food was not one of them. For the first time in years, ham could be purchased in under five minutes – for 60,000 zlotys a kilo, the price of a Polski car in the early 1970s; sugar and flour were so expensive in Warsaw that local bakers were considering buying their ingredients abroad.

From Plac Michiewicza, we set off in the direction of a central square entered by a long boulevard, both honouring Stalin. I had seen them on the large plan and wanted to photograph this phenomena, knowing it would soon disappear. But we were already too late. The name plates had been prised from the sides of the buildings and the clean brickwork strips stood out against the dark walls as if waiting for the old names to be reinstated. It was the obvious acknowledgement to all the people who had maintained at least a token of dissent by only calling the local landmarks by what they had been known as before the war.

We followed the anonymous avenue through a pastiche of Romanesque, neo-classical, Renaissance and Byzantine architecture, the level of restoration flowering to near perfection as we reached the Old Market Square, with its Italian town hall rising above the arcaded shops and enclosing an open square paved in stones shiny with rain. Outside the town hall there was a replica of the original wooden pillory erected by the good burghers of Poznan from the money collected in fines imposed on the prostitutes caught 'wearing too much make-up and clothes of excessive elegance'.

## Iris

On one side of the square a demonstration was in progress. Groups of young people wearing green and white badges were milling around a platform that held a microphone and loudspeakers. Large placards made statements in bold print that we could not understand. A girl dressed in the universal uniform of blue jeans, running shoes and denim jacket handed us a pamphlet that proclaimed '*Tak Mozesz Oszczedzac Energie!*'. I realized that they were celebrating Earth Day with millions of others around the world.

At that moment, a streak of lightening ripped open the grey skies and the drizzle became a deluge. We ran for cover to a nearby café along with the young demonstrator and her boyfriend.

'Are you from America?' she asked in very good English.

'Yes. How did you know?' Until then I had not said a word.

'By your clothes. They are so nice.'

I smiled. I had brought nothing stylish on this trip. We had not wanted to look affluent or stand out in any way. I had even bought a cheap digital watch to wear instead of my gold Cartier watch. I had comfortable walking shoes on my feet and the tweed jacket and corduroy trousers I had changed into at the hotel did not seem so 'nice'. Clifford was wearing a dark green sports jacket he had bought at a street market in London. Still, everything was relative and we apparently stood out as foreigners.

The four of us shook off the rain and sat down at the only empty table. We introduced ourselves and Sonia helped us order tea and biscuits. The inside of the café was smoky and damp and smelled of wet boots.

'Where did you learn to speak English so well?' I asked her.

'We learn it in school. English and Russian. I prefer English. I pretend not to speak Russian.' She laughed.

Wladyslaw, her friend, who chewed his fingernails, said he spoke English also and was studying engineering. He hoped to go to America, but did not know how he would find the money. In spite of being very thin and not very tall, his thick pullover sweater seemed much too small for him.

'How did you become interested in Earth Day?' I asked.

Sonia answered, 'My parents took me last year to visit the village where they were born near Katowice. My father had always told me how pretty it was, in a beautiful forest, with many lakes where they swam as children. When we got there, my mother started to cry. It was so ugly. The trees around the town were dead. The lakes were covered with green slime. The town was dirty. There was a chemical plant. Yellow smoke was coming out of big chimneys. The smell was horrible. I heard of Earth Day at school. I signed up to do something.'

Wladyslaw shook his head in agreement. 'We have the worst of everything. We have no consumer goods but we get stuck with all the pollution.'

'We just came from East Germany. It's just as bad there,' I said.

'But they have West Germany, who will help them. I am afraid for Poland. We have many problems and very little help. The Communist Party is still very much in power, only now they call themselves the Polish United Workers' Party and lots of the old ministers remain in important positions. Even Solidarity can't get rid of them.'

They both looked serious and concerned. The problem of politics, economics and pollution were very real for them, not abstract items read about in the newspapers.

The bill arrived. Wladyslaw put up a good fight but we insisted on treating them. He looked relieved.

## Clifford

There was a long line of cars trailing down the road from the main service station outside Poznan as we left the town the following day. I had no intention of stopping. I noticed Iris's theatrical shake of the head and patted her gently on the knee. 'Don't worry,' I said, 'There'll be another. . . .'

'I think we should wait and fill up now.'

My soft laugh was designed to inspire confidence, although I drove slowly to conserve gas. Just in case. The morning was warm and the air was fused with the smell of pollution. Factories dominated the landscape outside the city, each linked to the others by tall silver pipes that lay over the earth like an umbilical cord. Street lights like giant question marks, three out of four lacking fittings, lined the so-called 'expressway' and disappeared ten miles from town when the dual carriageway became a single lane track. The traffic thinned out as the industrial belt gave way to farmland although there always seemed to be an enormous truck charging towards us when I pulled out to overtake a horse-drawn wagon, the most common mode of transport.

The central plain was pleasantly tedious. Cows and goats tethered by ropes lifted their heads from the grass along the side of the road to watch us pass. The fields were full of women bent double over the new crops and working in long skirts and white bonnets. There were no chateaux, as one would see in rural France, no country mansions. Poland had suffered more in the last war than any country in Europe. Not only were six million of its people, half of them Jews, exterminated in the concentration camps, but the Nazis also demolished virtually every building that stood in their path on the long march to Warsaw.

The needle on the fuel meter was hovering in that vague area just above the quarter tank level as we reached the town of Kostrzyn and I pulled into a small garage with a sense of triumph. There was no queue. The attendant, a portly man with lots of grey hair swept back from his brow, cleaned the bugs from the windscreen, pointed to his supply of oil in rows of transparent plastic bottles and gestured forlornly at the three pumps when I said the one word he did not want to hear: *benzyny.*

'*Nie benzyny,*' the attendant said hopelessly.

Iris was leafing efficiently and with stern irritation through our Berlitz book and paused at the perfect phrase – Where is the nearest filling station? '*Gdzie jest najblizsza stacja benzynowa?*' she asked.

The man smiled. He ran his hand through his hair, as if to emphasize its beauty, and then pointed along Route Two with a little flutter of the fingers. He said something warm and assertive and I gathered that there were many filling stations along the way.

There were. At Golina, Konin, at Koto and various towns and villages. They were all generously endowed with engine oil and all were out of petrol. The car struggled on valiantly but just outside Krośniewice it began to make the gasping noises I imagine a man dying of thirst might make in the desert. I used its last breath to pull off the road on to a patch of grass. Two goats came to investigate.

'I won't say a word,' Iris said.

'I forgot to fill the spare can in Berlin,' I now told her.

The colour drained from her face. 'I said I won't say a thing,' she said again.

I took the jerry can from the boot. It was a beautiful day. I could see for miles. Not that there was anything to see. The trucks and the horse wagons had disappeared and, quite suddenly, the only sound in the silence came from the hum of the insects hovering over the fields.

'Lock the car,' I said through the open window.

Iris raised the electronic window, depressed the locks and made no reply.

After leaving Iris, I had been walking for a couple of miles when I came to a large tree that stood at a junction. The battered signpost read Leczyca. A wagon hugged the shade; a dirty white horse chewed grass, while the driver chewed the stem of his pipe. He eyed me with vague curiosity from under the brim of a broad hat and then said something that related to my predicament. He glanced at the jerry can. 'Out of petrol,' I said and bunched up my shoulders.

We continued the conversation for some while; he in Polish, I in English. Then, making space, he motioned for me to join him on the narrow bench. I climbed on board. It was like being in a boat; the wagon had a curving hull and was rounded fore and aft. It carried, however, not fish, but an assortment of hoes, rakes and scythes, all with shiny wooden shafts polished smooth by decades of sweat and toil. The iron heads were solid, not pressed out by a machine, but forged and beaten by a blacksmith. They were such beautiful tools I could imagine them decorating a wall in an English country house.

When the driver jerked the reins the horse bellowed, a roar more of complaint than anguish, and we set off at a leisurely trot between fields of dark soil where teams of oxen pulled ploughs; the way of life could not have changed a great deal since the Middle Ages. Long trailing branches swished at our faces as we passed through a thicket of mature trees and birds rose noisily from the undergrowth at the sound of the horse's hooves clattering on the stone track.

My companion grunted something and spat as we approached a group of peasant women. I thought for a moment about Iris. Even if she did not know it herself, she was probably safer there on the side of the road in Poland than she would have been standing outside her own building on East 72nd Street.

The horse slowed and swung the wagon through an open gate into an untidy courtyard where a regiment of geese, chickens and two haughty peacocks stamped among the incongruous piles of car parts, rusting tools and old tyres. The driver climbed down. The house was a rambling, L-shaped, single-storey disaster the owner had no doubt put up himself, tacking new bits on according to inspiration and cash. Certainly, no architect had ever interfered. Inside, we sat on facing chairs and, after studying the room, I turned my attention to my host. He was a tall man, broad-shouldered, with a

pot belly and long dangling arms. He had a moustache befitting a revolutionary and thick clumps of reddish hair sprouted from his ears and nose. He
communicated with his wife by what I assumed was mental telepathy for,
within a few minutes, she appeared from a connecting door carrying a tray
containing two small glasses of vodka.

The woman was grotesquely fat; in fact, all the married peasant women,
with their round red faces, short strong arms and bodies like loaded potato
sacks swathed in layers of skirts and aprons, could have been sprung from the
same mould. On their heads they wore bonnets of medieval vintage and their
large features expressed alternatively a childlike joy or severe disapproval as if,
like Swiss weather clocks that march out a wooden figure dressed each
morning for either sun or snow, their moods moved between violent
extremes. She was happy and grinned at her guest. I grinned back.

'*Na zdrowie!*' said the man and he drank his vodka in one hit.

My attempt at repeating '*Na zdrowie*' was greeted with squeals of laughter
but I drank the vodka down in one and that made up for my lingual
shortcomings. The man barked out fresh orders to his wife and then looked at
me with a little shake of the head, a gesture that belongs to misogynists
everywhere. I now noticed that one of his eyes was a good bit higher than the
other and the hat he had forgotten to take off followed the sloping angle of his
luxuriant eyebrows. He knocked the dead tobacco from his pipe, refilled the
bowl and lit up.

We sat in silence for a while and when I pointed at my watch, my host said
something in such an agitated tone that it made me wonder if he knew what I
was doing there. I started to wonder what I was doing there myself. I decided
to give it ten more minutes. Then I planned to walk back to the car.

I used the time to study the room more carefully. It was sparsely furnished
with new, very poor quality things: steel-framed chairs, a matching table, two
airport-style easy chairs covered in old rugs that smelled of dogs, a linoleum
floor with a wood pattern that imitated the grain on the farm tool shafts in the
wagon outside. On the mantel piece above the fire-grate there was an orange
alarm clock with a thunderous tick, a plaster elephant with chipped feet and a
marriage photograph of the happy couple, my pipe-smoking companion
bearing the same massive moustache and with his hair slicked back with
grease. His young bride was plump even on her wedding day.

I was finally about to come to my feet, when the woman reappeared with
two more vodkas and two plates of food: soft dumplings filled with
vegetables, doused in oil, sprinkled with salt, and delicious. It was lunchtime
and I was starving.

The woman vanished again. We ate the hot dumplings with our fingers and,
with the second vodka inside me, any doubts I may have had about my

taciturn Good Samaritan had changed into a great love for him, the Polish people and the whole of mankind. He stood suddenly and stretched his long arms. '*Benzyny*', he said gravely and I followed him out to the courtyard.

The horse grumbled as we climbed on board and the wagon rolled lazily back down the same track, like a small craft negotiating the currents of the sea. The driver held the reins loosely in his palms. The sun warmed my face. I felt at peace with the universe.

We reached the junction, turned right, away from the car, and, after another two miles, we came to a garage. I showed the attendant my petrol coupons and he laughed. '*Dolari, dolari,*' he said, rubbing his thumb and first finger together. I gave him a $5 bill and he filled the jerry can.

It took another thirty minutes to get back to the car. I waved to Iris as we approached. I was pleased to see her although, the nearer we got the more I realized, she did not share my good spirits. She was relieved, not pleased. I had been away for three hours.

## Iris

I could see a wagon coming slowly down the road. Two figures sat on the driver's seat and one of them looked familiar. It waved. The conquering hero was returning. He would not get a warm welcome from me.

I was furious with Clifford for allowing us to run out of gas. I had urged him to fill the tank before leaving Poznan but he had laughed his 'don't be a silly little woman' laugh and assured me we would not have problems. I had not known that the emergency can in the boot was also empty. I felt he had let me down.

After he had left, I had studied the map, filed my fingernails, fiddled with the radio, and when the occasional car passed, had tried to look like I was there by choice and enjoying myself. After a couple of hours I must have dozed off because suddenly, I had realized that someone was tapping on the glass. I had stared into one of those wide Polish faces that grinned like an imbecile. A middle-aged man, with sandy, unkempt hair and bad teeth, had motioned for me to roll down the window. He must have been mad.

He had parked his small, rusted truck in front of our car and then had tried to open the door.

'Okay, okay,' I had said, forcing a smile. I had quickly found the dictionary and looked up the Polish word for husband. I knew that 'travelling companion' would only confuse him.

'My – *maz, maz* come now.'

I had looked up the word for now and found *teraz*.

'*Maz teraz, maz teraz,*' I had chanted, hoping desperately that he would go away.

It had worked. His leering grin had closed in on itself like a punctured dirigible. I had just had to say '*maz teraz*' once more, and he had shaken his head and walked slowly back to his truck and driven away.

It was a further hour before Clifford returned. The one-horsepower vehicle he was riding in finally pulled alongside the car and Clifford swung himself down and lifted out the jerry can from the back. He was in very good spirits.

'Can you believe we were only four miles from the next service station? There was plenty of gas. They'd just had a delivery.'

He took a $20 bill from his wallet and handed it to the farmer, a peasant with an inscrutable expression who shook his head and said, '*Nie, Nie.*'

Clifford insisted. '*Tak, tak,*' he said, and put the bill in the man's pocket. It was more money than he could earn in a month.

A few minutes later we were on our way. A frosty silence prevailed. Finally Clifford asked, 'Did I do something wrong?'

'I'm afraid our views on travelling differ radically, Clifford,' I replied coldly. 'I'm obviously much more serious about it than you are. I like to be organized and plan ahead. Most of all, I do not like to run out of petrol. I've decided to fly back to New York tomorrow.'

I could see he was upset.

'That's great. Where does that leave me? It's a little late now to find a replacement for you. This is the sort of trip that needs two people. Someone has to stay with the car in case it breaks down, while the other goes for help.'

'This car sitter is flying home.'

'Everything has been going smoothly so far, but at the first little inconvenience, you chicken out. I should have known better than to bring a spoiled New York social x-ray on this trip.'

We did not speak again until we approached the outskirts of Warsaw. 'Shall I drop you off at the airport?' Clifford asked politely.

'No. It's too late in the day for a flight. Let's find a hotel for tonight and I'll make the arrangements tomorrow.'

I unfolded the map of Warsaw and tried to locate the Victoria Intercontinental. The receptionist in Poznan had told me it was the best hotel.

'It will be too expensive,' protested Clifford.

'It has a garage.' I knew he was paranoid about the car or parts of the car being stolen and, while he did not seem to mind personal discomfort for himself or even me, there was nothing he would not do to ensure the safety of his Range Rover.

It took us an hour to find the hotel. Many streets were one-way and clogged with traffic. I could tell by the confusion in the lobby that they were not short of clients. Nevertheless, I marched confidently up to the front desk and asked for a room.

'I am very sorry. We are fully booked to the end of the month.' The smartly dressed, green-eyed young woman looked genuinely sympathetic.

'Do you have any suites available?' I asked, without flinching.

'Sorry. We are fully booked. Even over-booked. Try the Europejski across the square.'

There was nothing left to say except thank you. I stalked out to Clifford who had meanwhile arranged to have the car washed by three young men with buckets and brushes.

'Ha! No problem finding a room, eh?' I kept walking and went straight to the Europejski. This time the reception clerk took great pleasure in telling me that there was not an empty room in all of Warsaw.

'But why?' I asked.

'It is always like this,' he replied haughtily.

It was the first I knew that the world was beating a path to Warsaw. It was now a challenge to find a room, and I knew that, contrary to his predictions, we would, but it did take some doing.

We stopped at the Orbis tourist agency. The uniformed girls were smiling and friendly and handed us a list of all the hotels in the city. When I suggested they telephone for us they became vague. They only had one line and it was out of order. We had to drive around ourselves.

We worked our way through the list, passing swiftly from deluxe, to expensive, to moderate and, finally, exhausted, we arrived at the Polonia. It was Clifford's turn to make the approach while I waited in the car. He came out with a thin smile, not of success, but not of failure, either.

'They're full here, too, but the clerk said he would tell me where to go if I tipped him ten D-marks.'

'Did you?'

'Of course.' He started the car. 'The Grand Hotel. Here's a diagram of how to get there.'

I examined the list the tourist office had given us and, sure enough, at the very bottom was the Grand Hotel.

Some hotels have enjoyed golden days, fallen on hard times and become shabby. Traces of former glory can still be found in a beautifully panelled elevator or the generous dimensions of a bathroom. The Grand must have been shabby the day it was finished. All the furniture was modern, cheap and falling apart. The lobby was small, dingy and filled with people, mostly men, who were smoking and drinking.

The man behind the counter was expecting us. He announced that he did not have a room after all. Clifford took a $10 bill from his pocket, laid it on the counter, and asked him to check again. The man put on his glasses, squinted at some papers, and in a very surprised voice said that yes, he did have a suite.

'We'll take it,' we both said together. There were smiles all round and the $10 disappeared under the counter.

Having a suite in a third-rate hotel is the same as having a room. There is just more of it. The beds were lumpy, the sheets were too short for the mattresses. The light bulbs that worked threw out the morbid glow of candlelight in an empty church. The bathroom tiles were broken and I saw a few cockroaches scurrying into the cracks when I peered around the door. The sitting room contained a black and white television that was inoperative and two straight-backed plastic chairs with slash marks and burn holes. There was a wooden wardrobe splattered with paint spots and, inside, no hangers.

The suite was as bad as it could be and, to rub salt in the wound, it did not come cheaply. There are few hotels in Warsaw, considering it is the capital of Poland, and, as accommodation has become harder to find, the prices have gone up. To rub the salt in still harder, Westerners are obliged to pay in badly needed foreign currency at a much higher rate than Polish nationals. Visitors, normally officials, from the Eastern Bloc countries are charged a sum that is between the two. In other words, as with airline seats, two people with identical rooms can end up paying wildly different amounts depending on their passports.

'I like it,' said Clifford. 'It has character.'

I kicked my shoes off and lay down on the lumpy bed. Warsaw. One does not come here for sightseeing. Most of the city was destroyed during the Second World War, and, with a few exceptions, rebuilt in a grey, functional style. A Stalinesque Palace of Culture dominated the skyline, and the joke was that it had the best view in the city because, while you were in it, you did not have to look at it.

I started to make plans for the next few days. A friend of my sister, a university professor from McGill in Montreal who was on a sabbatical in Warsaw, was writing a history of the Polish people. I thought I would call him tomorrow and invite him for dinner. Another day I wanted to visit the birthplace of Frederic Chopin. Then I remembered. I was supposed to leave tomorrow. But, mysteriously, my anger at Clifford had evaporated.

He was sitting in the dismal drawing room of our suite reading a book. I was not quite sure how to go about it and still save face. 'I'm starving,' I said. 'Let's book a table at the Victoria Intercontinental. If we can't stay there, at least we can eat there. Also, I'd like to see if they have any English newspapers.' I smiled.

He did not look up. 'Hmmm. Yes. Whatever you want.'

This was not going to be easy. I took a deep breath. 'I'm sorry. I over-reacted.'

He lowered the book.

'I was frightened, you see. That half-wit had tried to get into the car.' My voice trembled.

He was across the room in two bounds. He put his arms around me. 'Poor baby,' he said, rocking me gently.

I closed my eyes and let myself be soothed. I wondered if caviar would be on the menu. I felt like having some.

People were lined up to enter the Canaletto, billed as the best restaurant in Warsaw, but we sailed by them when we said the magic word: 'reservation'. Experience had taught us that a reservation was always necessary, even if the restaurant was empty.

A man was sitting alone at the next table and started talking to us. I could tell from his accent that he was Italian.

'How do you like Warsaw?' he asked. Before we could answer, he told us his feelings about the city. 'This is the worst place I ever been. I travel all over Africa, the Far East, but here, is lousy. The service, the food, everything. You know, they have casino upstairs? To enter you must have tie, jacket. Inside same thing. Bad food, bad service, dirty.'

I started to say something, but he interrupted. 'They like still to be formal. But to be formal, you must have quality. Here, no quality.' He left some bills on the table and, to our relief, left.

He had been too harsh. The Poles were struggling out of the past into the future, and they still did not have the resources to get it right. They would, eventually. Meanwhile, I was enjoying the friendliness of the people. I applauded their superhuman efforts to survive, their spirit.

Caviar was on the menu – Russian, black and $10 (£6) – a fair price by New York standards. I ordered a portion. The waiter immediately informed me that they were out of it. 'But,' he whispered confidentially, glancing quickly around him, 'I can sell you entire tin for $15. You will have four times as much.' He opened his jacket to reveal several small blue and silver cans of the best caviar. 'I will open one. You can eat it now. All for $15.' He smiled.

I tried to imagine a waiter at Le Cirque or the Four Seasons making his own deals with the customer. I couldn't. A whole tin was too much to eat, but I did buy a few to take back to New York.

At the end of dinner a different waiter came to ask us if we would like to buy some real Cuban cigars. We told him that we did not smoke. He thought that we should buy some anyway as they were such a bargain.

Everyone had something to sell. After forty-five years of Communism the people knew only how to endure, not to compete. We found a bribe-taking mentality on every level which was irritating, and, to us Westerners, somehow immoral.

We left the restaurant, the caviar heavy in my handbag, and Clifford went to collect our coats.

I noticed several young women, all with thick manes of fair hair hanging loose in the latest fashion, and dressed as if they all belonged to the same club, in short, tight dresses and very high heeled shoes. They were approaching the men in the lobby and it did not occur to me that they were prostitutes until I heard one man say, in an unmistakable American voice, 'Gee, I don't know. How much?' I was curious to find out what the girls charged, but did not know how to ask. I stood waiting for Clifford to reappear and hoped no one had an inclination for brunettes in tweed jackets.

## Clifford

At the corner table, a man in a striped suit played cards with a buxom woman in a yellow cocktail dress. The three desk clerks were bent over a pile of Swiss francs. A man who looked like a heavyweight was selling record albums. 'For collectors. Very cheap. Good jazz. Very cheap,' he whispered from the side of his mouth and then he winked salaciously like a trader in child pornography.

The various businessmen and unattached girls moving through the wreaths of blue smoke in the hotel lobby at nine in the morning appeared to have remained there since our return from the Canaletto at eleven the previous night. We elbowed our way through and, when we reached the exit, the doorman barred the way. 'American cigarettes,' he hissed. 'You sell. I buy.'

'We don't smoke,' Iris replied brightly, striding by none the worse for her ordeal on the plain.

There was another crowd waiting for us outside.

'Change money?'

'Taxi?'

'Guide? Ten dollars . . .'

'Camera film . . . thirty-six exposures.'

'Buy jeans? Sell jeans? Swap jeans?'

We negotiated the steps and set out at a brisk pace along Krucza and across Al Jerozolimskie into the maze of narrow, rain-dampened streets where the buildings had the melancholy air of stage sets in an amateur theatre, the paint peeling, the plaster façades cracked and crooked as if the old quarter had been thrown up in a hurry by unskilled workers – which it had been.

Warsaw, more than Dresden, more than any city in Europe, can truly be described as the phoenix that rose from the ashes. Straddling a broad curve in the Vistula, the small fishing village that came into being in the Middle Ages grew slowly into an important market town. Fortifications were erected in the fourteenth century to protect the noble mansions and golden-domed churches, and in 1596 it became the capital. The arts and sciences flourished. Copernicus proved the planets circled the sun. Chopin composed his music.

It was after a four week bombardment by the *Luftwaffe* that the city fell to the Nazis in October 1939. During the occupation, which was to last for more than three years, the citizens were systematically transported to concentration camps, beginning with the Jews, who had been herded into a walled ghetto, a city within a city.

With the Red Army advancing from the east, and after the unsuccessful uprising by the Warsaw survivors, the Germans finally commenced their withdrawal in January 1944. Hitler had one last order for his commander in Poland. It was a brief telegram: Destroy Warsaw, Stop.

Starting at the centre of the capital and numbering the blocks in sequence, the bomb squads first torched the buildings to burn the interiors and roofs. Then they went from house to house, street by street and, laying thousands of tons of precious explosives, they levelled every building. None were missed. The churches were flattened, the palaces, the statues of Copernicus and Chopin. They demolished the bridges, the avenues of trees, the cobblestones, all crushed into dust beneath the iron rollers of panzer tanks. It had taken seven hundred years to build Warsaw. It took two months to destroy it. It was carefully recorded on film.

When the invasion of Poland began, one and a half million people lived in the capital. When the bomb squads pulled out, it was totally empty. The Russians liberated the ruins and, slowly, the people drifted back. The survivors from the concentration camps returned. The soldiers who had fought in foreign lands returned. Refugees came from their hide-outs in the countryside. Using the stones that lay beneath the ashes, using photographs and memories and money raised by Poles all around the world, they built a new Warsaw on the foundations of the city they remembered.

It is not a beautiful city but a memorial to itself. We admired the rebuilt statues and monuments as the labyrinth of streets gradually unfurled at Rynek Starego Miasta, the old town square, where we met Andrew, who offered to be our guide. 'My fee is $5 (£3) and I will remain with you for as long as you require my presence,' he said and bowed in the quaintly formal way of older men in central Europe.

He had wisps of white hair over his ears and a tobacco-stained moustache. He was wearing an over-sized suit of wartime vintage and a tie with a design I knew without being able to place. 'You speak English very well,' I said.

He again bowed his head. 'Thank you,' he acknowledged. 'I learned in England. I was a pilot in the Royal Air Force. The Polish Squadron.'

Now I recognized the tie. I employed his services, we made our introductions and he started to point out the various buildings: the museum, the

Barbican Gate, the bronze mermaid nearby on the riverbank. 'There is a legend that a mermaid told a man whose name was Warsz that a time would come when there would be a great city around the spot where he was fishing.'·

I asked Andrew how long he had been a guide and he smiled. 'One week,' he answered. 'We are free. We can do what we want. For forty years I worked in a factory. I am retired but still I must work.'

'Why did you work in a factory?' asked Iris.

'It is like this: they put the peasants in administrative posts and the intellectuals worked with their hands. I was well-educated and an officer and worked on a production line making metal fixtures. Communism, you must understand, was a joke.'

He lit a cigarette and stared out across the grey surface of the river. We wandered back to the main square and, when I asked him what he thought about German reunification, he weighed his words carefully before he answered. 'When I was a child, my mother gave me a toy car made in Germany. They were the best, you see. My father, when he saw the car, crushed it beneath the heel of his boots and said I should only have Polish toys. He did not want to help the German economy. They were rebuilding after the Great War. Now, they are rebuilding again.'

'Does it frighten you?'

'No, not me. I am too old to be frightened.'

I gave Andrew $10 (£6). He bowed and we parted company.

There were a lot of tourists milling around the sites, which I found inhibiting. I liked to be the only stranger in town. There was a large tour group, all of whom bore the same pale blue shoulder bags and lapel badges with the letters 'SAS'; Scandinavians, I assumed. The souvenir stands were doing a fair business with postcards, woodcarvings and paintings of Warsaw 'that take about five minutes to finish', said Iris. There were horse carriages for hire. I saw one beggar, an early victim of the free market economy. He had a cardboard sign. It reminded me of New York.

We crossed Rynek Starego Miasta to the museum. It cost 1,000 zlotys (10 cents (6p)) to enter and was almost empty. The original German film of the destruction of Warsaw was being shown with a French commentary. After we had seen it, and feeling thoroughly depressed by the experience, we moved through the various rooms to view the rather sorrowful collection of artefacts dug out of the ruins: chairs, silverware, damaged pots and dusty portraits, cracked porcelain, wounded statues, flaking books. The floor was a mosaic of old, highly-polished stones. We were obliged to wear big grey slippers over our shoes and we slid about like drunken ice skaters. It cheered us up.

We were greeted outside by a thunder roll like a roar of canon and as the rain began to fall we chased through the souvenir stands to a café. Paintings with price tags filled the walls and the Rolling Stones were singing 'I Can't Get No Satisfaction' over two home-made speakers that occupied the far corners. We lined up at the counter and then joined a family from Pittsburgh: Jas, who had left Poland eight years earlier and was returning for the first time with his American wife, Janette, and their little girl, Sophie, a two-year-old with yellow curls and the confidence that comes from being constantly the centre of attention. She wandered around the large room being admired. The atmosphere, as well as the clothes the local people were wearing, was reminiscent of the sixties, ten years on from East Germany.

We sat there with our coats steaming and exchanged tales of the road. Like us, Jas and Janette had arrived in Warsaw without a reservation and, like us, they were at the Grand Hotel, on the same floor in suite 310. Unlike us, they were not paying $150 (£90) a night – but $60.

'I made an arrangement with the manager. I pay him $50. And then $10 for the room.'

'The room costs $10?' I was incredulous.

'That's nearly 100,000 zlotys. I'm Polish, don't forget,' Jas explained.

Iris and I glanced at each other with raised eyebrows. She looked determined, not defeated. Sophie was sitting on a small dog under the next table and her mother went to rescue her. Jas shrugged an apology. He was plump with fair hair, a wide face and blue eyes. In his eight years in the United States he had become a doctor of physics and was starting his first job teaching the following term.

'This world is new to me as well,' he said. 'I left as a student. I have come back with some dollars and everyone wants to take them. They think we are rich and I suppose we are.'

'I'm bored with getting ripped off all the time,' Janette inserted and Jas patted her on the hand. She was small and thin. He was a gentle giant. Sophie was a bit of both.

'It is not the fault of the people. It is the system. The government gives the people nothing and they must get what they can just to survive,' Jas told his wife.

'Some people managed to get rich,' I said.

'Sure, the nomenclature. The heads of the Party, not the members but the bosses, were like members of an exclusive club,' Jas replied. 'No one really knows how they got so much power. What we did know was that they had one objective: to stay in power. It is a simple equation: power equals wealth.'

'The same as the good ol' US of A,' added Janette.

Jas laughed. 'Now, I will tell you a Polish joke,' he said. 'What is the difference between Communism and Capitalism? Capitalism is the exploitation of man by man. Communism is the reverse.'

Janette did not smile. I had a feeling Jas was a Republican hawk, the result of growing up in Poland, while his wife was a liberal Democrat suddenly confused by what was happening in Eastern Europe. On the other hand, she had probably heard the joke before.

When we left the café the storm clouds had blown over and the dealers along Al Jerozolimskie packed the pavement, even blocking the windows of the state-run stores, which were drab, half-empty and waiting for the changes to filter through their doors. Poland was going through its own private 'big bang' jumping feet first into the free market, while the planned, Marxist economy was not being dismantled, but was being left to wither away of its own accord. It was an experiment that was being closely followed and nowhere more so than in Moscow.

It was still the early days, but the experiment appeared to be working. There was meat in the shops for the first time in years; farmers were selling their vegetables from the back of wagons; stalls were laden with electrical goods from West Germany and cheap cotton clothes from the Far East. Other would-be entrepreneurs, as new to business as the retired pilot, had displays that were so pathetically small, that even had they sold out I cannot imagine that they would have earned enough to buy a decent meal: an old gypsy stood behind a dirty wooden box with six toothbrushes; a fat peasant woman held a solitary embroidered blouse; a sallow-faced boy with his first moustache had two T-shirts, both small in a land of large people. I bought a packet of four batteries from a man who was so thrilled to have a customer I wasn't too upset when I put them in my cassette-player a week later and found they didn't work! The batteries were red and gold with Chinese writing on them.

A man with long greasy hair approached with an armful of used girlie magazines. He had a shifty look on his thin face and his voice was drowned by a grey helicopter that passed overhead. It had twin blades and red markings. No one glanced up. The people were preoccupied. The whole of Warsaw was one big market place. Everyone was selling, buying, bartering – in the streets, in hotel lobbies, over restaurant tables, across the back seats of taxis. The smell of hamburgers and fried onions wafted along with the exhaust fumes. The merchants and their stands were colourful but repetitive and I was suddenly more interested in the glowering monstrosity engulfing us in its shadow from across the boulevard.

The Palace of Culture is so ugly, like the early works of Bauhaus, that time can only render it beautiful. It dwarfs the surrounding buildings, a soaring mountain of concrete that rises in diminishing blocks to a tall spire like a look-out tower. At the very top there is a giant red star like an all-seeing eye, which still peers down at the city, but the Big Brother portraits have gone and the only visible nameplate was an unassuming sign for the United Workers' Party – *nom de guerre* of the new Communists.

The palace had been erected by Stalin in Stalin-mock-Gothic (what else?) amid the post-war hovels of the homeless. It was christened the 'Cathedral of St Josef' by the people, who loathed it, despised him and grew to resent the sleazy strip club opened in the basement for Party mandarins and visiting VIPs.

## Iris

We returned to our '$10' suite of rooms and I telephoned Andrew Kawczak, a professor of philosophy at McGill University in Montreal. He was taking a sabbatical and had wanted to return to his former friends and life in Warsaw. Miraculously he answered the telephone. Unfortunately, he had pneumonia.

'My dear, I would have liked to meet you and your friend, but my doctor says I must stay in bed for another two weeks. Now tell me, how do you like Warsaw?'

'Very much. I imagine that you must be startled by all the changes.'

'Not really. There was always an underground organization working against the Communists, but they only represented about ten per cent of the people. It needed the other ninety per cent to become disgusted by the nomenclature and their *apparatchiks*. But in a way you are right,' he laughed hoarsely, 'when it finally happened, we were not prepared for the enormity of the changes that took place.

'The system had created a new class with unbelievable privilege that had nothing to do with Communism or Socialism. A group of ruthless oppressors emerged, and controlling the army, police and media, they exploited the people for their own ends.'

'What do you think will happen now?'

'It is difficult to get rid of these people and it is going to take a long time. When people are used to privilege they are reluctant to give it up. Now I am afraid because the politicians want to sell off government-owned industry into private hands. But whose hands? Who has the savings put by to purchase shares? Only the nomenclature who have been tucking money away in Switzerland for years.'

'Still,' I said, 'I've seen so much trade going on in the streets. The people seem to be taking very well to free market enterprise.'

'Most of the entrepreneurs one encounters on the streets are people born with a street dealing mentality. They were trading before Solidarity, only then it was clandestine. There has always been trade in caviar, Japanese cameras and foreign currency. The difference is that now this mentality is being applauded.'

'Have you ever met Lech Walesa?' I ventured.

'Yes. He is a good man. But he overplayed his hand by insisting that he be made president. Had he waited, it would have fallen into his lap.' He began to cough. 'Excuse me,' he choked out between bouts.

'Professor Kawczak, I hope I haven't tired you.' I was distressed.

After a few minutes he was able to resume our conversation, but in a much weaker voice. We soon said goodbye.

The Grand was so depressing we walked back across town to the Victoria Intercontinental for tea. The dining-room was filled with groups of businessmen who used it as a meeting place. They clustered around the room at tables, spreading out files and conferring in a mixture of languages. Some groups had certain characteristics that identified them immediately. The Americans were all lean and fit, drank water and did not smoke. The Germans were heavier, boisterously confident and drank beer. The French were noticeably elegant and smoked continually. The Italians had the best shoes and laughed the most. The Japanese always had the biggest table because there were more of them. One, perhaps the boss, had his shoes off and sat with his legs crossed under him, Buddha-style, on a chair.

At another table an older man, unmistakeably English, with silver hair and an impeccable suit, sat dictating to his attractive secretary and drinking scotch. I heard him say 'let them feel we value their contribution . . .', but I had a feeling that he did not value it at all.

## Clifford

The next day was dreary. The coffee at breakfast was cold. Iris looked festive in a bright yellow rain jacket.

I offered the gaggle of crooks and businessmen $20 for the reappearance of my windscreen wipers, which had gone missing overnight, and they gathered around with sincere expressions to suggest other services that would relieve me of just such a sum. The cigarette dealer who doubled as a doorman heaved our bags into the boot and stared down at the zlotys I gave him as if his palm was covered with the unmentionable. 'Dollars?' he protested. I shook my head.

I started the car and drove into a heavy mist. We passed the Holiday Inn and the Hotel Marriott, signs of an American-orientated future, the two glossy skyscrapers flanking the Palace of Culture. Rain was waiting for us on the outskirts of the city, light at first but then growing heavier.

'We'd better pull over,' Iris said.

'It's all right. If you keep a steady speed, the rain streams off.'

'Travelling requires no point or urgency. It is like a pilgrimage. The purpose is contained within the journey itself.'

She sounded so pompous. 'What?' I said.

'I'm quoting you,' she replied. 'You're going to kill us both.'

'Is this an argument?'

'Yes.'

I pulled over. Old cars like competitors preparing for a vintage rally were parked on and around a muddy quagmire where another impromptu market was in progress. We set out under an umbrella and it was some time before it dawned on me that the miserable piles of junk set out on plastic sheets were actually automobile parts: mufflers, mirrors, tyres, pistons, axles, carburettors, steering wheels, seats, clocks and meters, whole engines without bodies; bodies without engines. And windscreen wipers.

Was a Fairy Godmother watching over us? I had made a number of telephone calls from the hotel that morning, a frustrating and fruitless experience. Apart from vehicles made in Eastern Europe, the only foreign car parts available in Warsaw were for Volkswagen and Mercedes. Naturally! It seemed pointless to allow something so minor to interfere with the trip. It had been raining so much, it was due to stop, if only by the law of averages; and, the following week, we would be in Czechoslovakia, where I would try again. Now, perhaps it would be unnecessary.

The wiper collection was extensive, new and old, rusty, bladeless, broken, armless. I sorted through under the dispassionate gaze of the vendor, a Godfather figure with a knife scar on his cheek and the stub of a Cuban cigar between his teeth. I looked up at him and he nodded wisely. Other men pushed forward, unshaven, in caps and greatcoats. They watched with growing excitement as the Godfather produced an oil cloth and unrolled it, and there, safe and clean, like a pair of giant ear-rings being displayed on a jeweller's tray, were a pair of windscreen wipers – my windscreen wipers: brand new, matt black, unmistakeable.

We haggled for a while but I had little enthusiasm for the sport and he knew he had a deal. Finally, I handed over three $20 bills. I pantomimed the fact that I did not know how to put the things on and the dealer left his stand to show me.

It had now stopped raining. Iris was grinning. Two gypsy children mumbling curses and selling bags of nuts approached. I bought some for a ridiculously low price. I tested the wipers and pulled away.

We quickly passed from the last outcroppings of tumbledown apartments into flat, rain-drenched meadows, the monotony of the landscape enlivened by pastel churches, some with frescoes decorating the outer walls and all crowned with silver domes that shone in the dull light. The going was slow. Animals clogged the roads, the herdsmen leading them oblivious to the traffic.

Close to the town of Radom, there was a market similar to the one we had just left, with the difference that there were no cars, only horse-drawn wagons laden with metal objects: copper tubing, balls of wire, ancient refrigerators with their motors hanging out on coloured wires like intestines, gas ovens, car doors, bizarre sculptures that could have found a home in a museum of modern art. The drivers whistled short, sharp signals and the horses moved delicately through the mud, their faint movements easing the wagons together so that the men could do their business. Strong arms passed rusting and seemingly identical loads back and forth and calloused hands exchanged notes in small denominations, as small as 100 zlotys – 1 cent.

Like the wagon that had taken me to the petrol station on the way to Warsaw, those at Radom were shaped like boats, a design passed down through the generations as if the peasants on the central plain had some nostalgic yearning for the strip of sea between Gdansk and Szczecin. I took one photograph, instantly felt guilty, and put the camera away. It was condescending, somehow – we in our car, the men at the market trading unwanted scraps from a poor society for mere pennies.

We ate our peanuts. They were rancid. We had stopped to see if there was a bar to have coffee but there was nowhere. There had been nowhere on the journey: no cafés or pull-ins. We had filled up with petrol the previous day and it was just as well. Outside the major cities most of the garages were closed. The bulk of the oil came from the Soviet Union and supplies were often delayed, the result of bungling and bureaucracy, nothing more sinister. Poland could have bought its oil on the international market but not at the subsidized rates provided within the Warsaw Pact.

Instead of coffee shops, there were roadside picnic areas with cement furniture and piles of rubbish over every surface. They were situated in windswept, desolate spots and contrived to look oddly surreal against the primitive surroundings, the wooden ploughs carving neat lines in the dark earth and barefoot boys leading teams of oxen. It was a scene that had remained unchanged throughout the century, except for the antennas riding over the rooftops. Poland had one television channel and it appeared to be showing the same movie on the various occasions that we switched on in different hotel rooms when by some miracle, after warming up for about ten minutes, the thing was working.

Apart from the television antennas, the only other intrusion on the countryside was the traffic, the tiny, Polski-Fiat 600s beetling by like wind-up toys, and the trucks, slow-moving beasts travelling in a cocoon of noxious gas. The very notion of lead-free fuel was science fiction.

The road became much busier as the fields thinned into small, neglected towns. It started to rain and the veil of mist we had left behind in Warsaw reappeared in the distance as Cracow rose over the plain like a city floating in the clouds. Smoke-stacks of every conceivable size and description poured out streams of waste and seemed more ugly and threatening after driving through rural villages where the air may not have been any cleaner but at least it had seemed that way.

The rain, rather than washing away the clouds, congealed the pollution into an inky vapour that smeared the windscreen and grew like a pair of bushy eyebrows along the top of the arches made by the wipers (bless them). No rain that I had seen before left a motor vehicle so grimy.

It had not been our intention to dwell on the problems of pollution but they were ever present on our journey from Berlin to the Black Sea, a legacy of Communism that is going to be more difficult to cure than the ailing economies. The forests were dying. The rivers were dead. The buildings were crumbling. For a thousand years, foreign invaders had been sacking Poland but, where the Russians, Prussians, Austrians and even Adolf Hitler had failed to destroy the cathedral and medieval castle on Cracow's Wawel Hill, chemical poisons were succeeding in eroding the intricate stonework.

The hill was surrounded by narrow roads that I came to know rather well as we drove in circles searching for our hotel. Finally, I asked a taxi driver to lead the way and, when we arrived, he refused to take the fare. His palms nursing an enormous belly, he was grinning at the USA decal on the back of the car.

'You American,' he said. 'Its best country in the world. I live in Canada. My wife in Canada. Canada, best country in the world.'

He helped me carry the luggage into the hotel lobby. Iris checked in, while I was led to the bar. The fat driver had his arm around my shoulders as if I were his new best friend. 'Vodka,' he said. 'We take vodka.'

I paid for the drinks and listened to stories about Chicago and Toronto. The bar was full of smoke. The lobby was full of smoke. Smoke was the great equalizer. The Party chiefs smoked. The workers smoked. The gypsy children smoked while they discussed the price of peanuts. The air smelled of smoke and the walls were the colour of smoke. Iris returned with a decrepit porter and, a cigarette lodged in his teeth, he waddled off with the bags.

## Iris

When I was a child I had a book of fairy tales that contained a story about an old alchemist who lived in Cracow. I had spent hours pouring over the illustrations of an impossibly beautiful city with turreted ramparts, castles and churches. It had all seemed so remote and far away. Yet, there I was, standing in the middle of the Market Square, the heart of the ancient city, and I was not disappointed. It was everything I had dreamed it would be.

It was the first time on our journey through Poland that we had seen a town that had survived the Second World War intact. The Germans had been ordered to raze it to the ground, as they had done so efficiently in Warsaw, but had been scared off by the advancing Red Army before they had been able to do much damage.

The old part of Cracow is an artistic jewel that contains seven centuries of Polish architecture. In 1978 the UNESCO World Heritage Committee placed it, together with the nearby Wieliczka Salt Mines, on a list of the twelve most significant world monuments. The job of preservation is enormous, however, because nearby are the massive Nowa Huta steelworks, which spew out tons of erosive pollution every day and have done more damage in the past two decades to the town than the preceding five centuries.

Cracow is a university town. In 1492, when Christopher Columbus was discovering America, Nicolaus Copernicus was attending the renowed Jagiello-nian University and was beginning to suspect that the sun, and not the earth, was the centre of the universe. The youth and gaiety of the students strike a happy balance with the serious, sometimes dismal history of their surroundings.

We walked around the square and down the side streets, going into several of the old college buildings. At one end of the square, women were selling flowers from a market as they have been doing for centuries. We stopped for coffee in an elegant café. A series of small ornate rooms with high ceilings painted in gold and red opened one on to the other. Panels of mirrors with gilded frames reflected the light from huge crystal chandeliers. We found a table and sat back on red velvet chairs to admire our surroundings. Next to us a group of chic old ladies, dressed in the classic styles of the 1940s, wearing hats and gloves, sipped tea and gossiped with their friends. I was struck by what youthful faces they had, with lovely, wrinkle-free skin that looked out of place on their bent thin bodies.

We emerged to find a heavy rain beating down on the cobblestones. There was no lack of shops. The streets were lined with them as in any regular Western city. Merchandise was nicely displayed, although on close inspection it was always the same sort of inferior goods we had seen since leaving West Berlin. A surprising number sold wedding dresses and veils, perhaps because it was easy to put together a bit of white satin and net and fulfil a girl's dreams, at least for one day. Shoes and handbags were plentiful and many stores sold only religious articles. Almost every window had a picture of Pope John Paul II.

The following morning we hired a guide to accompany us on a tour of the Wieliczka Salt Mines. She was fat, gap-toothed and panting for air as she apologized for her tardiness – she had kept us waiting half an hour.

'I am sorry to be late. I live far away. My name is . . .' she paused. Her eyes flicked over us. 'Just call me Jane.'

I was dreading the tour. I had not told Clifford, but I suffered from mild claustrophobia. Still, it was not every day that I had the opportunity to visit salt mines that had been in continuous operation for over seven hundred years. My curiosity overcame my hesitation.

It is hard to believe that once salt had a value equal to gold. Until the invention of refrigeration, salt was essential in the preservation of food. It was used in the tanning process and in the manufacture of gunpowder and was vital to every person. The Wieliczka mines contributed greatly to the wealth of Cracow and provided the financial basis for all the fine buildings, churches and the university.

In spite of her size, Jane was energetic and moved with nimble grace. 'Wait here,' she commanded, without explanation, when we entered the reception building at the mine. She returned about twenty minutes later looking disappointed. 'I am sorry, but we must walk down. There is an elevator, but they say we cannot use it.' I felt she had been thinking more of herself than of us.

We started walking down narrow wooden stairs that zig-zagged back and forth until I lost track of the number of turns. Descending with us was a group of schoolchildren, and their shrieks and giggles of delight at the adventure distracted me from my fear. Down, down, down we went, to almost 400 feet before we reached the first landing. It really was extraordinary, an underground world extending a further nine levels to 1500 feet and comprising 200 miles of routes. Visitors were only allowed into the first three levels.

Even though we had a guide, it was necessary to follow a miner through the corridors and chambers for our own protection. We joined another small group and started off after him into the eerie netherworld of the mine.

With us was a pretty Japanese girl, twenty-two years old and studying music at an academy in Brussels. She was using her Easter break to see Eastern Europe and was travelling alone by train.

'Are you nervous about travelling on your own?' I asked her.

'Oh, no,' she laughed. 'I feel safer in this part of Europe than I do in Brussels, even Tokyo!'

An English couple, from Yorkshire, materialized in the gloom. The man was holding a flaxen-haired girl, scarcely more than a baby, who was cross and fidgety. The mother said her parents had been born in Cracow and they were visiting relatives. She totally ignored her child and it was the father, a big, rough-looking man, who gently and patiently cared for her.

On every level there was a chapel where the miners prayed at the beginning and end of each shift. It did not take much imagination to understand why. Although modern working conditions are as good as can be expected, they were horrific in the past, with many casualties. In 1690 a group of miners staged a revolt. Retaliation was swift and brutal: four were impaled; seven, including one woman, were decapitated and quartered; and four other women were whipped at the pillory.

We passed through twenty worked-out chambers, including one, called the Chapel of St Kinga, that was as big as a cathedral, with an altar and numerous life-sized statues of saints, all carved from salt by the miners and illuminated by salt-crystal chandeliers. On the level below, we passed two lakes complete with piers and boats, and the huge Staszic Chamber, where the Germans used slave labour to manufacture aeroplane parts during the Second World War. Another chamber contained a theatre, bar, and even a tennis court for the use of the miners.

The deepest level housed a museum that displayed the tools developed over the centuries to extract the salt. I felt sorry for the generations of horses that had been used to operate the machinery. They were kept in underground stables and never saw daylight. The bottom level also contained a sanitarium for people with respiratory illnesses but this we were not allowed to visit.

When no one was looking, I touched my tongue to the wall of a corridor as we passed through. It was salt, all right. By the time the tour was finished, I knew all I ever wanted to know about salt mining. There remained only the little problem of returning to the surface. 'Do we have to walk back up?' I asked Jane. In Poland any inconvenience was possible.

'No. We go now to the elevator.'

We followed her down a winding passageway and up a ramp to what looked like a cage. We were packed in tightly with several other people. A bell rang three times and we were hauled up at amazing speed through the blackness. I closed my eyes tightly. After what seemed an eternity, we reached the surface. The sun was shining. Everything looked fresh and promising.

Jane had moved to Cracow as a child. She was a metallurgical engineer by profession but had given up her job earlier to care for her husband and two children. She had been a part-time guide for the past ten years. She spoke six languages fluently, including Russian, Italian, French and German. She had a sophisticated grasp of the political situation in her country.

'Here, we never had Communism,' she explained on the ride back to town. 'We had a Red aristocracy. The people in charge had no morals and no sense of responsibility. They got rich, and now, with the changes, they will get richer. Those who were poor will remain poor.'

'But there were some good things, no?' I asked. 'Wasn't there guaranteed housing for all, free medical care and education?'

'Not true!' she shot back, her face flushing with indignation. 'People had to wait twenty years for an apartment. It is not unusual to see three generations living together in two rooms. To get an operation, it was necessary to bribe an administrative official at a hospital. The same for a place in the university. The doctors themselves are paid less than a factory worker.'

I asked her how much an average family earned in a month, and she told us that her husband, a mechanical engineer, had a good salary but a take-home pay of the equivalent of only $125 (£75) per month.

'The government takes so much in taxes,' she explained. 'As much as eighty per cent.' She would earn 14,000 zloty for our three hour tour, or $1.40. We had paid $50 to Orbis.

## Clifford

They were waiting for me in the bar when we got back to the hotel: Kazimierza, the taxi driver, had brought his young cousin, Tomas, and sat there fondly stroking his paunch. Tomas was blowing plumes of smoke from his nose and at the same time was sucking on his cigarette so that the tip glowed like a beacon. After tramping through a salt mine for three hours my throat felt as if it were made of green rock crystal it was so dry.

'Vodka?' Kazimierza asked.

'Just a small one. And some water.'

He glanced at Iris. 'Maybe later,' she said and returned to the room to read up on Cracow. She was very methodical.

'*Na zdrowie,*' I said.

Kazimierza knocked back his vodka. His skin was dark and when he smiled fans of white lines opened around his eyes.

The bar was full. It was furnished with black plastic sofas that made vulgar noises and thick curtains blocked out the daylight. Tomas was drinking coffee. He drove a taxi at night and by day he studied English and French at the Philological College.

'Life is impossible here. That is why I study languages,' he said. 'I go to America.'

'America, best country in the world.'

Tomas impatiently shook his head and turned to me with an intense expression. 'But now I do not know. We have a chance to rebuild my country. It is up to the young people. The old ones are tired. The old ways are fixed in their heads.'

He looked around the bar and I did the same. Everyone had the grey, bloated look that comes from overeating and, staring into space, they seemed to illustrate man's love of irony. The rich in the Western world starve themselves to stay thin, jog and don't smoke, while the poor stuff themselves, don't exercise and smoke like the Lenin steelworks.

'You must be happy to have your freedom at last?' I said.

'Of course,' Tomas replied. 'We are waiting forty years. Now we must make it work.'

'Why did it take so long?'

'Russia.'

'Russia,' Kazimierza echoed.

'There were many uprisings – 1952, 1956, 1964; many, many times. But we were always afraid of the Russian tanks.' Tomas paused. 'The Russian tanks,' he said again and crushed the empty cigarette packet on the bar. 'It was Mr Gorbachev who allowed the Polish people to get rid of the oppressors. He is a great hero.'

When Iris reappeared, Kazimierza stood and kissed the back of her hand. Tomas offered to drive us to the main square. 'No charge,' he said, but we wanted to walk.

I carried the bag. It was made of canvas and green leather and contained numerous compartments concealing passports, money, credit cards, travellers' cheques, an assortment of lip balms, the odd book and three pairs of glasses that served Iris's needs for reading, distance and sun. Apart from lugging the bag of treasures with us wherever we went, I always wore a shirt with breast pockets that held a few dollar bills in one side and the local currency in the other. The idea was to split our valuables and, if we were mugged, there was a chance the instant cash would serve to protect the 'mother-lode'.

The street was grey and the sky overcast. There were out-of-date election posters peeling from the walls. The trees were sagging, heavy with rain. Black crows stamped through the garbage, which had been swept by the wind into shop doorways. *Rambo II* was playing at the cinema.

As we walked along, following the tram lines towards the city walls, we must have made a sight just as interesting to the local people as they were to us. Catholic men in eastern Europe do not carry bags. Although, just as Kazimierza had lived up to his royal name by regally kissing Iris's hand, the people clung on to the quaint manners of another time and another Europe. We had given a lift to an ancient peasant waiting on the side of the road outside Radom with a broken spinning wheel and, when we stopped in his village, he had ceremoniously done the same thing. He had also given me a cardboard token and, punching his palm with a broad finger for emphasis, he had explained what I was meant to do with it. Naturally, I didn't understand a word but, later, I discovered that the Polish government, never having built a satisfactory transport network, encouraged hitch-hiking by giving motorists fuel discounts with their hitch-hiking tokens. I kept mine as a souvenir.

The Poles also seemed to enjoy the way we walked arm-in-arm. It marked us as foreigners, which was unfortunate when we wanted to blend into the background, but it did have compensations. We were often shuffled into the best seats in bars and restaurants and, when they were full, the waitresses flustered around with the bills to make a table free as quickly as possible. There were other times when the service was painfully slow and the people positively rude. 'Nomenclature,' Iris would whisper and we would keep an eye out for a sneaking glimpse of a Rolex. We were crossing the final frontier of tourism. The last of the barricades were crumbling and, more often than not, we were welcomed as ambassadors from a world from which the people had been excluded and which they were now eager to rejoin.

We sat in the large main square. There were no cars. No billboards. Coloured umbrellas covered the flower stalls. We had coffee and watched the crowds going in and out of the cloth hall. The air was still. We remained quiet.

A pigeon dropped a message on my shoulder. 'It's lucky,' Iris said and I thought it would have been luckier still had it fallen on her shoulder. The sky had grown darker and the calm was ruffled by a chill wind that put life into the red and white flags outside the Church of Our Lady. They snapped to attention and made the sound of flamenco dancers clicking their fingers. The pigeons had taken to the air and were flying in all directions searching for cover beneath the eaves of the buildings. As the last one vanished, the rain began to fall with astonishing violence and rivers erupted among the cobblestones.

We took cover under an archway, where we ran into the English couple we had met earlier in the salt mines. The baby was sucking a dummy that hung on a green plastic chain.

'I thought we were in fa' a drop,' the man said.

'April showers,' I suggested.

'Aye, 'tis tha'.'

We exchanged a few more pleasantries and, the moment the rain eased, we hurried away in opposite directions.

From the distance, I could hear music and we followed the sound to a busy square where two gypsies were playing a duet for violin and guitar, while a third collected money in a damp cardboard box. The guitarist, a young boy with long black hair, was gazing at his partner with a look of rapt, almost religious devotion. He was an older man, very small, with malformed legs and a smile that was decorated with a cigarette. He held the violin, not under his chin, but against his chest. His long fingers danced over the strings, which he bowed like a cello, and they sang a melody that seemed Spanish or Hungarian, something haunting, even hypnotic.

We remained rooted to the spot for a long time. Some artists were unveiling their paintings in a row behind us. The people crossing the square stopped for a few minutes to listen to the music and carried on before the third gypsy accosted them with his empty box. I gave him 10,000 zlotys, a dollar. He threw out his chest, brought his heels together and saluted.

We left the square and passed through a high gateway that led to the road running around the city walls. Factory workers were rushing for trams that would take them home to the apartment blocks that ringed the suburbs beyond Wawel Hill. We were on our way back to the hotel. It was getting late and, after walking all day, we both had good appetites; Iris always did and, that night, it was going to be useful. We were dining at the 'best restaurant in Poland'.

## Iris

On one corner of the Market Square, in a medieval building with a cream-coloured façade, is the Wierzynek Restaurant, considered to be the finest in Poland. As long ago as 1364 Polish kings were wining and dining visiting royalty at its noble premises. Our first evening in Cracow we had arrived at the door, only to be told by a golden-haired receptionist, strangely attired in a green satin suit with a matching pillbox hat worn at a low angle over one eye, that it had been fully booked by a large party from Warsaw.

'What about tomorrow?' I had persisted.

She had looked vague and said they were again fully booked, she could not accept a reservation, there was little hope, but if we wanted to try around nine o'clock in the evening, well, maybe . . . her voice had trailed off.

We appeared promptly at 2100 hours, Clifford even wearing a tie, and me in my standard black skirt, black shoes and stockings, black sweater and black jacket, relieved only by a bright silk scarf around my neck.

The blonde vision met us at the entrance. A glimmer of recognition seemed to enter her eyes but we could not be sure. She had a new costume – a lemon suit with a cape instead of a jacket and another matching pillbox hat, this time with a long feather sticking out from it. She told us to wait downstairs in the bar and she would see what she could do. There were several others ahead of us. We ordered vodka and prepared to be patient.

'Should we have bribed her?' I asked Clifford.

He shook his head. 'I don't know. I had a feeling it was the wrong thing to do. This isn't Warsaw.'

Every fifteen minutes she appeared at the top of the stairs, looking like a young Zsa Zsa Gabor, and scanned the masses huddled below. Who would be chosen? Who would be called to follow her up the stairs to unknown delights? Who would remain behind? Her eyes would rest on two or more people. They would rise from their seats and, trying unsuccessfully to hide the triumph in their faces, disappear up the staircase.

A noisy Italian family entered the bar; father, mother, teenage son and daughter. They greeted her like a lost relative, showering her with compliments on her dress and appearance, all four of them fawning over her as only Italians can.

'If they get a table before we do,' I whispered, 'I'm leaving.'

To the Valkyrie's credit, she did not play favourites, and we were called in order of our arrival. Our turn eventually came, and we were beckoned up the stairs to the best restaurant in Poland.

We were ushered into a magnificent dining room, double height, with a display of medieval swords, breastplates and helmets arranged on one wall. Opposite, arched lead glass windows stretched from floor to ceiling. Polished wooden armchairs were placed at tables covered with white damask cloths and perfectly set with silver, china and tall candelabra. A small vase of flowers completed each table. They were plastic. Outside in the square was one of the world's oldest and most elaborate flower markets, and here they used artificial flowers.

Most of the tables were empty but rapidly filled with the remainder of the people waiting below. Last to enter was the Italian family, looking subdued. A group of waiters materialized and fanned out around the room. Our waiter was the oldest and very impatient with our attempts to decipher the menu, written only in Polish. The specialities were wild game. After quite a struggle I ordered a white bortsch with sweet berries, served with cheese pastry, to start, followed by roast boar with all the trimmings. Clifford enjoyed his wild mushroom soup and venison steak. We shared a bottle of very good red French wine. Unlike most of the restaurants in Warsaw, we were not obliged to pay in foreign currency. The bill came to 88,000 zloty, less than $10.

## Clifford

The vast plain stretching over Poland like a drum skin comes to an abrupt end along the southern border, where the Sudety and Carpathian mountains meet in a tall crown of snow-capped peaks, Vysoka Tatry, the High Tatras.

The drive had taken us away from the grime of the lowlands in a serpentine climb through meadows speckled with wild flowers – bluebells, buttercups, poppies, the armies of white crocus in patches like unmelted snow. Shepherds with long crooks across their shoulders stood motionless on raised knolls of stone watching their flocks of mountain sheep, proud, lithe animals with coarse wool hanging almost to the ground. The ewes were swollen with lambs that would be born any day; the rams had the short, curling horns always depicted on the sign of Aries.

A deep, narrow valley lined with the rock sculptures left by the restless glaciers of the last Ice Age finally unwinds itself at Zakopane, a resort town of neat chalets with painted shutters and ornately carved gables. A wooden church, built by pioneers and rebuilt frequently during the past two centuries, faces the post office and around them stands an assortment of small hotels and lodges booked solid during the skiing season which comes to an end just as the spring lambs are taking their first tentative steps.

'You were right.'

'I was?'

'Definitely.'

The esoteric snatch of conversation referred to my suggestion that we skip the Black Madonna at Czestochowa, in the opposite direction to Zakopane. I do not object to visiting churchs and museums; they form the skeleton on which the flesh of a journey is hung. But it is the flesh, communication with the people and the present, that is more important.

Zakopane had a scrubbed look about it. It had stopped raining and the sky was blue and cloudless. Most of the skiers had gone and the streets of the town and the tracks leading out of it were filled with grim hikers wearing ankle socks over their high socks and all seemingly carrying the same canvas knapsacks, shapeless things with bulging pockets and no supporting frame. We stared up at Mount Gubalowka and, guiltily, we headed for the funicular railway.

'Up and down? Just up? Or just down?' asked the ticket clerk, trying English after I had failed to understand his German. He leaned forward on his elbows and tried again in French.

'Up,' I finally answered.

'Two. Just up,' he said and handed me two tickets as fine as tissue paper.

The little railway groaned its way slowly to the summit, where the spectacular view, more Himalayan than Alpine, was second only to the taste of good clean air, the first to fill our lungs for weeks. It was cold but invigorating. The Vysoka Tatry rise to over seven thousand feet, a ring of jagged teeth that kept the Ottomans at bay during the era of the Turks. Beyond the mountains was Czechoslovakia, our next destination. There was a border crossing at a nearby pass but we planned to follow the country roads back to Wroclaw, scene of a hundred bridges and, with its claim of being the most beautiful city in Poland, sure to have its fair share of painted madonnas.

A thick, springy carpet of pine needles nursed our feet on the path down from Gubalowka. Black butterflies with golden markings hovered among the bushes and two eagles on motionless wings circled overhead. The sound of a mountain stream drifted up through the trees. It felt good to be using my legs after days in the driving seat.

'*Dzien dobry.*' A veteran hiker in a red woolly hat greeted us with a booming 'How do you do', and trudged on up the track at the slow steady rate of his heart beat. He was wearing long leather shorts of timeless vintage and the handle of a small knife poked out Highland-style from his knee socks.

'In case of bears,' whispered Iris.

Apart from the chamois, marmots and lynxes roaming the hills, the brochure we had picked up at the lodge where we were staying had promised the 'occasional glimpse of wild bear'; something occasional enough not to interfere with the skiing industry.

We saw several grand villas and hunting lodges built by Polish barons before the Second World War. They were well-maintained within mature gardens and behind high fences of more recent construction. The deeds of ownership had passed from one aristocracy to another and they seemed to be waiting for a third to unlock the gates and breathe new life into the shuttered rooms. 'I wonder who will buy these houses?' Iris said, reading my thoughts.

'Perhaps the occupants will,' I replied. 'They're the ones with the money.'

We reached a fast-moving stream, where the tops of boulders, like bald heads, rose just a few inches above the water. Iris's pink smile immediately vanished. 'Don't even suggest it,' she said. 'I'm going back up.'

'You don't have a ticket,' I reminded her.

'I'll buy one. Or bribe someone.'

A man, standing with his two hands clasped to his waist, listened to our conversation and then grinned. 'English,' he said. I nodded. 'I thought you were Germans. Never I talk with the Germans.'

'Never?' I continued.

He held up his palm. 'Never,' he repeated with finality.

He now glanced at Iris. 'Easy,' he said simply. 'Easy.'

He took a length of rope from his canvas knapsack and tied it to a tree. 'Follow', he said to her. He then skipped across the stepping stones and hitched the rope to a tree on the far bank. 'Come,' he shouted.

'Go,' I said.

'Is this a conspiracy?'

She braced herself. I took the green bag of valuables. 'Go as quickly as you can,' I said.

She took the rope loosely in her palm and, slowly at first, then gathering speed, she moved across the boulders with all the grace of a ballet dancer. I untied the rope and followed.

'Easy,' we each said and then we spent the next hour together tramping down to Zakopane. Theo was in his thirties and taught mathematics at a college in Cracow. He was tall and bearded with lots of curly dark hair, and though his English was reasonably good he used it with economy. I wanted to know why he did not like Germans. 'Silesia,' he said. 'Silesia?' I prompted. 'Silesia,' he said again. It was hard work.

We forded two more streams, swollen by the spring rains, and parted company when we reached town.

It was later that I discovered why the Silesians had little fondness for the Germans. It had begun six hundred years ago, when roaming tribes of Goths had sacked the territory and slaughtered half the population. They were later conquered by the Bohemians and the Habsburgs; Frederick the Great then annexed the region for the Prussians, who controlled it until the end of the First World War. After the war, the nationalist rebellion was brutally crushed and Silesia remained part of Germany until the fall of the Third Reich in 1945. The Germans who had remained were expelled and the area was repopulated by Poles from the Ukraine.

Modern-day Germans have tried very hard to live down their predatory reputation but it could take just as long for it to be forgotten as it was in growing. The earliest account of their ruthless aggression was recorded two thousand years ago by the Roman historian Tacitus. It was in the woods at Teutoburg that an army of German tribesmen led by Arminius lay in wait for three Roman legions. The Germans ambushed the legionaries and their massacre was such that Rome never again attempted to extend its empire beyond the Rhine. The slaughter was described by Tacitus as the '*furor Teutonicus.*' The Germans are tough, hardened warriors given to drinking and fighting and they are, he wrote, 'fanatically loyal to their leaders'.

The image has endured the centuries and the fear, in abeyance while Germany was divided, was on the rise again. Europe's destiny had been guided by the two rival superpowers and while East Germany's emancipation may have been met with a general air of enthusiasm in the West, in the East optimism was mixed with an equal share of doubt.

The mountains slipped and curved into ragged foothills. The trees thinned and the alpine pastures filled with wild flowers became tracts of crumbling cement. The villages, fading into the grey of the landscape, crouched around squat churches as if afraid of the encroaching battalions of chimneys, foundries, sweatshops. Poland's agricultural system, unchanged since before the invention of the automobile, had been neglected for Stalin's centrally planned economy based on industrialization. Towns without hearts and no memories of the boom years had grown up around steelyards and mine heads, the squalid spreads of cheap housing thrown up in the shadows of factory walls eliminating the need for travel. Home, work; home, work! Stalin's vision had been limited.

The famous Vistula, beloved by Chopin, and the Odra, converging on Katowice, ran black with waste. No fishermen perched on their banks. No small boys dived in under the afternoon sun. Coal slag in heaps bigger than apartment blocks formed dark impenetrable cities outside the cities. It is not difficult to believe that eight per cent of the world's supply of coal is dug out of the ground in Silesia and to understand why the Germans had always been so reluctant to give it up.

We stopped in Opole. The people had coal dust ingrained in their faces. Coal dust coated the air. But there was meat in the shops and fruit was appearing for the first time in years. A man with a crushed hat and a bristled chin was standing on a ladder pasting up a poster which showed a man on a ladder whitewashing a red map of Poland. We were stopped on the corner by two young men in blue boiler suits. 'Hello, do you speak English?' one of them asked and when I admitted I did he grinned like an idiot and walked off practising the same question: 'Hello, do you speak English' . . . 'Hello, do you speak English' . . . the words growing fainter in the distance.

Some fat ladies in aprons were yelling abuse at two men – a father and son by their appearance – selling albino strawberries that needed a month in Jamaica. Girls in smocks, their hair tied up in bright squares of cloth, gaped at us and giggled. A line of schoolboys, most with fair hair and blue eyes – a legacy of the expelled Germans – snaked by carrying huge, oblong-shaped cases on their backs; their grey socks rolled down over scuffed shoes, their short trousers and square jackets big enough to last another few years.

Opole was a grim little town with soot-blackened walls and filthy trams but no one wanted our blue jeans or our Deutschmarks. We passed through the broken streets unmolested, paid a few cents for some spotty apples and drove on towards Wroclaw.

Beyond the town, patches of green had made incursions on the cement. Horse wagons replaced the bug-like cars. Strange trees with clumps of leaves like canon balls dotted the road. I had never seen the variety before and wondered if they were merely new to me or a hybrid born of pollution and new to the planet.

## Iris

Wroclaw, an attractive town in south-west Poland, was our last overnight stop before leaving for Czechoslovakia. I must confess that I had never heard of it, but there I was, strolling along the banks of the Odra river, about to cross one of its hundred bridges. We had spent the last several days since leaving Cracow exploring the southern part of the country, and all the pieces of the Polish puzzle were falling into place in my mind; the turbulent history, with its succession of kings; the countless invasions and rebellions; the political, ethnic and economic problems; and in modern times, two devastating wars and the destructive results of Communism.

That morning, the road had taken us past Auschwitz, and we had stopped to peer through the gates at the most notorious Nazi concentration camp of all. It had been a sunny day, but suddenly, it had become overcast. Vast clouds had moved towards us, lowering as they approached. A grey pallor had clung to the fields.

I had read about the mountains of eyeglasses and false teeth, the gold fillings, the gas chambers where millions of people had been murdered. The camp at Birkenau is nearby. When the Nazis fled in 1945, they blew up the gas chambers and the crematoria. The ruins have an eerie, sinister look about them. The camp is huge; it could accommodate 200,000 people. They worked as slave labourers until they were too weak to work and then they were herded into the gas chambers, electric elevators raising the bodies to the ovens. Each chamber held 2,000 prisoners. It was more efficient than Buchenwald. It is thought that up to four million men, women and children were slaughtered at Auschwitz and Birkenau.

Children under the age of thirteen are not permitted to visit the camps. We had stood there for a long time. It had started to rain. We had looked through the fence, looked at each other. We had got back into the car and driven on.

After crossing at least a dozen of Wroclaw's famous small bridges that span the many canals and tributaries of the river, we stopped for refreshments at an ice-cream parlour. Unable to understand a single word on the menu, we were rescued by two girls, obviously students, sitting at the next table.

'Have kiwi ice-cream,' said one. 'It is new.'

'I prefer peanut flavour,' said her friend.

Diplomatically, we had a scoop of each. The four of us chatted briefly before they left, gathering up their school books, throwing their jackets over their shoulders and looking exactly like schoolgirls everywhere. Clifford and I were left to concentrate on our ice-cream.

'You know something strange?' I asked him. 'The kiwi and the peanut taste exactly alike!'

'I find that neither of them have much taste at all,' he replied.

I thought how typical this was of Poland in general. So many things were almost perfect, but in the end, just missed. The women were almost beautiful, but their hair was too blond, their bodies too voluptuous. The men, almost handsome, smoked too much and grew heavy at an early age. The food was almost good. Some of the bigger hotels were almost well run. The people did not seem ready to give that extra effort. I thought of the irate Italian man in the restaurant our first evening in Warsaw. I could understand better his exasperation.

Poland suffered greatly under its Stalinist bosses. In the last forty-five years the country had been sacked and pillaged much as it had been by the roaming tribes of Goths in the middle ages. Debt is conspicuously high and inflation, allegedly under control, is never far away. Unlike East Germany, there is no older brother waiting to bail it out and, unlike East Germany, the Communist apparatus remains, the tip of a largely unseen political iceberg.

# Czechoslovakia

## Clifford

Boys on racing bikes swished by, the riders contorted over the handlebars as they forced their way up through a pattern of low hills as green and as rounded as a child's drawing. The bicycles were new, high-tech; the cars that passed were clean. The bulbous silver dome I could see across the valley floated over the peach-coloured stucco of a church. Later that same day we saw churches in orange, apple-green and dark blue, Christianity in a new range of colours.

We had crossed the border into Czechoslovakia, a lone vehicle on an empty road, the same as when we had arrived in Poland, and we went through the same drawn-out and dreary set of formalities. The officials wore side arms, grim suspicious faces and asked questions that were pointless, mechanical more than malevolent. There was a photograph of Vaclav Havel above the immigration office door but the officers, whatever their feelings about their new playwright president, must have embraced the former system to have got jobs in the first place. Just a few months before we crossed the frontier, while the Western world was chiefly concerned about the movement of cocaine and heroin, these men were still busy confiscating *Playboy* and the *Wall Street Journal*.

I liked the look of the church. It could have been growing on the hillside, something creamy and edible. We were in Bohemia. The hills around us, bounded by the Sudety Mountains and the Moravian Heights, gave out coal, lignite, iron ore, graphite, silver and Europe's major supply of uranium, essential for nuclear power. The plateau stretched between the peaks is cut by the Elbe and the Moldau and produces cereal, including the hops that go into Plzen – the original Pilsner. With its arms industry, including Semtex, the plastic explosive beloved by terrorists, the giant Skoda car works, the steelyards and holiday spas, Communism in Czechoslovakia generated sufficient wealth for some of it to spill over into the lives of the working people.

You could see it in the racing bikes. We had finished our picnic – bread, cheese and some apples bought on the side of the road – and watched them flash by, the riders' shirts in the bright hues of tropical fish. Swish, swish. They raced by in ones and twos and then a whole group, following the leader, skidded to a halt around the car. The young boys who wore the red shirts of the Nachod cycling club, spoke a little English and grinned as they panted for breath. I asked them if they were taking part in a race. 'No, we race on Tuesday,' one of them replied. He was tall and skinny with lots of fair hair tumbling over his collar.

'It is May Day,' one of his companions added.

'It is a big celebration in Czechoslovakia?'

'This year it is the biggest,' the skinny boy answered. His face had grown serious.

'This year?'

'Yes. Czechs and Slovaks are free.'

'And are you happy?'

'Yes. We are happy.'

His friends were becoming restless and the group soon left, all shouting goodbye in English as they vanished around the corner, leaning into the bend and pumping up their thigh muscles.

A delivery van went by and once more there was silence. I locked the car and we walked across the valley to a village of granite cottages and unsurfaced roads. We admired the small peach-coloured church. We watched a woman scrubbing her doorstep. She had white hair and wore a grey pinafore. We heard the sound of heavy, ponderous footsteps and turned as an elderly man, also white-haired, approached us. He was wearing a green loden coat and carried an ebony walking stick that had a bone handle held by an engraved silver ring. We exchanged a few words in German, of which none of us could claim great fluency. '*Deutsch?*' he then asked.

'No, we are from the United States,' Iris told him, and he took a long time thinking about her reply. Finally, he lifted his chin and threw back his shoulders. 'Patton,' he said. 'General Patton.'

The woman scrubbing the step glanced at us and then went back to work, singing quietly to herself. We shook hands with the man and he marched off, swinging his cane and thinking back those forty-five years to when the war had come to an end.

The Americans had arrived to liberate Czechoslovakia at the same time as the Russians, something remembered by the older generation, although it was not taught in the schools. The Americans had left when the job was done, but the Russians were only now, at this very moment, on this very day, commencing the long withdrawal. On the road that morning we had pulled over to watch a convoy of Soviet army vehicles as they moved with painful slowness in the direction of Wroclaw. The trucks were identical, hundreds of them, like reflections in a mirror, high-fronted, brutish, the young soldiers leaning over the tailgates uncertainly. 'There is no place for us behind,' had been the wartime motto of the Red Army, a slogan that now seemed less a battle cry than a prophecy. There was nowhere for the soldiers to go when they got back to the Soviet Union, no jobs, no housing. They had looked gloomy and were probably on their way to Lithuania or Azerbaijan. The whole empire was breaking apart. The convoy had taken more than thirty minutes to pass. I was unable to find out whether it had started from Czechoslovakia or Poland, but it was probably Czechoslovakia, where five full divisions of Soviet troops had been stationed since the Prague Spring of 1968, the year of the Soviet invasion.

Until then, Czechoslovakia had maintained a close, even warm relationship with Russia. Communism had not been foisted upon the people but had been chosen by a narrow margin in the 1946 election. While Western Europe was busy rebuilding itself with American aid, the Czechoslovaks had little trust in the Western democracies – historically, with very good reason.

Czechoslovakia had been proclaimed an independent republic on 29 October 1918, after the collapse of the Austro-Hungarian Empire. Its past, like that of Poland, had been dominated by the whims of acquisitive neighbours; its boundaries and rulers had changed frequently through the centuries. The landlocked plateau had originally been inhabited by Celts and, later, the Germanic tribes and the Slavs. It had never been part of the Roman Empire and, though smaller than the state of Pennsylvania, the region was really three countries: Bohemia, Slovakia and Moravia, with two distinct peoples: the Czechs and the Slovaks.

Following *Anschluss*, the annexation of Austria by Nazi Germany in March 1938, Hitler had turned his attention to Czechoslovakia. On 30 September that same year, Britain and France signed the Munich Dictate, the infamous appeasement agreement that surrendered the Czechoslovak borderlands to Germany. Hitler's tanks rolled in to claim their gift and did not stop until the whole of Czechoslovakia had been seized. It was to be the Führer's swiftest and most economical victory. The United States at this time was going through one of its periodic spells of isolationism and, like Britain and France, was sitting back and watching General Franco's German- and Italian-backed Nationalists usurp the freely elected Republican Government in Spain.

After suffering the ills of Nazi occupation for three years, Czechoslovakia was placed under the command of the notorious Reinhard 'The Hangman' Heydrich. His reign of terror was brought to an end in May 1942 when he was assassinated by two agents sent by Eduard Benes, the head of the Czechoslovak government in exile in London. The Germans in reprisal surrounded the village of Lidice, 15 miles from Prague, murdered all the males, including the children, and deported the females to concentration camps, where the majority died.

As a result of the massacre, the resistance grew stronger and the anti-fascist feeling was such that the burgeoning Communists attracted universal acceptance. After the war the Party formed a coalition with the Democrats. It was doomed to fail and, with the hand of Stalin like a puppetmaster in the background, a Soviet-style system came into existence. Land reform began in

1948 and all businesses employing more than a handful of people were nationalized.

The usual blend of repression, propaganda and state terrorism inherent to and typifying Stalinist Communism came to a sudden and surprising end in May 1968 when Alexander Dubcek was made the Party's First Secretary. He engineered what for the time was an unprecedented programme of social reform; political prisoners were released, decentralization of the economy commenced, censorship was abolished. The short-lived era became known as the Prague Spring and it drew to a close in the dark hours of 20 August, when 250,000 Red Army troops occupied Czechoslovakia with token contingents from all the Warsaw Pact countries except Romania. Nicolae Ceauşescu withdrew from the alliance in condemnation of the invasion, a step that was to win him friends in the White House and a Knighthood from the Queen at Buckingham Palace.

The Czechoslovaks that summer day in 1968 met the invasion force with the same passive resistance with which they had greeted Nazi Germany. Girls in mini-skirts gave the soldiers rose stems. Young men with Beatle haircuts stood in front of the tanks, empty-handed, their arms outstretched in that querulous gesture that cuts across all cultures. One of Prague's young students, Jan Palach, burned himself to death in protest at Russia's aggression, but his protest and all protest was to no avail. Five Soviet divisions pulled in and they remained in support of the new Party boss, the 'realist' Dr Gustav Husak, a man so devout a Stalinist that he later put up the greatest resistance to the reforms initiated and encouraged by Mikhail Gorbachev in Russia and throughout Eastern Europe – an economic and social package that, ironically, was virtually identical to the Prague Spring changes two decades before.

Dubcek was exiled to a minor post in the forestry commission – gone were the days of Siberia – and, while the regime led by Husak grew harsher than anything the Czechoslovaks had known since the days of Reinhard Heydrich, a small group of writers and intellectuals kept the flame of dissent alive by smuggling their work out of the country and having it published abroad. They formed Charter 77, in 1977, a bill of human rights that would mark the signatories as enemies of the state. One of its leaders was Vaclav Havel.

He was imprisoned on three separate occasions, the last being in November 1989, when he was held under guard in hospital in Prague. The Velvet Revolution he had helped to create was reaching its final stages. The people wanted change. They had grown tired of lies and restrictions, the rhetoric, the wealth and double standards of the party glitterati.

One morning, still in hospital, Havel was awakened by the sound of his own name being chanted outside in Wenceslas Square. He got out of bed, went to the window and thousands of supporters cheered his appearance. He was released from confinement and his prestige and energy formed the Civic Forum, spreading a wide social base around student unrest to forge the weapon that would bring down the Communists.

On Friday, 17 November, fifty thousand demonstrators were attacked by riot police in white helmets, reinforced by special troops of the Red Berets. A general strike on Monday, 27 November, combined workers and students throughout the nation. Church bells, car horns, factory sirens and riverboat hooters were sounded at noon. The centre of Prague was jammed. The Communist Party admitted that it was 'partly to blame for the situation'.

Three weeks later, in a series of dramatic scenes he could have written himself, Vaclav Havel was President.

In Poland, it took ten years to end totalitarian rule; in Hungary, ten months; in East Germany, ten weeks. And in Czechoslovakia, they were saying, it took just ten days.

## Iris

Although I was prepared to love Czechoslovakia without reservation, we had a series of negative experiences within the first few hours of crossing the border.

The first happened immediately. We had passed through Customs and immigration and went to change our dollars into korunas, the local currency. The woman who sat on the other side of the glass wicket, packed tightly into a floral print dress, smiled sweetly as she took our money and recounted it, licking her fingers after every bill. I found it curious that no exchange rates were displayed. After doing some calculations in pencil on a piece of paper, she handed back what we assumed was the correct amount.

It always takes a while to get used to a new currency and, after we had finished admiring the engraving and the colours, we got around to counting it. Somehow, it did not seem enough. I asked her what exchange rate she had used, but she pretended not to understand. I ran back to the car to fetch a copy of the *Herald Tribune* that we had kept from West Berlin while Clifford stood fast at the exchange window, the money lying like a diseased fish between them. We checked the rate in the newspaper and did our own calculations. We showed her the figures. She had given us exactly half. Wordlessly, her mouth drooping, she made up the difference.

We stopped for the night in Hradec Králové, historically important as the capital of East Bohemia. The old buildings crouched humbly among high-rise apartments and modern office blocks, all functional and rather dull. We found a hotel that looked acceptable, went in to see if they had a room for the night and came face to face with another example of bureaucratic inefficiency.

About twenty people were patiently waiting in line at the reception desk, but no one was there to help them. We asked two girls, who were sitting further along the counter under a sign that said 'Keys' if they could assist us.

'No,' said one lethargically. 'My colleague will help you.'

'Where is your colleague?' I asked.

'There.' She lifted a limp arm to indicate a boutique across the lobby, where a group of Hungarian tourists were noisily buying glass vases and dishes. Taking the cash, writing out receipts and wrapping the purchases was a very pretty, very busy young woman, wearing the same red uniform as the Key girls.

I went over. 'We would like a room for tonight,' I called.

'You must wait,' she smiled back. 'You must go and stand in line at the reception desk.'

There was nothing else we could do. Everywhere we looked we saw hotel staff in smart red uniforms, standing around and talking to each other, while one woman seemed to be doing all the work. No one else in the line seemed to find this absurd. They were all Czechoslovaks and stood clutching their identity cards in silence. After checking in, we bought a map of the city and had to ask three times for the change.

Our room, when we finally reached it, was clean, modern and the size of a cabin on a boat. A very long list of rules and regulations was on the back of the door, written in several languages including English. The clientele were referred to as 'citizens', and the citizens were told, for example, 'The citizen can accept in the room the visits only with consent of authorized person of accommodation establishment after booking the visitor in the visit took since 8 a.m. to 10 p.m.' and 'Between 11 p.m. and 6 a.m. the citizen is obliged to keep the night rest.'

The last turned out to be wishful thinking because the hotel was across the street from the railway station, and we were treated to the clank of trains coupling and uncoupling all night, as well as a loudspeaker announcing arrivals and departures. Even worse, in spite of all the warnings for the citizens to be quiet, the hotel had a discotheque on the top floor that pounded out music until 2.30 in the morning. I phoned downstairs to complain, but the man at the desk said, 'What can I do?' I could visualize the shrug of his shoulders at the other end.

Prague is famous for its lack of hotel rooms. We had been told by several people that only a fool would go there without a confirmed reservation. The next morning two fools slung their bags in a car and headed down the road to the capital.

Prague had been a market town until 1355 when its ruler, Charles IV, was made Holy Roman Emperor and it became the foremost city in Europe. A golden age of Gothic construction followed. A few centuries later, under the Habsburg dynasty, a second period of baroque building took place. The city escaped almost unscathed from the Second World War and modern development has been severely controlled. The result is a city of breathtaking beauty, with hundreds of years of magnificent architecture, flourishing parks and public squares, 'The prettiest gem in the stone crown of the world', as Goethe wrote after his visit. Like Rome, it is built on seven hills. The Moldau river curves gracefully at their feet, spanned by sixteen bridges.

We made our way to all the hotels in or near the centre and found that, even with our newly acquired skill of offering bribes, they really were fully booked, with no last minute cancellations. One hotel advised us to go to the Cedok tourist office and more or less throw ourselves on their mercy. This we decided to do. There was an eerie lack of traffic on the streets, which I found strange for a Monday morning. The next day was 1 May, a national holiday, and I realized the Czechoslovaks must be taking the day off, making what the Spaniards call a *puente*, a bridge over the Monday, to make a four day break. We found the office and it was closed.

We were standing in the street wondering what to do next, when I noticed a tall, broad-shouldered man hurrying towards us, his reddish hair bright in the sun. He, too, was surprised to find the Cedok office in darkness. Then he noticed us.

'Are you, perhaps, seeking a room?' he asked, hesitantly.

'Why?' I answered.

'Because I have a room in my house. Very nice. Not far. I come to tell the people here, but . . .'

All restrictions on tourists staying in private homes had been lifted the previous month and people were trying to earn extra cash by renting accommodation.

'Does it have a bathroom?' I inquired.

'Oh, yes.'

'Is it big?'

'Oh, yes.'

I was stalling for time while I decided whether to accept his offer or not. He looked like a decent person. Clifford had remained silent.

'There is space for your car, also, behind the house. It will be safe.'

That did it. He climbed into the back seat and directed us through the silent streets. It seemed pointless to ask about the price until we had seen it.

His name was Otkar Mach and his English was good. He told us that he and his wife, Sylvie, often rented to foreigners and added brightly that the week before they had had a Polish dentist and his wife. Clifford and I exchanged glances. We were not impressed.

After several minutes he told us to turn into a narrow driveway between two dusty buildings. His apartment was on the ground floor of the one on the right. Things did not look favourable. Now we would have to go through the motions of inspecting the room, and telling him we would not take it, without hurting his feelings.

The door was opened by an athletic woman of about thirty-five, her brown hair combed back from her face to form a crown of short curls. Her husband spoke to her rapidly in Czech and she greeted us in English.

'Please come in and let me show you the room. Perhaps you will not like it. Or maybe you will need time to decide. Follow me, please.'

She was making it easy for us.

They both looked as if their favourite pastime was mountain climbing, and, later, I found that it was. Two little girls, their hair in pigtails, peeked at us from a doorway.

We followed Sylvie through the living room. I noticed that everything was spotlessly clean, although the furnishings were sparse. A brown unyielding sofa was guarded by two matching chairs. One wall was covered by shelves that were packed with books. I trust people who read books.

By the time she threw open the door to 'the room', I was not surprised to find that it was really quite satisfactory, which was fortunate as we had no other option. There were two beds, each with the usual duvet and big square pillow covered in snowy white cases. A painting of a mountain range, jagged peaks silhouetted against an impossibly blue sky, hung on a wall. A pile of towels was neatly folded on a cabinet in the tiny bathroom. She showed us another door that led directly to the street and a place where we could park the car. It cost $25 (£15) a day, breakfast included.

'We'll take it,' I said.

## Clifford

A great festive swarm of young people with banners and placards spilled across the road at the top of Wenceslas Square and we found we were trapped in the middle of a vociferous but peaceful demonstration. They were students occupying the streets of Prague to demand that the Old Guard Communists hand back the money secreted away in Switzerland.

It was May Day: chaos and colour; fireworks fizzed across the sky. Rock bands and orchestras floated above the multitudes on wooden stages, their music running into each other like rivers to the sea. A girl kissed me on both cheeks and then did the same to Iris. She was wearing a tie-dye T-shirt in red, white and blue, the national colours. On a metal electricity box someone had sprayed: 'It's Over! Czechs are Free!'

It was in English, a message to sum up the mood, the emotion, the relief. There were no hooligans; no drunks. No one was arguing or throwing their fists around. The crowds mobbed the main thoroughfare and all the small roads that meander their way between Wenceslas Square and the Old Town Square, an open arena that was filled with antique churches, chiming clocks and another stage with another rock band. The raised arms of towers, turrets and spires could be seen above buildings with pastel façades, rococo swirls and leaded windows gilded by the spring sunshine. It seemed as if a war had just ended, and perhaps it had.

Students are a good source of English and we asked one couple if there were to be any parades that day. 'No, not this year,' we were told. The speaker had a romantic beard, shoulder-length hair and sensitive features composed in a look of absolute triumph. He was with a skinny girl, all in black. 'Are you happy about what is happening in Czechoslovakia?' I asked her. 'So happy,' she said simply.

In East Germany, I had constantly had the feeling that we were trespassers at a private party. In Prague, it was different. I felt welcome. The whole world was welcome and appeared to have turned up.

Grandmas with polished, pre-war shoes strolled by on the arms of handsome grandsons. Girls, just like their mothers in 1968, were wearing micro-short mini-skirts that clung to their slender figures. We had left the avoirdupois behind in Poland. The Czechoslovaks are a cocktail of Celts and Saxons with a pinch of Slavic exotica: high cheek bones, almond eyes, tiny noses. Almost everyone looked like a *Vogue* model. A young man disguised behind a death mask and carrying a hammer and sickle led a group of suitably attired companions, each bearing a different effigy of the various former leaders. The last carried a decapitated Stalin.

A bobbing, bouncing procession of Maharishi devotees in saffron robes played tablas and cymbals as they chanted '*Hari Krishna . . . Hari Rama . . . Hari Hari . . .*' – all so reminiscent of the peace rallies and love-ins and happenings of the sixties, and yet there was something more exhilarating in Prague that morning, something profound and potent. Freedom had taken a long time coming to Czechoslovakia. The Velvet Revolution had only begun in November, a tumbling domino in the pattern that was sweeping Marxism from Europe. The people who remembered 1968 must have been afraid that the changes were temporary and that any moment the Russian tanks would arrive in the capital. By spring the revolution had gone too far. The changes were forever.

Below the mounted statue of King Wenceslas, there was a circle of raised stones that held the rippled mountains of thousands of spent candles. Fresh candles were burning. It was a tribute to Jan Palach. There was now a Jan

Palach Square in Prague, replacing what for four decades had been Red Army Square. Many of the street names were going through a fresh metamorphosis. The Czechoslovak writer, Milan Kundera, once described a character who was born at one address, grew up at another, and married at a third. 'All the time it was at the same street,' he wrote. 'They just kept changing its name, trying to lobotomize it.'

Now the changes were for a different reason. The Czechoslovaks were no longer raising memorials to their oppressors but to their emancipation. There was a Square of the Soviet Tank Drivers, soon to be renamed; although, the November 7th Street required only a little tinkering with the date. It had commemorated the Bolshevik Revolution of 7 November 1917; it could now mark the Velvet Revolution of 17 November 1989. Some enterprising subway travellers had that week pasted the name Forum Station over Gottwaldova Station – Klement Gottwald had been the founder of Communism in Czechoslovakia.

At the Jan Palach memorial, I saw an older woman and a younger woman both openly crying. Immediately next to them, another group of students were collecting signatures for a protest demanding the arrest of the old Party hierarchy and a hastening of social and economic improvements. There were protests everywhere.

There were countless posters for Civic Forum and portraits of the president were omnipresent, like those of John Paul II in Poland. I saw an old man, bent over a walking stick, wearing a pin with Havel's photograph and the sight was strangely moving. I wanted to wear a badge myself. There were posters for a candidate representing the new party sprung from the loins of the defunct Communist Party. On every one the blue eyes of the good-looking man had been drawn over with swastikas. Czechoslovak Communism was really just Fascism, Otkar Mach had said in the car the previous day.

The cafés were full, the ice-cream stands had long queues and the people were content just walking in the May Day sunshine doing absolutely nothing. They did not want to see parades of tanks. They did not want to hear tributes to their leaders. They did not want to hear how much the state was doing for them.

With the *Hari Krishna* singers moving on down the long narrow square and the approaching sound of a screeching guitar that seemed to recall Pink Floyd's *The Wall*, attention suddenly shifted to a snaking file of people all carrying blue and white banners with the words 'Eurotrain 90' on them. Two hundred students from all over Europe, including the Soviet Union, had set out from Brussels to tour a dozen European capitals with the message 'One train, one youth, one Europe, one future', we learned.

Our informant was a pretty dark girl with the sweet voice of Walt Disney's

Snow White. She told me about the trip and, when I asked her where she was from, her features wrinkled with that admonishing look the young have for those unable to see the light so clearly visible to their own eyes. 'Europe,' she answered, and I felt suitably chastised.

Apart from the banners, flags, posters, the students dressed in mocking parodies of past luminaries, there had also been a scattered explosion in Czechoslovak fashion. It was totally eclectic: punks with spiky hair, red and green, gold and blue, like parrots; hippies in garish bell-bottoms; yuppies with button-down shirts; the *Krishna* girls in saris. We managed to obtain a seat at a pavement café and the waiter was the spitting image of Elvis Presley, all the way from the heroic quiff to the pointed-toed shoes. We ate gritty ice-cream and bought the first edition of a new democracy paper, and then another that lampooned the former organ of the Communist Party, in Czech, which we were unable to read, although it gave us a chance to talk to the people selling it. Everyone wanted to talk to us. We were guests, after all.

A punk in military fatigues with a stuffed goose strapped to his back goose-stepped by and all the people in the café stood and cheered. Goose, *husa* in Czech, is the root of the name Husak, the disgraced 'realist'.

'He cost us twenty-one lost years,' the newspaper-seller said and he spat on the ground. Dr Husak, he explained, had been awarded the Order of Lenin, Russia's highest honour, by Leonid Brezhnev, after clearing demonstrators from Prague with armed riot police on the first anniversary of the Red Army invasion. 'We hate him. We hate all of them,' said our friend, spitting once more. 'Our president wants to forgive them, but I think in this he is wrong. We must arrest them, put them on trial and then put them all in jail.'

Our rest break at the café was interrupted by the occasional sly hiss of a money-changer, which seemed out of place, but was a useful reminder that for all the festivity, corruption and dishonesty, the crutches of Communism, remained a way of life. After almost getting cheated changing money officially at the frontier and again when buying a map in Hradec Králové, at a garage on the way to Prague I had been robbed by a master. After filling the tank, I had been informed that foreigners had to pay with petrol coupons – contrary to what I had been told at the border. The attendant had taken my passport 'to check the visa' and had then proceeded to lock it away in a drawer. He had told me that I would have to go back to the border and purchase the coupons with hard currency. He had been straight-faced, a poker player. I had offered to pay in dollars. I had then offered to pay double, writing the figure down on a scrap of paper to make it clear. The man had crossed the figure out and doubled it again. 'It is your problem,' he had said in English. I had had four options: Return to the border (without my passport); go to the police (pointless); go to my embassy (pointless); or pay up. I had paid up. 'Now it is my problem,' the man had said and had handed me my passport.

Between the songs being performed by the rock band there were speeches. Suddenly, we heard English being spoken over the microphone and went to investigate. On the stage was the American civil rights activist Allen Ginsberg. He had been crowned 'king' of the students' May festival in Prague twenty-five years earlier and, sent packing by the Communists, this was the first time he had returned to the city.

He warned the silent crowd that filled the square against blind imitation of the West as Czechoslovakia returned to democracy. 'The way of American capitalism is not the only way,' Ginsberg said. 'No-hope Communism, no-hope capitalism – everyone's lying on both sides. There is another way, the third way, and that is ecology, green and muscle power, and maybe meditation.'

He threw up his arms and the applause was long and enthusiastic. The Maharishi followers had quietly listened and now, with cymbals ringing and the tablas drumming the same bright familiar rhythm, they began dancing in procession back through the press of people towards Wenceslas Square.

## Iris

Following the giant party that had been May Day, we spent the next few days in a frenzy of sightseeing, setting out each morning on foot to explore as much of the city as we could, walking until our legs ached. Spring had finally arrived. It was warm and sunny. Everyone seemed unusually happy and Prague shone like a worn coin under a clear blue sky. The city had been called the golden heart of Europe and for good reason – in addition to the warm, champagne-coloured stone, many buildings and churches are literally trimmed with gold.

We started our exploration in Wenceslas Square, the centre of modern Prague and not so much a square as a broad boulevard, lined with trees and venerable hotels. One of the main attractions is the Old Town Square and the neo-Gothic Town Hall, which contains one of the finest outdoor astronomical clocks in the world. Every hour wooden statues of Christ and the apostles act out a miniature pantomime, and we joined the crowd below to watch. They show themselves at two little windows above the clock and then withdraw as a skeleton, the figure of Death, tolls the hour. Judas Iscariot is always left outside as a punishment for his betrayal. We saw the clock strike twelve noon and then entered the fourteenth-century tower and climbed the many flights of stairs to the roof, from where we had a panoramic view of the city.

At the other end of the square is the Tyn Church, begun in 1380 by German merchants, and the most enchanting church I had ever seen. The original Gothic steeples soar to the sky, but they are enchanced by a ring of mini spires, each crowned with a golden ball, which were added a few centuries later.

We walked across Svermuv Bridge and climbed through the wooded park that encircles Hradcany, a complex of Gothic and baroque palaces and churches that dominates one of the seven hills above the Moldau. As we approached, it seemed to draw away from us, so that for a while, we appeared not to get any closer. Eventually, the optical illusion gave way and we passed through an arch where two guards stood ceremoniously to attention. The main palace is still the centre of political power and official residence of the president.

I remembered reading that Vaclav Havel had said that one of the best things about being president was that he could redesign the uniforms of the palace guard, and I wondered if the smart livery – a blue jacket, grey trousers, white gloves and a scattering of brass buttons and gold braid – was his work.

At the end of a long afternoon, we sought out the house where Franz Kafka was born, in the narrow cul-de-sac of Golden Alley, below the fortress walls. It was this castle that he had in mind when he wrote *The Castle*, the story of a man who travels from another part of an unnamed country to take a position at the castle and who, upon arriving, is neither expected nor made welcome.

Another morning we struck out across the river towards Mala Strana (Lesser Town) to see the parks and palaces of the old nobility. We crossed the Charles Bridge, commissioned in 1357 by the industrious Charles IV, and the only bridge in Prague until 1841. It has always been lovingly maintained and for some time has only been open to foot traffic. Mala Strana contains foreign embassies, museums and administrative offices, although it is also popular with students, artists and writers, who live in the crumbling back streets. Groups of young painters were selling their work on the bridge. We stopped to look at the display of one hungry-looking man and bought a pair of street scenes. His eyes lit up. 'Thank you very much. Thank you very much,' he said when I paid him. 'It is difficult to be an artist in Czechoslovakia.'

'It's the same everywhere,' I told him.

'You know, Van Gogh never sold a painting in his lifetime, and now they sell for millions and millions of korunas.'

I did not have the heart to tell him that now they sold for millions and millions of dollars.

That night we returned to the Mach house, wilting with fatigue, at midnight. They were still up, took one look at us, and said that what we needed was a glass of slivovice. Otkar went to get glasses while we waited on the uncompromising chairs.

'How do you like Prague?' asked Sylvie, pouring the plum brandy.

'We love it,' I replied. 'You are lucky to live in such a beautiful city.'
She smiled thinly.

'Maybe not so lucky,' answered Otkar. 'The city is beautiful, yes, but life is difficult. The harder we work, the less we have. Before, I could support Sylvie and the girls, but now, she must work or we have a hard time.' He frowned.

'What work do you do, Otkar?' Clifford asked.

'I am a history teacher. I teach boys and girls from fourteen to sixteen years.'

'Do you like it?'

'No, I hate it. You would not believe the history I must teach. If I complained, I would have no job. But now, finally, since the beginning of this year, I can be honest.'

'Oh, Otkar.' I did not know what else to say, as I visualized him spending years of his life teaching what he knew to be a lie.

'For me, it is easier,' said Sylvie, refilling my glass. 'I work in a bank. All day I sell petrol coupons to foreigners. It is a stupid job. Soon, I think, it will exist no more.'

I hoped so. That day we had waited half an hour at a bank before we could purchase a supply of coupons.

'Sylvie is clever,' said Otkar, putting his hand on her shoulder. 'It was her idea to rent the room. We moved the girls into a corner of the kitchen, and we make a little extra.'

'Shhh, Otkar. You tell too much,' his wife said reproachfully.

So that was it. We were in their daughters' room.

'They are young,' said Sylvie. 'They don't need so much space. Anyway, we do it for them. We must save money. We would like to open a restaurant.'

'I cook, you see,' explained Otkar. 'It is my hobby. I have enough of teaching, and now Sylvie and I want to have our own business.'

'He is a good cook,' said Sylvie. 'You would not believe the *svickova* he makes.'

'What is that?' I asked.

'I will make for you,' Otkar said. 'Tomorrow. Your last night here. You will be our guests. Please, I will be honoured.'

When we arrived back at the house on our last day, I knew from the tantalizing aroma drifting into our room that we were going to have a memorable culinary experience. Promptly at eight o'clock we presented ourselves in their living room.

While we waited for Otkar to put the finishing touches to the feast, we sipped a local wine and nibbled on a plate of hors-d'oeuvres – thin slices of *przska sunka*, smoked Prague ham, wrapped around miniature gherkins.

I was interested in the role of women in Czechoslovakia and remarked to

Sylvie, when Otkar was in the kitchen, how nice it was that men and women shared the household tasks. She made a face and said that it was not usually so. Even if a woman worked, she was still expected to do all the domestic chores and care for the children in the traditional way. There were many divorces and single women raising children on their own. 'Otkar is special,' she said, and I did not doubt her for a moment.

Otkar appeared with an apron folded over his arm and announced that all was ready, and we seated ourselves around the kitchen table. The little girls were asleep in their parents' room.

We began with a clear soup that had small pastry dumplings floating on top. The *svickova* turned out to be pieces of beef with spices and vegetables, braised in the oven and served with a cream sauce. It was sensational. We finished with pancakes stuffed with fruit and soaked in chocolate sauce. Later, over a tiny glass of the whisky which we had brought them, Clifford toasted the chef and wished them both luck with the restaurant.

I asked Otkar where he wanted to open his restaurant and he looked momentarily confused. 'Wherever the authorities decide, I suppose,' he replied.

'But now you are free to decide yourself,' I said.

He laughed once again. 'Yes, it is true. But it takes a long time to get used to it. We were both born after the war. We have only ever known Communism.'

## Clifford

The porter at the Grand Hotel Pupp had a bandage around his head and one arm in a sling. He led the way along the high-ceilinged corridors talking non-stop as I carried the bags. He told me in a confidential tone that he was King Karel of Bohemia, a direct descendant of Charles IV, the Holy Roman Emperor, and that he would soon be going to the capital to claim his throne. 'I have little faith in democracy,' he remarked. 'What we need is strong leadership.'

The king spoke English with an impeccable French accent. His blue uniform was a polyglot of stains that had probably been issued the last time the room he showed us into had been decorated. He led the way to the bathroom. '*Très elegant*,' he said, waving his good arm through the air. The bath was as large as a rowing boat and there must have been half a ton of brass and copper tubing like spaghetti circling the walls. The monarch winked and leaned close to whisper, 'It is made for a couple.' I gave him a princely two dollars and he left with a bow.

The bath fit for a king was rust-stained. The towels were plentiful and worn out, like the town outside. We had driven through the Böhmerwald, the

Bohemian forest, to Carlsbad, the spa of the courted and kingly – Bismarck and Metternich came here to intrigue; Beethoven, Paganini, Brahms and Liszt were inspired walking in the hills; Schiller, Tolstoy, Peter the Great, Karl Marx and Yuri Gagarin – all came to sip the mineral water and tread the ornamented boulevards, cracked now and grubby, like the *belle époque* hotels, and yet retaining a certain quality, as you can see the beautiful girl in the features of an older woman.

Throngs of people, mainly elderly, a few German and Austrian tourists among the Czechs, strolled along clutching porcelain cups made with a spout in the handle and filled with the elixir that has made the spa the most famous in the world. The vistors taking the cure drank continually as they walked along, while they were talking or sitting on the public benches, or eating pastries at the outdoor cafés.

We bought two cups and joined the parade, filling up at one of the public fonts below a long row of arches that drew the eye into infinity like the paintings of de Chirico. 'You can add a little something,' the man next to me said in German, opening his jacket to reveal a flat silver flask. He had a round stomach and a red round nose. I asked him if it were his first trip to the spa and he told me he had been coming every year for twenty-five years. 'To clean the liver,' he added.

We wandered back through the arches to the Museum Karla Marxe and learned that Marx, always chronically ill, had taken a rest cure in Carlsbad on three occasions, the last being in 1876. The museum, functional and falling apart, was deserted and I could not help but wonder how long it would be before it was closed down and reopened as the Museum of the Velvet Revolution.

Still clutching our cups, we walked on the high banks of the River Tepla on the Yuri Gagarin Colonnade. A statue of the cosmonaut, 10 feet high and in black stone, shows mankind's first man in space peering into the heavens, a glazed look about his smooth features. He twice visited the spa, in 1961 and 1966.

Behind the statue, a messy outbreak of glass and steel, a rare intrusion on the town's pretty architecture, houses the great jet of steaming thermal water that gushes from a mineral spring a mile underground. The spa was discovered, inevitably, by the busy Charles IV, or rather, by his dog. While the monarch was out one day hunting stag, the animal vanished with a hissing yelp and, when the king found it, the dog had been cooked in a boiling spring. The king ordered the first baths to be built in the village of Vary in 1358 and the town that came into existence was regally renamed Karlovy Vary – Carlsbad. Nearby is Marienbad – Mariánské Lázne – another spa that developed in the second half of the nineteenth century and, smaller and perhaps more refined than Carlsbad, was favoured by the elderly Goethe who while on one vacation

worked on his epic poem the 'Marienbader Elegie', which he wrote for the
young beauty Ulrika von Levotzow.

Inside the glasshouse, we discovered that the water appears from the ground
at a steady 72 degrees Fahrenheit, 10 gallons a second, shooting almost 40 feet
into the air.

The waiter in the beer hall that night had the rare distinction of appearing
genuinely to care about the comforts of his customers. All in black, he moved
among the tables with the ease of a leopard, a round silver tray held aloft as if
he were performing a cabaret act. I asked him if he approved of the changes in
Czechoslovakia and, drawing a breath, he replied with a little shake of the
head. 'Too slow, much, much too slow,' he said. He put two drinks down in
front of us. 'We have an old director here . . . all the directors are old and they
do not want any changes at all.'

Iris told him he should open his own restaurant and, closing his eyes, raising
his shoulders in an exaggerated shrug, he drew another long breath. 'I want to.
I have a friend and we want to have a place together. They offered us an old
castle, just out of town, but we must repair it and then lease it from the state,'
he said. 'We do all the work – they take all the money!'

He disappeared and then hurried back to our table. 'The Red Men are still in
power. It is still not safe for me here,' he said. 'It would be better if my friend
and I could leave and go to another country.'

'But now you can,' Iris remarked.

The waiter winced and his thin body seemed to contract and become even
thinner. 'There are so many papers, so many forms. It is not so easy,' he told
her. 'And, if we go away, we cannot come back.'

'Why?'

'They will make it difficult for us. They do not like people who want to live
abroad,' he answered. 'We must be careful.'

He left for the kitchen and returned with our meal: two enormous bowls of
boiled pork and dumplings, and two more beers that soon became another
two. The Bohemians call their beer *nas chleb*, our bread, and it is almost totally
different from the insipid lagers we see truckers quaffing in our television
commercials. It is golden, rich with natural ingredients, brewed with spring
water and, when you have had enough, you take one more to guarantee the
famous Czechoslovak hangover. For some it is a meal in itself, and it occurred
to me that the ancients taking the mineral cure might have been better off with
a daily glass of Budvar.

Like Prague, Carlsbad is impossibly beautiful. The hills roll away from the
winding course of the river like green sand dunes. Long walks follow paths

that give the peculiar feeling of descending, even while you are climbing; and, plunging through lush masses of trees, branches and thornscrub, you could almost be swimming underwater in a tropical sea. The trees appear to be in good shape, which is something of an irony considering half the Böhmerwald has been destroyed in the last decade by acid rain, which, like desertification, will reach out and claim the spa towns if nothing is done to control pollution.

Czechoslovakia is a fairyland kingdom with its castles, blue lakes and mature forests. What the country needs is a good Madison Avenue advertising agency to start selling it as a major, or *the* major, tourist destination in Europe. It has the potential. England, Germany, Austria and Hungary have their castles; Italy has its palaces and Roman ruins; Spain the corrida and Greece the Acropolis. But they all pale beside the gilded, crenellated, spire-infested, pastel-hued strongholds that rise above every dominant peak in Czechoslovakia. The towers and turrets appear in the distance like soaring sculptures and, winding slowly up the unmade roads to the fortress walls, what always greeted us was an agreeable surprise: silence; no tourists, no parties of schoolchildren. Perhaps a deep moat filled with ancient carp, a drawbridge that led to a pair of studded oak doors and a door-keeper like some forgotten relic who pointed out the iron spikes on the raised portcullis before taking us on a conducted tour of his empty domain. On one mountain top half-way between Carlsbad and Prague, a hobbling man with masses of white hair, plus-fours and knee boots told us the history of Czechoslovakia from the time of the Celts and, when I asked him how long he had been there, he replied with a fey smile, 'Forever.'

It was the last castle we saw that day. We were becoming blasé; there were so many of them and, as we drew closer to Plzen, our attention shifted from medieval architecture to the grey-yellow pallor that clung to the sky. The hill villages, as gorgeous as theatrical sets, as remarkable as the castles, retreat into slovenly agglomerations of asbestos and pre-cast concrete, the rows of mean windows like pages of postage stamps making the sole difference between the apartment blocks and the factories. Every breath tastes rancid. There is a stillness, a closeness, something that makes the hairs on the back of the neck stand up. The hill people are jolly and the workers on the plains are so sullen and unkind, they seem like a different race. In East Germany, pollution had been noticeably bad; in Poland it had been bad. In Czechoslovakia, it was worse. The steel, glass, porcelain and chemical works pump out toxic poisons that, untreated and uncontrolled, gather in clouds that hang motionless above the rooftops until the rain brings all the waste back down again. There are no sea coasts, no sea breezes, no outlets; just high mountains that chill the air and hold the gases like a saucepan lid over the entire country. We walked in the forests and, outside every large town, the shrubbery looked forlorn and the trees were dying, the branches lifeless, the leaves malformed and punctured as if attacked by parasites, the softwood evergreens more blighted than the deciduous hardwoods.

It is clearly Civic Forum's intention to put checks on pollution and adapt the nation's entire economic structure. But it is not going to be easy. Not one of the 5-year agricultural plans introduced by the Communists reached the projected target and, with 96 per cent of the land collectivized, even with modern farming methods, incredibly, production levels have remained lower than in the years before the war. True to Stalin's vision, the economy has been rooted in heavy industry, with almost half Czechoslovakia's foreign exchange earnings coming from the arms trade. Present customers include Libya, buying 150 tanks a year; Ethiopia, while suffering constant famine, pays $1.9 million (£1.13 million) each for all the L-39 jets it can get; China takes more tanks; and assault rifles, hand-grenades and small arms are shipped to Angola, South Yemen, the Congo, Abu Nidal's Fatah Revolutionary Council, the Italian Red Brigades, the Irish Republican Army and the Palestinian Liberation Organization.

Before the Velvet Revolution swept Dr Husak from power, there were guerilla training camps all over the country and so many clandestine arms dealers in Prague, the élite unit of Red Berets spent much of its time guarding hostile factions from each other. They all stayed at the same Communist Party hotel, closed now, although, while the United States and the USSR continue to reduce their arsenals, Czechoslovakia is locked into a web of contracts that ensures the steady production of weaponry for the foreseeable future.

## Iris

We left Carlsbad without any specific destination in mind, knowing only that we wanted to see as much of the country as possible in the next few days. Czechoslovakia is a wanderer's paradise, rich in history and natural beauty. Southern Moravia alone has over seven thousand protected monuments and another eleven thousand cultural relics, and the other nine regions are equally endowed.

Towards evening we arrived in Piešt'any, north-east of Bratislava. In the distance, the green foothills of the Tatras, dappled with forests and farms, rose to the horizon. Although Piešt'any is the most popular spa in Slovakia, it was never on the international circuit like Carlsbad and Marienbad, and the small commercial centre was modern, dusty, and not particularly attractive. The best thing about the town, I decided, was that there was very little to do and nothing to see; no castle to be explored, no ancient cathedral to be checked out. It was a good place to rest for a couple of days.

The second best thing was the spa itself, situated on a long, narrow island covered with mature trees in the middle of the river. Clusters of hotels, sanatoriums and treatment centres, modern and nineteenth-century, were linked by tree-lined roads. We walked over a footbridge to the island. Along one side there were small shops selling souvenirs, mostly embroidered blouses and tablecloths. A plaque at one end announced that the bridge had been destroyed by the 'Fascist Army' and rebuilt in 1956 'for the benefit and health of the working-class'.

All the patrons of the spa, riding bicycles on the traffic free roads, strolling on the river bank, or just sitting on the park benches, looked old, poor and contented. One had a momentary vision of what Communism could have been – working people enjoying a yearly vacation at a spa, indulging in mud baths, water treatments, rest and exercise.

We sat on a bench, too, and it was not long before an elderly woman, her neck wrinkled like an armadillo and her silvery blond hair in tight little curls, stopped, scrutinized us for several seconds, and then posed the guess, 'American?'

'Half and half,' I replied. 'He's English, I'm American.'

'I can always tell, although I don't see many nowadays.' She spoke in perfect, German-accented English. She informed us that she was eighty-three and a baroness, 'a long time ago. They took everything. Our land, houses, everything.'

'Will they give the people back their property?' asked Clifford.

The woman shrugged. Her eyes were old, pale blue and with a twinkle in them still. 'My mother used to say that it was easier to give than to take. She was wrong.' She laughed. 'Anyway, what would I do with it now?' Abruptly, she said goodbye to us and continued her promenade along the avenue of silver birch trees.

## Clifford

There was an orange, battery-run plastic clock on the wall in the bath-house at the Irma Palace, this token of modernity being the only change that appeared to have taken place this century. The original timepiece, set between two high Gothic arches, had stuck at ten to two, the metal face growing liverish with rust, the curvaceous iron arms that had once danced in a circle of Roman numerals in a motionless state of permanent surrender.

The bath was an oval-shaped pool dissected by a wall of white tiles that divided the sexes. The pool was very hot, hotter than bath hot, and was continually topped up through copper pipes that fed a trio of bronze satyrs. They had horns, small beards and features that could have been designed by

Hieronymus Bosch, their lascivious grins gushing out the steaming water which comes from deep in the earth's core and contains natural chemicals and sulphur.

I lay back, completely still, and watched the antics of my companions. Old men become as little boys when they have no clothes on, and when one of the bathers discovered a way to trap air in his palms and, using the vacuum, to shoot sprays of water over the wall, the others were quick to join in. They were rewarded by the delighted squeals of the women on the other side. Iris was not among them.

Gradually turning lobsterish with the heat, it was exactly fifteen minutes later, according to the orange clock, when, fully cooked, one of the attendants hauled me out and sent me naked along the corridor to the massage rooms. The ceiling rose in a steep rounded arch; grotesques leered at me through the gloom, gnomes and gargoyles that perched on columns and hid themselves in dark recesses. At the end of the corridor, I entered the massage parlour, which was lined in walnut, each cubicle inside being large, marble-floored and marked by a pair of sculptured pineapples.

A man in white appeared looking like a sumo wrestler, very fat, very serious and holding in outstretched arms a linen sheet of great quality and age. He wrapped me in the sheet, then in a thick, ivory-coloured blanket and, my arms pinned to my sides, lifted me on to the leather-topped bench where I was left for another fifteen minutes.

I was warm and immobile like a grub in a silky cocoon. I stared up at the vapour swirls above my head, my reverie interrupted every few minutes by the same man who came to exchange the same piece of dialogue.

'Hot, *ya, gut?*'

'*Ya, gut,* hot.'

The massage followed. I was first covered in an off-white jelly that smelled of mayonnaise, and then manhandled like a carcass of dead meat in an abattoir. The fat wrestler turned me one way, then the other, thumping my calves, thighs, lower back, spine, shoulders, arms and neck. '*Nervoizh,*' he kept saying, and I mumbled the reply, 'Not before I came in here' in English, which he did not understand.

Another man materialized briefly in the steam. 'Hot, *ya, gut?*' he said.

'*Ya, gut,* hot,' I answered. I decided to sign up for German lessons the moment I arrived back in England.

The beating continued. I was about to scream for mercy but as the thought passed through my mind it was over and, still stark naked, I was sent to the shower room. I felt dazed, and it was all but impossible to wash off the massage cream. The soap was as hard as a brick and no amount of rubbing raised a lather. I gave up, dried and dressed myself. The muscles in my neck were killing me.

The burly masseur was waiting outside, a smile, of mockery I thought, lifting the corners of his mouth, his palms resting on the bulging lip of flesh that spilled over his belt. I gave him 5 Marks and he crushed my hand shaking it. '*Velmi dekuji*,' he said.

'No, thank you,' I replied.

I left through a door different from the one through which I had entered and found myself in a long corridor filled with bent old people waiting on benches or wandering along the black and white checked floor like lost chess pieces. No one spoke. They all carried forms, a preoccupation in Czechoslovakia – my passport details had been entered into a giant dusty ledger before I had been allowed to take the treatment.

The corridor turned into another corridor just as long and, as I passed the old people, I had the feeling that they must have been there forever, growing old with the building. When I eventually reached the main doors, they were locked. For just a second I considered smashing a window and leaping out, an urge I somehow managed to control. It was lunchtime and everything closed for lunch in Czechoslovakia, even some of the restaurants. I found an old woman cleaning the floors with a filthy mop and, reluctantly, she produced a bunch of keys and set me free.

## Iris

Clifford flung himself down beside me on the grass and groaned.

'What happened? You look awful.'

'I didn't know the correct word for "mud". I was boiled and beaten. I'm lucky to be alive.'

We bought tickets for a cruise on the Vah River. I thought a sea voyage, or the closest thing to it, would hasten his recovery. A handful of us were scattered over the upper deck, about to leave the shore, when at the last minute about a hundred more people came thundering down the gangplank. It was an interesting crowd – workers and their families holidaying in the spa town and dressed in their Sunday best. Most of the Slovak women wore colourful peasant clothes and had their heads covered with a scarf that looked like a nun's wimple. The dresses were tightly-bodiced and had waists embroidered with flowers. The dirndl skirts and aprons were remarkably short, ending just above the knee and usually revealing thick, elephantine legs.

We all sat on the open top deck in two neat rows. Recorded music filled the gaps between the commentary of a female tour guide, who spoke only in Slovak. I was struck by how quiet everyone was, like obedient children in church. Most were couples and many knew each other, judging by the photographs they took with old-fashioned box cameras. Still, their passive enjoyment was impressive.

The boat trip lasted a couple of hours. There was not much to see and even the bucolic scenery was ruined by eight large cooling towers that loomed in the distance like a gang of bullies. After getting close enough to sample the foul air, the boat clumsily turned around.

The dining room in our hotel was surprisingly elegant, and even more surprisingly, most of the patrons were Arabs. At first I could not work out the connection. Why here, in a spa village buried in the hills? But then, why not? Various Arab countries had had their flirtations with Communism and Czechoslovakia was a major supplier of arms to nations that, for political reasons, were unable to buy from the West.

The waiters wore immaculate dinner-jackets; the food coming out of the kitchen was arranged on silver trays – an example of Communism's double standards on display once again. Clifford ordered a Pilsner Urquell.

'I am sorry. We have no Pilsner. Only Topvar,' said the waiter.

'Is it Czech?'

'No. It is Slovak.'

I asked for a bottle of white wine. The waiter recommended one. 'Is it Czech?' I ventured.

'No. Slovak.'

He disappeared and we never saw him again. The Slovakians, one-third of the country's fifteen million population, are fiercely nationalistic. They had demonstrated in Bratislava, the regional capital, when the Communist name was changed on 23 March to the Czechoslovak Federative Republic. The Civic Forum government had been quick to compromise and, after playing around with the idea of using a hyphen – Czech-Slovak – they had agreed to name the country The Czech and Slovak Federative Republic.

We were served by a series of different waiters and waitresses who, like cells in some secret organization, appeared to have no information about the others.

Our dessert waitress looked like a young Lauren Bacall and wore fantastic gladiator sandals in white kid leather. After bringing us our stewed pears, she vanished, like all the others before her. It was a man with iron-grey, swept back hair who presented us with the bill. I had noticed him earlier. He stood at the door and greeted some clients with obsequious courtesy, and was rude to others. Us, he had ignored.

I remarked to Clifford, who was busy writing in his notebook, that I thought we were the only innocent tourists in the Magnolia Hotel.

'Not that innocent,' he said, snapping shut his book, and pouring the last of the Topvar into a glass.

## Clifford

Getting lost in Trnava had been very straightforward and, at first, not at all unpleasant. The narrow lanes curl away from the centre and each turn seems to progress into the underside of something timeless and remote. The cobbled streets were virtually deserted. A gypsy woman in long skirts stopped to stare at us and then hurried into a doorway. I could hear music in the distance. A man was levering a tyre from a bicycle wheel. Two children in rags emerged from a courtyard and followed along behind us. A horse pulling a cart piled with scrap iron approached and we had to flatten ourselves against a building to avoid being crushed. I think the driver, slumped over and hidden under a trilby, had been asleep.

The labyrinth smelled of urine. It was dark and the hills beyond town were in shadow. Trnava, perhaps the oldest town in Slovakia, nestles among low peaks circled in mist on the rim of the Vah valley. It had once long ago been the cultural and artistic centre of Hungary, after the Turks pillaged Buda and before the shifting frontiers placed it in Czechoslovakia. The cathedral, part mosque and part Saxon chapel, with its brick-red onion domes and stained-glass windows, had served as the Holy See of the Archbishop of Esztergom for three centuries. It stands at the heart of the old quarter with the Church of St Nicholas, built in 1380, and two slightly earlier structures, the medieval hospital and the adjoining Church of St Elizabeth. The University Church of St John the Baptist, the finest example of baroque architecture in the country, contains sensuous, mystical carvings of extraordinary daring and, peering up at the outer façade, so richly scribbled over with stone motifs, it was not difficult to appreciate the psychological conflicts that had inspired the counter-Reformation.

We climbed the steps, bow-shaped with wear, spiralling our way up to the central tower and studied the Slovakian panorama while we panted for breath. The Turkish influence remains evident in the surviving minarets that prickle the pink-tiled rooftops although the bird's eye view destroyed the passing feeling of being close to the roots of history.

Encircling the town like an old city wall are Communism's careless streets of modern housing blocks, blank, featureless cuboids speckled by the polyester flags of the weekend wash. The developments were grey, gaunt and seemed unfinished, an illusion created by the total lack of landscaping, trees and bushes. Environmental groups had been illegal – they were reactionary – and the civic planners had never been told that people are happier and work harder in nice surroundings.

On the horizon, as visible from Trnava as they had been from Pieš´t´any, were the same set of eight giant cooling towers gently puffing white fumes across the sky; and, setting out over the hills in five columns was an endless procession of Eiffel Towers, the steel pylons bearing the high-tension cables that power the factory plants further south in Bratislava.

For some reason that appeared to make no sense at all, while the working population had been jammed into the anthill tower blocks, the buildings in the old quarter with their high ceilings and wrought-iron balconies had been forgotten, and were now neglected ruins, mainly empty, often windowless. Courtyards that must once have rung out with the sound of carriage wheels and horses' hooves overflowed with broken motor cars and rusting heaps of metal junk.

From the recessed doorways children came out to join our entourage. We had begun with two followers. Now there were seven bringing up the rear, although I had the uncomfortable sensation that they were subtly leading the way, drawing us deeper into the labyrinth. I could see the tower rising above the University Church but each turn that I thought would take us closer only took us further away. Then it disappeared.

'We're lost,' Iris remarked.

'At least we're off the beaten track,' I said.

We set off again, turning right, then left and found ourselves in a square of ornate shabby buildings that focused on a dry fountain. A group of men was sitting there without talking. They were gypsies, the same as the children, thin and ragged with the dead expressions of men who spend a lot of time doing nothing. Just waiting. One of the group, a younger man in a shiny blue bomber jacket and tight trousers, approached and spoke to me in German.

'Give me 10 Marks,' he said. He grinned. He had gaps in his teeth and bloodshot eyes. There were five men behind him, all smiling, one very old. The children had spread out around us, scowling malevolently.

'*Zehn Marks*,' the man said again.

'Don't be ridiculous,' I replied in English.

He rubbed his thumb and finger together and his eyes strayed over Iris's green bag with its precious load: cash, passports, car papers.

There was a brief silence, extensive with the whims of fate. The men were quietly amused. The children looked furious. I pushed my hands into my pockets. It was one of those situations where my options were severely limited and, whatever I chose to do, it would almost certainly be the wrong thing. If I gave the gypsy 10 Marks, less than £4, they would all want 10 Marks. And, if I gave then 10, why not 20; a hundred? The man before me stared into my eyes and then glanced once more at the bag as if to say 10 Marks would mean nothing to me. Which, relative to the circumstances, was true.

I was still running through my alternatives when the young gypsy drew the older man forward, pushed up his sleeve and showed me the faded blue tattoo on his lower arm. I could just make out the letter 'G' and an illegible number with six digits. The man had survived one of Hitler's concentration camps. What now was 10 Marks?

'*Ich habe nichts. . .*' I said, tapping my chest with my fingers. '*Nein Deutsch, Americano.*'

The gypsy shook his head dismissively. '*Zehn Marks,*' he repeated.

The children had remained utterly silent. The men sitting on the fountain rim seemed to be enjoying themselves, but passively, too lethargic to join in. I imagined they all had knives. Iris had pulled closer.

Finally, I took two 50-koruna notes from my shirt pocket. I gave one to the old man, who shuffled it away with alacrity. The other I held back. 'My car is next to the big church,' I said, shrugging the question mark.

The gypsy held out his palm. I gave him the note and he fired off some instructions to one of the elder among the children, a boy who led us back through the maze of narrow streets to the large square. The car was parked outside the University Church. I gave the boy 10 koruna. My total outlay had been eight Marks, a compromise.

## Iris

We were seeing parts of Czechoslovakia not seen by Western eyes for decades. Sometimes we strayed so deep into the countryside that we became objects of curiosity. The car came in for a lot of scrutiny. One day at a petrol station while Clifford was checking the oil an enormous group of men assembled to gaze at the complexities of the V-8 engine. One man wanted to know how much the car had cost and Clifford wrote the sum on the dust-covered door – a figure about one-quarter of the real price.

Slovakia had been a part of Hungary for a thousand years and Bratislava its capital for three centuries, until 1830. We arrived there on a Saturday afternoon and, as usual at weekends in Eastern Europe, everything was closed until Monday morning, the shops, banks, services and most of the restaurants. The streets were as quiet as they had been in Trnava and, while it certainly made driving easier, it was like entering a ghost town.

Having found ourselves rooms for that night, we set out to find the Danube, which was not as easy as it sounds. Bratislava had turned its back on the river, unlike Prague, where the Moldau was an integral part of the city. Above us, in the distance, we could see the ninth-century fortress that rests on the highest point on the riverbank, but all the streets leading in that direction were either dead ends or blocked for repairs. Eventually, seeing a bridge between two buildings, we climbed a barrier and picked our way across a construction site until we reached the water's edge. The bridge turned out to be ultra-modern with a single, sloping support pylon on the far side. The Danube flowed steadily by at our feet, indifferent to our efforts.

We walked through the park on the far side of the river, crossed back again on another bridge and wound our way through the cracked tiny streets of the old city. There was scaffolding everywhere and a lot of badly-needed restoration was in progress. The fifteenth-century Michael Tower, all that remains of the original city wall, stands in a cluster of baroque buildings which, though interesting enough in themselves, do not compare with the elegance and stunning beauty of Prague.

An old gypsy woman selling wild flowers in small bunches pressed one on me and, as I parted with a few koruna, she muttered what I hoped was a blessing, not a curse. I was becoming more interested in the gypsies as time went by and realized that almost everything I thought I knew about the people was entirely wrong. In Eastern Europe, they had survived outside the system, contributing nothing to Communism and drawing none of its benefits. They had been nomads for centuries but the iron walls that had marked the frontiers for the past fifty years had kept them in one place. They no longer roamed the countryside in colourful caravans but had settled in the neglected city centres, their poverty turning them into slums. The women often worked on road gangs and as labourers, the children begged, and the men did not appear to do anything at all.

We found a bar that was open and went in for coffee. It was strangely sophisticated with carefully restored art deco mosaics decorating the walls. The tables and chairs were from the same period, sparklingly clean, and I noticed even the customers were unusually well dressed. A television over the bar was broadcasting an official ceremony and lots of men in grey suits were taking a turn and reading speeches to thousands of cheering spectators. We recognized Vaclav Havel, short and smiling under his mop of fair hair. Soon, it was his turn at the microphone but, just as he began, the man cleaning glasses behind the bar turned the set off and pushed a tape into a cassette player. Bohemia had been plastered with photographs of the new president, but they had diminished and eventually vanished as we drove through the eastern and southern parts of the country. He was popular, but he was not Slovak.

The playwright-president, the 'Philosopher-King', as he was described on the cover of *Newsweek* on 30 April, had become my new hero – as he was a hero to most of his countrymen. Before leaving London, we had gone to see the *Vanek Plays* at the Lyric Studio in Hammersmith. They had given me a greater understanding of the way in which the dissidents had suffered and my heart had been stirred by their persistence and courage.

In *Living in Truth*, Havel had explained that on the surface Communism seemed to work: people attended meetings, went along with voting for the single party, cheered at May Day parades – and joined the Party when their ambition overcame their conscience. But the motivation behind every aspect of life was fear. Everyone, from the gypsies at the bottom of the heap to the lesser members of the Politburo at the top, lived with some degree of fear – and, despising the system, there were many who tried to destroy it through apathy, inefficiency and vandalism. Even the red and blue buttons that mark the hot and cold water taps in the hotel rooms were reversed often enough for it to be more than just coincidence. I imagined the small joy there must have been in imagining some out of town Party boss scalding his hands as he washed them.

Czechoslovakia had been the most orthodox of Stalinist states and this had created the greatest extremes: corrupt, dishonest officials in hotels, city halls, on garage forecourts – but balanced by kind, caring, generous people like the Machs, the castle historians and many others who had welcomed us to their towns and villages. In 1975, Havel had written that Communism carried the seeds of its own destruction and that one day it would come apart at the seams. How right he had been.

# Hungary

# Clifford

'Budapest is the one place where you can still make a fortune.'

George Kun was almost well-dressed, very well-mannered and had joined us at a pavement café where we were drinking mint juleps and eating a rare delicacy: a cheese and tomato sandwich. The sun was thrusting shafts of light through the clouds and the breeze was making the umbrella rock back and forth across the table. 'We could almost be in Paris,' Iris remarked and I was certain by the way George so enthusiastically agreed he had never been there. The Danube washed by below the promenade where we were sitting, a wide expanse of soiled dark water lined with ancient monuments and modern hotels. Barges in long files plied a path along the centre of the river and tour boats clung to the banks. A floating casino with garish signs was berthed in the shadow below the Elizabeth Bridge.

George had alighted on us like a man finding a diamond ring. 'I do hope you don't mind?' he had said and, pulling back a chair, his expression was both charming and apologetic. He looked like a young David Niven without a moustache.

'Why, not at all,' said Iris.

'I thought you were American?'

'I am,' she replied and a hint of relief flitted across his features. George introduced himself, gave us a card and said he did most of his business with Americans. 'They are always so quick to grasp things,' he explained. The card described George Kun as a property consultant – he found property and arranged through a lawyer to sell it to foreign clients. Large apartments in the old city could be bought for $30–$40,000 (£17,850– £23,800).

'You must put in a bathroom and new kitchen, but labour is cheap here. Not like New York – or Paris,' he continued. 'There are many builders. It is the one business you can start without a lot of capital.'

'Or expertise,' I suggested.

George turned to smile at Iris. 'The value will double in a year,' he said. 'And if you sell, you can take the money out of the country without any problems. No tax. No exchange controls. Budapest is a gold mine.'

It was more of a gold rush. The city was full of Hungarians returning with their wallets stuffed with American and Canadian dollars. One-third of the nation's fifteen million people had lived in exile and many were coming home to make their fortune. Without bloodshed or fanfare, the Communists those warm spring days were quietly vacating the government offices and passing the keys to the opposition leaders they had once persecuted. Behind them, they were leaving forty years of Marxist bureaucracy and the army of civil servants who had agreed to serve the new masters – with the same dubious competence, one assumes, with which they had served the old.

It was revolution Hungarian style: stealthily. The country had always been out of step with its allies and there appeared to be no hurry to get in step. There was to be no Polish 'big bang' for the economy: no quickie divorce from the Warsaw Pact like Czechoslovakia and the now vanished East Germany. Everything had been assigned, as it always had been, to the imbroglio of countless committees.

Private enterprise had been introduced by the reform-minded Janos Kadar way back in 1968 but, in more than two decades, only 15 per cent of trade had shifted from the confines of the centrally dictated economy. The people had been promised great changes but they were used to waiting. They were still waiting on lists for new refrigerators and waiting in line to buy bananas – although, at least there were bananas in the shops to buy. All those prodigal sons disembarking with ideas to turn a quick buck were at liberty to go into business but permission, papers and probably profits were at the far end of a broad expanse of administrative quicksand.

We left the café and George wandered with us along the waterfront. He proudly announced the names of all the new hotels as we approached them and pointed at the view they had across the Danube to Buda with a proprietorial air. We saw BMWs and Mercedes with Hungarian registration plates. 'Now we have our millionaires, too,' he said in the soft, reverent tones deserving of saints. We passed an old man, who looked like a war hero, playing a steel zither. I gave him some change and George peered at me over his shoulder with total incomprehension.

Vehicles were banned from the old town centre. The narrow lanes had only recently been resurfaced, the red and grey paving stones patterned with raised flower beds and wooden benches occupied by gypsy women hawking peasant blouses, woodcarvings, knitted sweaters and seed necklaces. The buildings had been restored and the ground floor shops were so up-to-date they had been rebuilt to appear antique. There was a surfeit of government craftware stores and a vanguard of foreign retailers with the foresight to think in the long term – Estée Lauder, Benetton, McDonald's and a Cartier's with prices marked in Swiss francs. 'So the people don't know how expensive everything is,' Iris told George.

He giggled and then took her arm to steer her around a particularly aggressive group of shrill women selling embroidered tablecloths. 'You shouldn't buy anything from these people in the street,' he whispered, guiding us towards a sports shop selling Nike trainers and tracksuits. George was seeing his changing world through the glossy tint of his designer sunglasses but, for me, those early hours in Budapest were both a disappointment and a relief – disappointing because we had not been inducted into the usual, farcical round of bureaucratic muddle, and relief for just the same reason. The hotels and pensions no longer reported the arrival of guests to the police. The staff at the Intercontinental were polite, cheerful and helpful. There had been no currency exchange forms – although the black market still thrived – no petrol coupons and no delays at the border. We had been hurried through immigration and, at Customs, the officers had been too busy dealing with a hapless Pole in a pea-green Trabant to give us a second glance. Bundles of clothing were being removed from his car and minutely examined. A year before, perhaps a month before, we would have been stopped and the Polish driver waved through. The Poles were the nomads of Eastern Europe, journeying like medieval merchants between countries, trading tins of ham for cigarettes, caviar and Cuban cigars, moving goods in plenty to places where there was a shortage and dropping off a little something at the frontiers, all very un-Communist and as normal as being asked to wear a tie at the state opera.

## Iris

I had noticed the differences immediately: the smart roadside stands selling a variety of vegetables, fruit, baskets of flowers; modern petrol stations, including those of BP and Shell, that appeared to be well-stocked and did not have long queues of bored, silent men pushing their small vehicles to conserve what petrol they still had in their tanks. There were pretty restaurants and the direction signs were clean and freshly painted. Hungary had always been the most liberal of the Communist states and it showed in every way.

In spite of a turbulent history of constant invasion and annexation, the country had retained a culture and an atmosphere that was very different from its neighbours and occupiers. Most of the credit for this can be attributed to its unique language, which bears no resemblance to the Indo-European tongues spoken throughout the rest of the continent. It is a member of the Finno–Ugric branch of the Uralic family – meaning, in simple terms, that it is virtually impossible to learn and, as Clifford remarked, 'Who really wants to?' Nobody speaks Hungarian except the Hungarians although, luckily, as we were soon to learn, they appear to be unusually gifted as linguists.

Budapest quickly became my favourite city. I felt a great wave of excitement as we followed the arrows pointing to the centre. Straddling a bend in the Danube, exactly half-way between Sofia and Berlin, it has one of the most spectacular situations in Europe. It is really two cities: the dramatic, historic Buda, majestically crowning the hills on the west side of the river; and Pest, newer and more commercial, the modern shopping precinct always jam packed with tourists, which meanders into a tableland of dull grey housing blocks, the leitmotiv of Communism, where the tourists never go. The Danube is the main street dividing the two. In 1872, together with a third town, Obuda, they united to form present-day Budapest.

The city looks exactly the way an old European capital should look: beautiful and damaged; timeless and self-assured. The outer ring of new buildings is an intrusion on the senses but, like an ugly scar on a loved one, in half a day it vanishes from sight. The traffic-free Corso runs along the riverbank. It is where people walk and lovers meet; there are restaurants and outdoor cafés, benches where people sit watching the boats go by and the clouds passing over the distant hills – so sensible, and yet, so unusual.

I had been surprised to learn from George Kun that seventy per cent of the city, including all the bridges, had been destroyed in the last year of the war. 'And there isn't one wall over forty years old that does not have bullet holes,' he had added. He had told us all about the uprising in 1956, crushed by the Russians. 'The restoration has been so extensive that none of this is evident.'

We had eventually managed to shake off George and had gone into a department store to try and replace some of the numerous items left behind along the way. We were in the middle of buying toothpaste when an American voice said, 'Hello. How do you like Budapest?' We turned and saw a very attractive woman with dark eyes and glossy black hair smiling at us. She could have been a beauty had she lost forty pounds.

'Well, I like it very much,' I replied, slightly puzzled. Clifford just nodded benignly and said nothing.

'I saw you checking in earlier at the hotel,' she explained. 'I was sitting in the lobby, killing time.' She then turned to the salesgirl and fired off a swift stream of Hungarian. She leaned close to my ear and her breath was warm as she whispered. 'You have to take care . . . if they can rob you, they will.'

The girl behind the counter carefully counted out my change and we took our new friend back to the Corso to have coffee.

Her name was Rosanne Lazar and she was from New York City. She was thirty-seven, travelling alone, and had just completed an emotional pilgrimage to Auschwitz, where she had lost nineteen relatives during the war. She had an urgent need to talk about her experiences and we were compulsive listeners.

Her parents had died within three months of each other the previous year. All her life, she had heard how they had managed to escape the Nazis and flee to America. It was in their memory and as her own, personal catharsis, that she had decided to visit the concentration camp and also the village, now in Russia, where both her parents had been born. She had heard the horror stories, seen the photographs and the films the Germans had made and had felt prepared.

'I'm a very stable person. I felt sure I could handle it. I mean, I never even knew my aunts and uncles or their children. They all died before I was born. But as soon as I walked through the gates, I started to cry and I couldn't stop. I sobbed the entire time I was there.' She withdrew a mansized handkerchief from her large, black alligator handbag and blew her nose.

'Then I hired a car and driver – in Poland, can you believe – and he took me across the border into Russia,' Rosanne said, mopping the tears from the corners of her eyes. 'You wouldn't believe how poor my parents' village was. I mean, real poverty. It was like nothing had changed since the Middle Ages. The people were diseased and crippled. I saw some with cancers and growths and they weren't receiving treatment. Almost everyone was an alcoholic – and who can blame them? I felt like becoming one after twenty-four hours!'

The record-keeper in the village, a man of ninety-two, had remembered her parents. He had cried and embraced her. The small inn where she had stayed had been so dirty and the food so poor and spartan she had left after only one night.

She told us that entering Russia had not been a problem but leaving had been a nightmare. The immigration officials had grilled her suspiciously for three hours because she had a Jewish surname. Other people in the line had pushed and shoved her for jumping the queue, not realizing that she was an American and leaving the country under different circumstances. Some of the people had been waiting at the frontier for over a week. 'It was chaos, madness. I thought I would never get out and, when I was finally allowed to go, all the people rocked the car and hit the roof with their fists. I was terrified,' she said.

The chauffeur had taken Rosanne as far as Cracow, where she had caught the overnight train to Budapest. A woman opposite her in the dining car had asked her if she were a Jewess. 'Can you imagine? No one uses that term anymore. I'm Jewish and so what,' she said and shrugged. 'I'm proud of it. But the way she said the word "Jewess", it was filled with such hatred.'

She sat back and her sigh became a discernible chuckle. She sat forward again. 'Then, guess what, in the middle of the night, I thought I was going to get raped. The conductor woke me to check my ticket, then he wanted to see my passport. I was in one of those little sleepers with nothing on. He kept leaning over, real close, and I was sure he was going to climb in the bed with me.'

She said that even now, in Budapest, she felt threatened and in danger from the anti-Semitic feeling on the rise once more in Hungary. 'It's crazy. They killed all the Jews. There's none left for them to hate,' she added.

I was fascinated and sympathetic. Rosanne Lazar was an appealing woman, articulate and intelligent; and in spite of everything that had happened to her, displayed a vivid sense of humour.

The sad truth was that during the last war, Hungary had participated in Hitler's 'Final Solution' with a good deal more vigour than any of the other countries. They had sent their entire Jewish population, more than five hundred thousand people, to die in concentration camps. The Germans had asked for six thousand people to be rounded up and deported each week, but in their zeal, the Hungarians had doubled the amount and requested more trains.

We quietly drank our coffee and then parted with promises to have a drink together before she left.

Later in the afternoon we walked across the Elizabeth Bridge to Buda and climbed the hill to see the castle where the Germans had made their last stand against the advancing Red Army. The castle had been rebuilt and little remained of the original thirteenth-century structure.

When we arrived back at the hotel, we found a message marked URGENT in our mailbox. 'Please come to the front desk,' it said. A solemn man, completely bald and wearing tortoiseshell glasses, asked us for identification. 'Why?' I wanted to know, slightly irritated. This was Hungary, after all. Without a word, he checked our passports and then took an envelope from a drawer. Our room number was on it. Inside, there were six $100 bills. 'They were buttoned in a pocket of one of the shirts you sent to the laundry this morning,' the bald man said.

## Clifford

With bells clanging and the iron wheels screeching over the rails, a trip on the yellow and white No. 2 along the Danube and across town was as good as a ride on a roller-coaster. We paid about 5 c. (3p) as we boarded the tram and took a seat directly behind the driver. The sun had left an orange streak over Buda. I could see the Liberation Memorial on Gellert Hill, vast on the skyline, a commemoration to the Red Army dead who fell in the seven-week siege that drove the Nazis from Budapest. Below the memorial, the sculpture of a group of Russian soldiers, mentioned with reverence in all the guide books, had quietly been removed.

The memorial itself vanished from view around the first bend and the No. 2 raced through the darkening streets beyond the restored quarter where we had strolled in the afternoon sunshine with George Kun before climbing the hill to the castle. We left the tram close to the university and watched the brightly lit carriages hurry into the night. Then there was silence. A diffused sprinkling of amber lights cast long shadows over the buildings and the sound of leather heels on the cobblestones gave the hour a melancholic air. 'It's cold,' Iris said, shivering as she drew closer. We turned a corner and the still was broken by the busy sounds of eating and talking that surrounded a low-ceilinged winery called 'Karoly'.

We found seats at a long bench and were immediately given a basket of bread and some dark wine in a red-clay pitcher. The walls were lined with pyramids of barrels. The tables had initials carved into them, and the atmosphere was brooding and festive, a guitarist picking out chords, half-hidden in the palls of cigarette smoke. We were handed a greasy card, the menu. We were unable to read it but I knew the food would be good. The best food is served in restaurants that are full and the 'Karoly' was packed with students.

'Order the bean soup, it's safe,' said a voice from across the table. It belonged to Imre, who pointed out the dish on the menu. He smiled. He had long hair tied in a pony tail and the strong, resolute features of a ballet dancer. He was with Sara, whose dark eyes moved over my face as if she intended painting my portrait. She was thin, all in black, the universal uniform, with a sharp nose and short cropped hair. We introduced ourselves.

The waiter came, a big man, bearded and wearing a grubby T-shirt featuring a picture of John Wayne in a cowboy hat. We took Imre's advice on the soup, and to follow ordered sausage and cabbage, a fiery affair with lashings of onions, peppers and paprika. We were drinking Egri Bikaver; light at first, it creeps up on you like a cat stalking a bird.

'We must have five glasses,' Imre said and, with all the solemnity of a priest at a wedding service, he took us step by step through the ritual: one glass: for health; two: for friendship; three: for love; four: for shame.

There was a pause. 'Five?' Iris prompted.

Imre refilled the glasses and we held them aloft. 'Five,' he said, 'and the Danube will be blue!'

We downed the fifth. Imre sat back satisfied. Sara lit a cigarette. She studied us minutely and never smiled once. 'You are English,' Imre said and I nodded in agreement. 'I see Mrs Thatcher has lost many seats in the provincial elections,' he continued, up to date with the news. 'Will she lose the next general election?'

'It is hard to say. A lot can happen in two years.'

'A lot has happened in Hungary in two years,' he said, glancing at Sara. 'You know, I think it is good to have a woman for prime minister. They need to be given a chance to prove themselves.'

'They are all chauvinists here,' she said impatiently. 'We have changed the government, not the way of thinking.'

As soon as we had finished the bean soup, the sausage and cabbage arrived, piping hot from the kitchen. Just in case it was inadequately flavoured, the tables were furnished with a three-piece set of condiments: salt, black pepper and an additional shaker of paprika, something we saw all over the country. Hungarians love paprika.

We filled our glasses and drank one more toast: to democracy. 'With freedom,' added Imre, his voice so serious it was clearly a subject he did not take for granted.

'With freedom,' said Sara.

We talked about economics, Imre's subject at university. 'Everywhere in Hungary we have managers who were chosen for their loyalty to the Party – unqualified men, ungifted, untalented, un – ' He threw up his hands. 'They are un-everything.'

I suggested that all that was changing but he was quick to interrupt. 'No, no, no,' he said. 'We have far worse problems in Hungary. We have been more liberal and for a much longer time. But all the managers chosen by the Party – we call them the Red Barons – those men are still in their jobs. It is impossible to get rid of them.'

'We make only bad things in our factories,' said Sara, and Imre continued for her. 'She is a designer,' he explained. 'But they do not want new ideas from the young people. There is no incentive when you work in a factory making things nobody wants. So nobody cares, nobody works.'

'We pretend to work and they pretend to pay us,' said Sara, an old joke and one of the few imports from Russia enjoyed by Hungarians. Everything else is condemned with utter contempt. If a telephone gives a busy signal or an elevator is broken, it is called a Communist elevator and, by inference, a Russian one.

We had another glass of wine and I was suddenly glad the glasses were small. The guitarist was singing 'Blowing in the Wind', Bob Dylan's protest song from the sixties. Sara's eyes had glazed over. 'Everyone who moved up the ladder under the old regime is suspect,' Imre was saying. 'There are some good men among the bad but it is too difficult to find them. It is better that they all go.'

I had lost concentration for a moment. Twenty years before, the same Dylan song had been played in the same sort of wine cellar where the customers had long hair and politics leaning towards the left. Then we had talked about nuclear disarmament and wanted the Americans out of Vietnam. I told Imre this.

'Of course,' he said scornfully. 'They say the grass is greener over the hill. We all want the opposite of what we have. It is human nature. But we have learned. We do not want Communism; we hate Communism, it is a failure – and, you know, we do not want to have your great loyalty to being consumers. It is the new opium of the masses. We want Hungarians to take the middle path.'

His words, so wise in one so young, echoed the message of Allen Ginsberg on May Day in Prague and it suddenly occurred to me that far from the people of Eastern Europe having so much that they could learn from us, there was much that we could learn from them.

We paid our bill: $2 (£1.20). I was already drunk as Imre poured the last of the wine from the pitcher. 'One more for the journey,' he said.

'To Mrs Thatcher,' said Sara and still no smile touched her features.

## Iris

'Clifford . . . Iris . . .' Rosanne shouted as she came running up to us in the lobby, panting with excitement. 'Have you head the news? Diana is coming. Here. To this hotel. With her husband!'

It all began to make sense: the red carpet running from the car-park to the entrance, the four maids in pink gingham working so hard with vacuum cleaners the noise was deafening; the photographers strutting around like big-game hunters.

'It's so exciting. I just love the royals,' said Rosanne, and it seemed heartless to remind her that the United States had fought a war to rid itself of the British Crown.

She was about to continue, but was interrupted by a fellow American, a woman who had invested heavily in chains of gold necklaces and had enough yellow hair to stuff a small pillow. 'Where's the press conference being held?' she said indignantly. 'They changed the location and they didn't inform me.'

Clifford told her that if she were meeting English journalists, she would find them in the bar. She hurried away, tossing her haystack of hair from side to side, calling 'Thank you' over her shoulder. Later that same day I heard her yelling into a telephone and discovered she was the gossip columnist for the *Los Angeles Times*.

'. . . and we're so lucky,' Rosanne was now saying. 'Here. Right here at the Intercontinental . . .'

'What time are they arriving?' I asked her and she lowered her voice to a whisper.

'It's a secret,' she replied. 'Nobody knows . . .'

## Clifford

We pressed through the crowd and made our way to the coffee shop where Miklos Voros was waiting for us, his eyes scanning the front page of a newspaper. He had been a delegate at various conferences in Europe and the United States, representing the Hungarian Alliance of Free Democrats, and we had been given his name by a mutual friend.

He stood and Iris was visibly taken aback. Miklos was tall, with jet-black wavy hair, piercing dark eyes and an intense expression. He was twenty-five, wore a leather jacket and black jeans and, like Imre and Sara, his English put my language skills to shame. There is an adage that a Hungarian who enters a revolving door last will come out first.

We had been reasonably certain the young man was Miklos Voros the moment we entered the coffee shop: the remaining tables and chairs were empty. Everyone was waiting for the arrival of Prince Charles and the Princess of Wales. I asked Miklos if he knew they were visiting Hungary.

'Oh, yes, of course. We have royal fever in Hungary, too,' he answered.

We ordered coffee and, after talking briefly about ourselves, the conversation moved quickly on to economics. I had just read that 90 per cent of Hungary's oil and gas came from the Soviet Union. Were the current changes going to create a problem?

Miklos immediately became more animated. 'Very much so,' he said. 'It was Hungarian technicians who built the refineries and we have a contract that guarantees supplies in exchange for forints. Now, all of a sudden, the Russians want to be paid in dollars.'

It had been feasible, he explained, for Hungary to buy crude oil from Iran or Saudi Arabia and have it refined cheaply in Romania. But nationalist violence on both sides of the border had brought the two countries to the brink of war. 'The Romanians are very aggressive people,' he added. 'They have been repressed for so long they are ready to explode. They want to destroy everything, starting with the Hungarian villages in Transylvania.'

Iris put her cup down with a bang. A spoon clattered to the floor. 'I imagine it is still safe for foreigners,' I said, before she could speak.

'Not for Hungarians.'

'No, but for us?'

'Yes, I should think so. There are many workers from the Red Cross and other charities going to Romania.'

I asked him if he was satisfied with the election results in Hungary; an alliance of democratic parties led by the dissident author Arpad Goncz had swept to victory over the Communists' renamed Socialist Party. 'Of course I am happy. We are all happy,' Miklos answered and again three deep lines cut into his brow. 'But we do not want to create another extreme; extremes are always possible in Hungary. Socialism is now a dirty word – people think Socialism and Communism are interchangeable and they are not. We want democracy, of course, but we do not want to lose sight of Socialist ideals: a health service, like in Germany and Switzerland, free schools and universities, pensions for the old, benefits for the unemployed. I like the United States, I love the United States. But we do not want Hungary to be the United States.'

His feelings expressed a certain doubt we had found throughout Eastern

Europe: a bogus Utopia had fallen and, from the rubble, it was a new Utopia the people – especially the young – wanted to erect. They did not want a free market economy to create a new rich and a new under-class. 'We are beginning from nothing. We have the opportunity to build a new nation that is fair and just. It is time for a new sort of politics – the politics of care, not confrontation.'

Miklos was a loyal supporter of Goncz, who had followed Vaclav Havel from similar circumstances – including a six year spell in prison – to become the head of the government. 'But I think he is more serious,' he continued. 'I can't imagine him going to night clubs with Frank Zappa and Jane Fonda.'

The lobby held a capacity crowd. A line of photographers like a firing squad hugged the ornamental barrier rope. The four maids were still vacuuming, sucking the colour from the red carpet. Iris had returned to her room and now reappeared in the lobby. Rosanne joined us.

'Diana's wearing pale blue. One of the reporters told me,' she said in the hushed voice of betrayal. 'She's just left the airport.'

Rosanne eased her way back to her position close to the front. Iris was clutching a slip of paper and had a business-like air about her. She was anxious to go.

The car-park had been emptied of vehicles and it was in the adjacent street that we managed to find a taxi. She gave the driver the address of the American Consulate at Szabadsag 12. 'Please to get in,' said the driver. He pulled away, made three left turns and came to a halt in under five minutes. We were outside one of the neo-baroque mansion houses opposite the Parliament building. The American flag, huge and spotlessly clean, hung at an angle over the street. 'No charge,' said the taxi driver, pushing the $2 (£1.20) I gave him into his pocket. 'You change money?' he added.

A man in a smart blue uniform opened the door and, inside, the woman sitting at the high wooden desk seemed to be expecting us. 'Hi, Mrs Gioia,' she said, coming to her feet. 'I'll take you straight through.' She revealed herself, uncommonly joyful in layer upon layer of tumbling flesh all neatly wrapped in a red tartan suit.

I turned to look at Iris. 'Who did you speak to?' I asked. She did not reply. 'Who did you say you were?' Still she did not reply. 'Who are you?' I finally asked.

'Come,' she said and I followed Iris and the fat woman along a corridor that smelled of fresh lemons. The doors were painted white with heavy brass fittings and the carpet below our feet was new, wine red, the same colour as the carpet waiting for the feet of the royal couple.

Charles La Prade stood and threw out a long tapering hand as we entered his office. It was a large room with a large desk and the assistant Vice Consul was a large man with a slow Texas drawl, a bright yellow tie and a grey suit etched with a fine check. He had an open, kindly expression and was one of those men who like to give the impression of being none too bright, a mask concealing a large intellect to go with his great size.

We sat and he asked a few, diplomatically-worded questions, establishing who we were and what we were doing travelling across Eastern Europe. His easy-going manner was disarming, which made me suspicious. I remembered reading somewhere that charm was getting what you want without asking for anything. And Mr La Prade was charming. He had friends in common with Iris back in New York. 'Gee, I miss the States sometimes,' he said and, looking genuinely doleful, he moved straight on to business. 'We don't exactly know what's going on in Romania,' he said. 'It keeps changing. There's an election coming up in two or three weeks, 20 May, I think it is. The head of the National Salvation Front's expected to win.'

'Do you think it is going to be dangerous?' Iris asked.

'I can't rightly say. Could be.'

'Then, so can New York,' I said.

The man, nodding his large head slowly up and down, studied me more carefully. 'If you stick to Bucharest and the major cities, you should be okay,' he said. 'The Romanians are not courageous people. They just get through, cheating and lying.' He opened his cupped palms as if to allow a butterfly to escape. 'Don't quote me on that one,' he added.

We talked for several more minutes about the problems facing Romania but nothing useful was said. The Vice Consul was able to agree with me that it was not particularly dangerous for foreigners, while confirming Iris's fears that it certainly could be.

'What's your advice about going in the next few weeks?' she finally asked.

'Don't,' he answered.

'And if we do?' I pressed.

'Take a few cartons of Kent cigarettes – and plenty of treats for the children.'

## Iris

The whole question of Romania was like a shadow. That part of the journey was still weeks away, but it seemed to be pressing down on me, interfering with the present. Clifford insisted we would be in no danger, but surely, Charles La Prade knew best? Don't go, he had cautioned. I repeated his words once again to Clifford: 'Don't go.'

'. . . without some sweets for the kids and some Kent for the smokers,' he replied. 'Fear is psychological. You should read Vaclav Havel.'

'I have.'

We had left the embassy, crossed the square and were walking around the Parliament building, a frilly lacework of white stone like a wedding cake. Twice in recent history it had been peppered by bullet holes, in the Second World War and again during the 1956 uprising. Immediately after the uprising, teams of workers had been sent out to undertake repairs, their explicit orders being to cover over the fresh pieces of damage, while leaving the original, manipulating history.

We looked for the old war wounds and the more recent repairs but the neo-Gothic palace had just been fully restored, not changing the past so much as wiping away the bad memories and preparing the building for all the bright young men like Miklos Voros now busy guiding Hungary on its new democratic course.

The sun was warm and the Parliament building stared at its mirror image in the still surface of the Danube. Miklos had told us that an enormous crowd had gathered to applaud the red star being removed from the central dome and I now looked up to see where it had been.

A ferry went by and the reflection in the river rippled and disappeared. Some children waved from the top deck. I waved back, and suddenly, at that moment, felt homesick. We walked silently back to Vaci Utca. I still had some last-minute shopping to do, an exercise that usually had a cheering effect. I was shaking off my negative mood, my self-doubt. It was all very straightforward: I was going to Bulgaria, I was now looking forward to seeing Bulgaria, and, as for Romania, we would just have to wait and see.

I wandered into Estée Lauder. It was full of people, although few seemed to be buying anything. Behind the glass counters there were three stunning girls in uniforms that looked about three sizes too small for them. They were so helpful in a land where customer service had only just been invented that I was not surprised to learn that they had returned that week from a training course in Vienna. Products by Hermes were being advertised but there was nothing on display. 'They will be arriving any day,' one of the girls told me breathlessly, her eyes sparkling.

Outside the store, two black Americans – I assumed they were American – were performing in front of a large crowd, one on bongo drums, the other break-dancing. Two policemen were watching the show without interrupting. Their sole job seemed to be to check that the postcard sellers had licenses, which they do; and not to check the gypsies, who do not. The gypsies scurried into shop doorways or hid their products under wooden benches as the policemen passed.

There were no banks in the inner city and no cash machines, but currency exchange was provided by taxi-drivers, hotel waiters and Arabs. Clifford had become very adept at this operation and always made sure he had the foreign currency safely in his pocket before parting with any dollars or Deutschmarks. A young Arab approached us with the usual offer, 'Change money?' Clifford asked him if he were a student.

'No,' he answered, shaking his head. 'I'm a businessman.'

'Where are you from?'

'From Syria,' he said, and he pulled out a roll of notes the size of a double hamburger. 'You want change?'

'Why not?' Clifford said.

They agreed on a rate for $100, and when they had both put their cash away, the Arab lost his stern countenance and warned us to be on our guard. Some of the money-changers tried to palm off Polish zlotys, 'which are worth nothing', he said, and others offered much higher rates, but were robbers, not businessmen. 'They hold the notes out and as you go to make the exchange, they grab your money and run away.' They looked for tourists laden with cameras and shoulder bags, he explained. 'You must be careful,' he said. 'Only come to me. I am always here.' It was sound advice, as we very soon discovered.

There are relatively few bars in Eastern Europe and, therefore, not only are they always full, you always have to share a table. We left the young Arab and joined Wolfgang, a stout German drinking double brandies one after the other, at a pretty café. We ordered coffee. He had given 500 D-marks to a man on the Chain Bridge and, just as we had been warned, the money-changer had run off. On the table sat a large camera bag, a giveaway.

'The Germans are the unluckiest people in the world,' Wolfgang said and he really did look sorry for himself. Clifford asked him why. 'We are trapped between Russia and France,' he replied, tipping back his brandy and shouting for a refill. 'Every nation in Europe expands to make an empire; the British, French, the Spanish, Russians, even the Dutch. But if Germany wants an empire, France and Russia are always in the way. Instead of getting an empire, we always lose more lands.'

Another double brandy arrived. 'But now, Germany is united again,' I reminded him.

He raised his glass and a crooked grin shaped like a letter S formed on his lips. '*Ya, ya.* Finally, we can build an empire,' he said.

'Where?' I asked.

'In Europe,' he replied. 'We build a financial empire. We buy Europe.'

He was in Hungary, he informed us, to acquire land. 'It will go up in value, ten times in five years. You see, even in this mad country it will happen,' he said. He raised his bushy eyebrows and leaned forward as if to impart a confidence. 'This country is an insane asylum. From the east railway station you get trains going west, and from the west railway station you get trains going east!'

**Dresden: the war could have ended yesterday — except for the Trabants**

**A gypsy fiddler in the streets of Cracow**

Warsaw's Rynek Starego Miasta, the old market square, which was completely rebuilt from the rubble of Nazi devastation using old prints and photographs as a guide

Yuri Gagarin greets visitors to the Carlsbad spa

**Prague: students deriding the Communist
past in the first May Day of freedom**

**Hungary — on the road**

**Budapest — the Parliament Building, beside the Danube, now in use again**

**Tidying-up in Pecs**

**Lenin's last days, Lenin Square, Sofia**

**A new party for democracy sets up shop in the centre of Sofia**

**Taking the bread home in Sozopol**

**Democracy demonstrators in Bucharest's University Square, taken from our hotel room**

**Doing the family wash in Transylvania**

We checked it out later and he was right. As for the two stations, they were masterpieces of old Hungary, lavish and light, with tall arches and fields of glass. There was even a zither player in the east station, mournfully serenading the passengers going west. The people hurried by clutching battered leather suitcases. A newspaper seller was shouting out the headlines. Pigeons sat on the rafters, scattering in a terrified grey mass as the huge locomotives screamed out into the sunlight, and resettling again when they had gone.

We made our way across Pest to Nyagati pu, the smaller, western station designed by Alexandre Eiffel, his fame from building the tower for the 1889 exposition in Paris having then taken him on a spree of commissions all over Europe. Trains were leaving for Moscow, Sofia, Bucharest, for towns and cities with romantic-sounding names I had never heard of and suddenly longed to visit.

## Clifford

Big Brother had been watching me ever since our arrival in Budapest. Dark brown, piercing, almost avuncular below nests of thick eyebrows, the eyes of Jo Stalin peered down from posters plastered on walls, windows, the sides of trams. There was a whole row of them at the station, just like the Pope in Poland and Vaclav Havel in Bohemia. It would have been understandable if the people had still been terrified of the monster but, in fact, something close to the reverse was true. He had been brushed aside, forgotten, become so irrelevant in modern Hungary that the posters advertised an exhibition of 'Stalin' memorabilia at the old palace in Buda, a national museum and one building, unlike the Parliament, that will not be going back to its former use.

We paid 10 forints for the ride up Castle Hill on the funicular railway and it was another 10 forints – about 10 c. (6p) – to see the exhibition. I asked for two tickets and the woman behind the glass partition engaged me in a long conversation of which I understood not a single word. I tried Spanish, '*Dos, por favor,*' then German, then French. And every time I switched languages, she repeated what she had been saying only louder.

Iris was flicking through our survival dictionary and came up with the words we wanted in Hungarian: '*Ketto kerem,*' pronounced '*kehter kayrem*', which made the ticket-seller laugh uncontrollably and, leaving her post, she led us through a pair of high wooden doors and we were admitted free of charge.

A gigantic, God-sized statue of Stalin had been removed from one of the city's main squares just a few weeks before and photographs of this joyful event had been enlarged and displayed in sequence at the entrance. More statues, busts and items of Stalin iconography filled shelves and walls; myriad flags, all in red, pictures of parades, the people carrying huge portraits of Stalin just as Catholics in small villages in South America carry the Virgin through the streets on feast days. The parades were a form of religious hysteria. Stalin had made himself into a myth, a symbol, worshipped by those who believed the propaganda and feared and despised by everyone else. Hitler had been adored by the Germans in the early days of his rise to power. But Stalin not only cut across national borders, he lasted so much longer and, even after death, people were afraid that he could reach them from the grave.

More galleries contained soldiers' uniforms, medals, paintings in the style of socialist realism approved of by the state and endorsing the fiction that the people were deliriously happy in their labours. From the upper floor, we had a better view of the lookout tower, a wooden box on four slender stilts, something innocuous yet sinister, a reminder of the concentration camps from the war years and the appearance of the Iron Curtain that came after.

Off to one side, at the end of a short corridor, there was a small, shadowy room lit by an old-fashioned standard lamp. The books on the shelves that circled the room leaned at odd angles, some upright on their spines, others stacked, some open. These were books that had been read and would be read again. The hat-stand contained a hat and an overcoat. The lamp cast a pool of amber light over a table covered with papers. A pen had been abandoned on a half-written sheet. The chair at the table had been pushed back and faced the door. I could imagine the midnight knock, the writer or poet or philosopher or some such class enemy being dragged away to some filthy basement and interrogated by mindless bullies. It seemed so unreal, so unlikely, so Hollywood. But it was real and the reality had still existed until just a few months before the exhibition opened. I stood there looking at the small library, a shiver passing through me one moment and a feeling of sheer wonder at man's ability to adapt touching me the next. There must be a lot of people who would prefer not to be reminded of the Stalin era but the display of mementoes served a sagacious purpose, the de-mystifying of the man. It was like getting back on a horse after a bad fall, something Hungary was ready for, even if elsewhere in Eastern Europe the same process was going to need a lot more time.

## Iris

Once you have climbed the hills of Buda and promenaded on the Corso in Pest, it is time to take to the main street and allow the city to reveal itself from the rail of a ship. Budapest is the Danube, the Hungarians say, and I daresay the Yugoslavs in Belgrade, the Slovaks in Bratislava and the Austrians in Vienna say much the same thing.

The sun was streaming through the window when we awoke and, from our balcony, the river looked almost blue. We hurried through our coffee and *croissants* and were early boarding the *Pannonia*, a double-decker excursion boat, for the day-long trip to Esztergom and Visegrad, two towns on the Danube Bend, the S-shaped curve where medieval kings built their fortresses and ruled over their unruly subjects.

Although we boarded the boat a good half an hour before it was to depart, the seats on the upper deck were already occupied by a party of Germans, all senior citizens with lots of bags, raincoats and cameras.

We fled to the lower deck and, in the stern, sat on a box containing life jackets, the only seating available. There were a few more distressed people taking shelter in the same place. We looked at each other. We smiled and exchanged names. There was Donna, an American woman from Washington D.C., with her son, Anthony, a music student studying in Budapest, and his Hungarian girlfriend; a young Japanese couple on their honeymoon, both dressed in a weird assortment of black leather and fake fur; and an elderly couple who, emphasizing that they were Dutch, implied that they may have been old, but they were not German and did not want to be associated with the party on the upper deck.

We passed the Parliament building, gleaming in the sunshine on our right side and then we switched to the left, the *Pannonia* cruising close to Margaret Island, an 8-mile slither of parkland that appeared to be the sports centre for the city.

The Danube, however, is not blue. For the most part, it is charcoal grey. Raw, untreated sewage and, worse, the poisons from numberless chemical plants, are all dumped into the flow along much of its 1,750-mile journey from the Black Forest in Germany to the Black Sea. The river has its own, inbuilt cleaning mechanism, but it has been excessively strained for two decades and is now on the point of total collapse.

Anthony told us about his apartment; he was renting a floor in an old building in Pest. 'To get to it you have to go through an amazing courtyard,' he said.

'A dirty alley,' his mother, Donna, remarked. She had a sweet face and curly brown hair.

'We have a lot of space and really high ceilings,' Anthony continued with enthusiasm.

Olga, Anthony's girlfriend, who shared the apartment, now told us that she wanted to be an opera-singer. She loved the high ceilings, and, when she was not exercising her voice, she was studying English. 'If I fail as a singer, I must become a teacher,' she said, glancing at Donna. 'There is no time for other things.'

Donna went to speak but her son got in first. 'Before I came to Hungary, I was only interested in music. I want to become a conductor,' he said. 'But here, you get involved in politics. You have to. Everyone I know in Budapest has a social conscience, everyone cares.'

Two hours later, we reached Szentendre and our gang of nine marched in step behind the fifty-one energetic Germans and Julia, our guide for the day, somewhere in the distance below a parasol with blue and white polkadots.

I adored the village the moment we entered and was not surprised to learn that it had been described as the prettiest in Hungary. It had been built by Serbian merchants fleeing from the Turks in the seventeenth century. Having found a deserted spot on the river, they put up elegant houses in a medley of styles that drew their inspiration from baroque, rococo and Louis XVI. The village harbours its own artists' colony and there are various galleries and studios where their work is displayed.

We dutifully trailed along behind Julia and listened to her running commentary, sometimes in English, sometimes German, and never very clear. We reached Marx Square and this prompted her to tell a story she had obviously told many times before. A little boy asks his father, 'What's the name of this street?' The father shrugs, 'Don't ask me, ask your grandfather.' He knows what it was before and that's what it will be again.'

She laughed and enjoyed the story so much we laughed with her. Julia was middle-aged, buxom, very short and blonde. Her comments were highly political but it was far from easy to work out what point she was making. She complained that for the past four years Hungarians had been taxed at the same rate as the people of Sweden, on salaries like those in Albania. The Germans rewarded her with another outbreak of laughter and we followed them into the Margit Kovacs Museum, a modern gallery filled with the fanciful creations of the sculptress who died in 1977. Julia told us that Margit Kovacs was now considered one of the 'most important artists of the twentieth century.'

The Red Army was leaving Hungary and three of its uniformed soldiers who wanted to visit the country's prettiest village before they left were sight-seeing with the rest of us. Two stopped and posed in the centre of the main square while the third took their photograph. Clifford had taken shots of the young soldiers buying ice-cream in East Germany, much to their annoyance. Now he went a stage further. He gave his own camera to the photographer and stood between his two companions, grinning and gesturing.

There was a long pause while nothing happened. The photographer held Clifford's camera with the tips of his fingers as if it were red hot and looked at him with sheer disbelief. He was not frightened or angry, but confused. The orders from above had become unclear. The soldiers had been in Hungary, as everywhere in Eastern Europe, to stop counter-revolution. Even the term sounded ridiculous now. Clifford, still smiling, finally went forward to point out the position of the shutter button and the boy pulled the camera away as if to say he knew perfectly well where it was. He took the photograph and returned the camera.

'English,' Clifford told him, slapping his chest.

The soldier slapped his own chest, much harder. 'Russian,' he said. The three of them hurried on.

Back on board, I was astonished to find that the crew had organized a very formal, very elaborate sit-down lunch in the main salon on the upper deck. The tables, covered in crisp white cloths, were set for eight and it took a good deal of persuasion before we were allowed to bring an extra chair to our table and make our group complete. I had a feeling that in the past people had rarely made such demands, however petty, and sensed that it was the small, insignificant changes – more than the sweeping ones – that were difficult to accept.

## Clifford

A cloudburst launched raindrops the size of gemstones that drummed a tattoo on the car roof. The detritus from swarms of insects fled to the shadowlands beyond the arcs of the windscreen wipers and my vision through the glass was the best it had been since the rainy days in Poland. The drum beats slowly softened into silence. The sun was breaking through and the pink, yellow and cream stucco towers of the churches on the Buda hills stood out like lightning flashes against the sombre sky.

I had a feeling of complete contentment watching the cottages on the outskirts of Budapest rush by. Green fields glossy with rain stretched out as far as I could see. After spending some time in a city, it was, as always, a relief to leave.

We were heading for Lake Balaton, 60 miles of hotels and camp sites that fill up with families from Hungary and Austria in the summer but in May still retain the peaceful mood of resort towns off-season. Pollution is killing the Danube but Lake Balaton, the only sizeable stretch of open water in the landlocked country, is vigorously protected. Even motor boats are banned. We walked along the sandy shore. Two windsurfers scored lines on the lake's surface. Some girls were sunbathing and a muscle man was doing press-ups.

The road south passes through the Hungarian bread basket and the villages looked ancient and prosperous. There were horses working in the fields but the roads in the rural areas had become go-cart tracks filled with miniature tractors as fast and as noisy as motor bikes.

We were looking for the site of some Roman ruins outside the town of Kaposvar but even the town had vanished from the signposts. I stopped to ask a group of people the way and they seemed terrified by the sight of the map. 'Kaposvar?' I asked hopefully and they shied away. I opened the concertina pages and pointed out Budapest, the lakes and Pecs, our destination, and slowly they became more interested. 'Kaposvar?' I said again, but the two women and the elderly man now holding the map between them were lost in their own private journeys. The man traced a work-soiled finger along the north shore of Balaton until he found Veszprem and, when he did, he gave a small cheer. 'Veszprem,' he said excitedly and one of the women echoed the word with all the joy of an immigrant sighting the Statue of Liberty for the first time.

They were so thrilled with their discoveries, I produced the map of Europe and showed them Hungary. They were excited when they first saw it – and became less excited when they discovered Yugoslavia, Bulgaria, Romania. The old man indicated different chunks of land and I named them for him. 'Italy,' I began. He raised his thick eyebrows and pointed again. 'Germany.' He nodded thoughtfully. 'Mmm,' he said. We found France, Spain, Britain, Ireland, and he repeated the words as if checking through the dusty files of his memory. Almost every country in Europe is larger than Hungary and the three peasants found this disconcerting. I ran my finger around the Soviet Union, the frontier disappearing off the sides of the map. 'Russia,' I said and they were visibly shaken by its size. Hungary was their universe. They had probably never even been to Budapest.

I returned to the problem of getting to Kaposvar and we discarded the maps as if they were devices of the devil. The man and the two women all pointed vaguely over rolling hills where grapes were beginning to grow on the vine and I gathered we were on the right road.

'*Koszonom*,' I said; thank you, about the only word in Hungarian I had managed to learn.

'*Koszonom*,' the old man repeated and he gave me his big worn hand to shake.

We arrived in Kaposvar thirty minutes later and decided not to stop. It is an ugly town surrounded by smoke stacks. Attempts to make the place look more cheerful have been made by painting the identical apartment blocks in different colours but the end result is merely gaudy and cheap. The Roman ruins nearby consist of a ring of white stones like broken teeth and a gypsy encampment surrounded by a high fence, not to keep the gypsies in or strangers out, but simply to keep everything hidden. The regulation pair of surly children appeared and I gave the boy and the girl 10 forints each and they cried for more. Iris gave them packets of chewing gum. Two men came up to look at the car and I noticed they had the same walk: throwing their bodies forward and using the momentum to drag their feet along. They were tired and agitated. One of the two asked for a cigarette, holding two fingers to his lips and puffing. I opened one of the packets of Kent and the two men took one each and appeared satisfied.

They sauntered off and the two children followed, lurching in the same awkward gait. The gypsies we had met were all gripped by some deep tribal depression, so unlike the band of wanderers who had willingly shared their food with Patrick Leigh Fermor, the eighteen-year-old adventurer who had walked across Hungary in 1934. On his travels, the gypsies he had met had roasted a chicken and pulled potatoes from the field. A fiddler had played and bare-foot girls danced, their jewellery jangling in time to a tambourine.

In Communist Hungary, it had only been the gypsy musicians who had been able to make a reasonable living. The previous night after our day on the river we had found a traditional restaurant where a gypsy orchestra dressed in red boleros and tight black trousers had played Hungarian folk songs. In file, they had left the stage and encircled our table. The leader had asked Iris what she would like to hear and, suggesting 'Moon River', they had broken into a soulful rendition of 'The Blue Danube'. 'They were going to play that whatever I asked for,' Iris had whispered. At the end of the performance, I had slipped a bill on the table and the leader had put it expertly into his pocket.

## Iris

Pecs (pronounced Paitch) was like finding a forgotten trunk in your grand-mother's attic, old, well-made and filled with priceless treasures. It was graduation time and students in fancy dress created a mood of elation. They were happy and this feeling seemed to have spread to the rest of the population.

It was the cleanest city we had seen since leaving West Germany, thanks to endless numbers of street cleaners, men and women, all in bright orange vests, who worked in teams going along every road and pavement. We saw one very old woman in an apron and scarf who had the job of keeping the main square clean. She attacked it as if it were her own kitchen. She swept small areas and stood back every few yards to check there was no dust or litter left trapped among the cobblestones. She seemed proud of her work, something I respected.

The square rose at a slight angle, and at the top end stood the Gazi Kassim Pasha mosque, built in the sixteenth century and now a Catholic church. A stern door-keeper smoking a cigarette studied us carefully before she allowed us to enter and kept her eye on us while we were inside. 'Have you noticed the women who look after churches always smoke,' Clifford said, and the woman waved her finger at us, saying 'Shush, shush.' I felt like a naughty schoolgirl.

We walked on in silence. The light was streaming in through stained-glass windows set high in the rounded walls. Lines of pews, all different lengths, to allow for the curve, faced the altar and a roughly hewn crucifix, which managed to complement the simplicity of the Islamic decoration, a bonding of the two religions. Off to one side, we found the mihrab, the Muslim prayer niche facing east to Mecca.

Clifford placed a donation on the dish at the entrance as we left and the door-keeper checked to see how much it was before she granted us a smile brimming with tobacco-stained teeth.

I held Clifford's arm as we dawdled along. The sun was shining, polishing the fronts of the buildings. We crossed the square again. The old woman was still sweeping, an old man on one of the benches looking on. I wondered as we passed if he were her husband and this was his entertainment, watching her work before she came home and cooked his dinner. He was wearing a Turkish beret, tight-fitting and going green with age. The afternoon sun had grown brighter and, against the background of a cloudless blue sky, Pecs had the appearance of a town on the Mediterranean. The domes of mosques and tall, elegant minarets rose above red-tiled rooftops and shady avenues where the eucalyptus and elm trees were in full leaf. A huge television mast soared in the distance, looking like a space rocket.

Cherries, apples, tomatoes and cucumbers from the local farms were being sold from boxes outside shops where the shelves were well-stocked and the housewives stood gossiping in little clusters. Geraniums filled window-boxes and stood in Ali Baba earthenware pots in courtyards that looked inviting and mysterious. Time seemed to have stopped here and the monuments left by the different invaders who had marched through the city on their way to Vienna, Buda and Bratislava were untarnished by excessive restoration and untouched by the tourist swarm that assaults Western Europe each year.

Pecs was originally known as Sopianae and served as the capital of Roman Pannonia for four centuries. The remains of villas and places of worship were scattered around the cathedral with its imposing set of four square towers. Most of the remains are now just piles of rock, each invader having pulled down the old structures to re-use the stones to raise up new temples in the glory of their own gods. One site that has survived since the fourth century is the early Christian mausoleum with its well-preserved frescoes of Daniel in the Lion's Den, and another of Adam and Eve in the Garden of Eden, showing Eve naked and wonderfully plump.

King Stephen, the Magyar chieftain who became Hungary's first king on Christmas Day in the year 1000, made Pecs a bishopric and, in 1367, the town became the site of the country's first university. High walls were erected to protect the citizens, but did not prevent the Turks from conquering the city in 1543 and staying on for almost a hundred and fifty years. The Turks built numerous small masterpieces of Byzantine architecture, which continue to give the old quarter an eastern flavour that Christian reconquest has been unable to obliterate.

The cathedral was begun by King Stephen and is considered the most important medieval structure in Hungary. Two of the towers were built in the eleventh century and the second pair was added a century later. Next to the cathedral, the Bishop's Palace is much later, an example of Hungarian baroque. With the catacombs below my feet, the towers and graceful domes in a circle all around me, and the television mast severing the sky, sixteen hundred years of architecture were on display from the spot where I stood. It was overwhelming.

In Kaptalan Street is the museum that houses the large collection left by the Op artist Victor de Vasarely to the town at his death in 1989. He was a native of Pecs, who worked in Paris and pioneered kinetic effects in painting. His canvases were huge, covering entire walls, the reproduction of identical shapes, often moving through shades from black to white, tricking the eye and confusing the mind.

We paid 10 forints to get in, a little over 10 c. (6p), the going rate for all the museums and libraries, and a sum that must contribute very little towards supporting the cost of maintaining the polished wood floors, the track lighting and the two plump little ladies in blue smocks who trailed around behind us making sure we did not steal anything. The Hungarians were a lot more careful with their art exhibits than the curators in East Germany.

## Clifford

They did not like people sitting in their restaurants writing in big black books. I had a table to myself; before me stood a large silver pot full of hot water, a single tea bag, a bowl of sugar cubes and a half moon of lemon (somewhat dry). The waiters, seedy men with Stalin haircuts, kept straightening the chairs, wandering by to steal a glance at what I was doing, before hurrying back to the kitchen.

One of them finally spoke to me, rapidly and in German. 'Room two-o-nine,' I replied, not understanding what he had said.

Another came with rudimentary English. 'What are you doing?' he asked.
'Having tea.'

He stared down at the black book. 'But . . .' He shrugged and looked very unhappy.

'My diary,' I told him.

He retreated, walking backwards as he went, like a servant departing royalty, and at dinner that night, we were given the best table (the only one with a flower on it) and food in such abundance it seemed a shame it was so bad we left most of it.

It was still early and our room was too depressing for anything but sleep. We made our way back to the main square, the sound of rock music growing louder as we approached. The mosque looked like a birthday cake. The arched windows were lit from behind by a yellow light that made a warm glow and isolated the cross crowning the domed roof so that it seemed to be hanging on invisible strings in the darkness. The cross was planted in a recumbent crescent, a design I had never seen before, Christianity quelling Islam, and with such aplomb they had found no need to demolish the mosque, simply sanctify it.

A student band was performing Hungarian rock for its young audience. When they finished, I asked the couple next to us why they were holding the concert.

'For nothing,' said the girl. I was unsure what she meant.

'Because we can,' her companion added.

They smiled. They both had dark hair and a darker complexion than their countrymen in the north, a legacy of the Turkish conquests. They drifted towards the stage, drinking beer from bottles. The music started again, a boy playing guitar and a girl singing in harmony. I recognized a song by Paul Simon.

Around the square, apartment windows were open and older people were leaning on the sills and enjoying the show. Live music in the open at ten at night. In the past it would have been considered reactionary, Fascist, a foreign plot; now it was a symbol of freedom, although I did wonder how long it was going to last. How long would it be before the people who lived in the square became sick of the noise and complained that their rights were being violated?

I heard the sound of bottles breaking on the grey cobbles and remembered the old woman working so diligently with her broom during the afternoon. She was going to have a lot of extra work to do in the morning.

We wandered back through town, passing a white stone synagogue in the same near-perfect condition as the mosque. The drinking men were making their way home, swinging from side to side, stretching out their arms in the affable way one feels inclined to embrace, even while knowing that it can only lead to problems.

Our room on the hotel's second floor with its pair of iron beds and antique eiderdowns, had a smell of stale vegetables. The small table between the beds was completely taken up with a huge radio in a wood casing. It took about ten minutes for the tubes to warm up and no matter how much I turned the dial, every station I found was playing Turkish folk music. It would have sounded awful on the BBC but was oddly appropriate as I stared out into the dark night. I could see the shadowy outlines of domes and towers, the ancient minaret where the muezzin had once called the faithful to prayer.

We had gone from the luxury of the Duna Intercontinental to the Hotel Piroska, a Communist relic with soiled rooms, shredding carpets, a gloomy bar with cracked, marble-topped tables and plastic chairs that had replaced the wooden chairs probably sold off to the antique dealers and smuggled out of the country to Austria. The bar was always full of men smoking small black cigars and drinking beer, although the local wines were much less expensive. They were there all day and they were still there late at night, huddled in groups over dense ashtrays with an air of purposeful intrigue, waddling from one table to another, their shoes pressed down at the back to make slippers, another legacy bequeathed by the Turks. Passing through the bar was like passing through a bazaar of infinite possibility. I had been offered change, naturally, but also French cigarettes, caviar, a pair of season tickets to the state ballet, Czechoslovak petrol coupons, a passport and the opportunity of adopting a two-year-old girl named Hanna. I had been shown her photograph.

In the year 1566, 2,482 Hungarian patriots manned the battlements at the Szigetvar fortress and for thirty-three days held off an army of 207,000 Turks. On the last day, when the fort was certain to fall, Miklos Zrinyi led the handful of survivors out of the main gates in a suicidal attack in which every man was slaughtered.

On those thirty-three days of the assault, the view the defenders could see beyond the marauding Turks must have been little different from the way it remains today. The fortress, high and solid, with its four corner bastions built in 1420, is surrounded by fields that are still worked by the horse plough introduced by the Romans. The rural south of Hungary is far less prosperous than the area close to Lake Balaton and Austria in the west. There are less mini-tractors and more horse wagons. The churches, liberally sprinkled over the landscape like tea cakes, come in an endless variety of pastel shades. Farm buildings nestle along the sides of the Mecsek hills, facing the sun and surrounded by mature trees that give the compounds a medieval appearance.

There are two million cars in Hungary; one million in Budapest. Allowing for a large number undergoing repair, there being a preponderance of Ladas and Trabants, the country roads are empty and the sight of the green Range Rover was often met by waving, smiling crowds and children who ran along the side of the road with us like children in Africa and South America. It was just as well we had stocked up on chocolate bars although, when we handed them out in the villages, I am not certain the children knew what the small packages were. In Hungary, more than anywhere in Eastern Europe, the difference between the capital and the countryside is extreme. Budapest is completely cosmopolitan and most things, if not everything, you can find in London and New York are available. Outside Budapest, there is another world and another century.

The type of clothes the people are wearing have changed, although only in recent times. The young boys are kitted out in shiny tracksuits, usually bright red, the colour of the national soccer team. Their fathers wear shorts, their huge bellies like sacks ballooning from unbottoned shirts. Some of the older men are more traditional in linen smocks and heavy trousers, the peasant uniform, with the women in headscarfs, voluminous skirts and aprons with bulging pockets. The young girls are usually skinny and petite, blonde and blue-eyed or brunettes with brown eyes, but their mothers are universally buxom, dimpled and double-chinned, round as spinning tops with short, bare legs and short strong arms that wield scythes and hoes with the accuracy and momentum of Swiss clocks.

We passed through villages with impressive, unpronounceable names: Ottomos, Matel Telke, Tathaza, Balsalmas, Vasatallomas, Hodmezovasarhely. The cottages were simple with water pumps in the yards outside, while the graveyards on the outskirts of each community were laid out in neat avenues of marble like a model of some wonderful city. We stopped in Balsalmas and, wandering among the gravestones, reading the dates, checking to see how many of the dead had acquired their three-score years and ten, we were invited into the church by the door-keeper, a peasant woman as plump as her neighbours.

The church was cream-coloured with a squat silver spire. The inside was spare and unassuming with a flagstone floor and whitewashed walls. Jesus on the Cross was clothed in a toga, something peculiar to Hungarian crucifixions, and on the back wall, behind a wooden baptismal font, was a mural depicting Jesus giving the Sermon on the Mount. The faces of the disciples were strikingly Hungarian, as was the landscape, a view that could have been sketched from the porch.

We made a small donation and the woman indicated that we should wait. She rushed off, crab-like on her short bowed legs, and returned with a gift of two pastries wrapped like a parcel in thick white paper. We added them to our picnic.

In the field beyond the graveyard, we watched two muscular men loading pitchforks of hay on to a haywain. It was being pulled slowly along by a decrepit horse with lugubrious features as sad as a cartoon drawing. The men saw me taking a photograph and both waved their fists. I threw out my arms in a gesture of apology and then they smiled. The younger of the two, a Tarzan of a man, invited me to join them in their labour and was surprised when I agreed. Iris took the camera.

Gathering the hay on the pitchfork requires the same skill you need for eating spaghetti. You have to dig in, rake to one side and then twist the strands in a coil. The hay gathered, you must heave it in one sure motion towards the heavens, which I did, without the remotest jot of success. The loaded pitchfork can weigh more than fifty pounds and, lurching from side to side, it quickly scatters and more hay goes down your neck than on to the back of the wagon. The two men found my humiliating efforts hilarious and thus, with shared laughter, we became friends.

## Iris

Szeged, our last stop in Hungary, emerged from the plains, a spread of small factories and housing blocks. From the outskirts, the town looked grim and grimy, but later, walking through the old streets in the city centre, it came to life, ancient and tangible. I realized again how important architecture is and how our ancestors were wise to pay so much attention to balance, harmony and detail.

We easily found a hotel and were given a room that seemed dedicated to dreariness. It contined two narrow, lumpy beds at odd angles to each other on opposite walls. Although the Communist governments encouraged people to reproduce, they clearly did not want them to do it in hotels. The colour scheme was monochromatic: the embossed nylon carpet, mohair armchairs, headboards and wallpaper were all in various shades of brown. Outside, the Tzige River flowed below the balcony, also brown.

We walked along the river bank and stopped outside the Leanykollegium, the music academy, to listen as someone played Bartok's piano pieces taken from the folk music he collected among the hill villages between Hungary and Transylvania, and which he thought were pre-Christian in origin. Through an open window we could see a young woman engrossed in mastering the compositions. We continued on our way and on a street named Lenin Korut, passed under a bridge made of tall arches. A stone sentry, wearing the Nazi uniform of a Fascist stormtrooper, was carved into the supports at each end. It was another reminder, if any were needed, that unlike Czechoslovakia and Poland, Hungary had entered the war in 1942 on the side of the Third Reich, with dreams of gaining back the territory it had lost in the First World War.

We retired early, and the next morning, under a leaden sky, left Hungary and prepared for the long drive through Yugoslavia to Bulgaria. Clifford had parked the car under a very large tree, heavy with white blossom. During the night it had rained, and in the morning, we found the car covered with a sticky sap that had washed down from the leaves, as well as what were once white petals. Looking like a float in a Mardi Gras parade, we drove three hundred and fifty miles south and spent the night in a little town in Yugoslavia just across the border from Bulgaria. Greek music filled the warm air. Our dinner was cooked in olive oil. Turkish coffee was served to us in the morning. We had arrived in Southern Europe and new civilizations were in the wind.

# Bulgaria

## Clifford

A tall, hydraulic crane was standing motionless behind the statue of Comrade Lenin. The statues of Communist heroes were vanishing from the squares of Eastern Europe like lost chess pieces but Lenin, the king, still stood there, intense, yet slightly puzzled on a cement plinth above the streets of Sofia; 30 feet high in a long, Russian coat, his chin was raised in an imperious gesture, his body leaning forward as if he had been captured mid-step.

Lenin peered across the Largo, the city's central boulevard, and what met his gaze was Communist Party House, the reason for that puzzled look, I imagined. Built in the 1950s, it is a Greek temple crowned by a tower in Stalin Gothic. The portico is blessed with six lofty Doric columns that form a grille leading to a fan of brickwork in Regency style. The tower narrows into a spire that, like a Christmas tree, is decorated with a star, in this case, a red one. There were no flags flying over the building in May, although the concrete hammer and sickle on its façade was still in evidence. The new Socialist Party had just taken on the keys, the hats and the faces of the former Communists, a stratagem that, with the control of the media, was to assist in its narrow election win over the Union of Democratic Forces the following month. Lenin was then to be quietly removed, unlike the famous landmark across the Largo. That went with high drama. On Sunday 26 August 1990, 15,000 demonstrators were to gather in the Bulgarian capital to complain about the red star on the building and, one thing leading to another, they then ransacked it and put it to the torch.

Lenin seemed rather a sad figure, alone in the small square that bore his name. That part of the square was silent but all around the city was a bubbling cauldron full of activity and change. Crowds gathered around news sheets pasted on walls, the men at the front reading aloud for those at the back and those unable to read. Fly-posters for a whole plethora of new parties competed for space. One group, clearly too poor to rent an office, had set up shop under an arcaded passage where two men sat at typewriters hammering out policy as fresh as a fish caught and dropped straight into a cooking pot. Voters were giving their names and addresses for future support. The election was coming up on 10 June and the people in the capital were carefully considering the different candidates; it was their country cousins who voted for the crypto-Communists.

One of the men in the group, barrel-chested and with a moustache, was handing out leaflets and repeating the same words over and over again, one of which I understood: Chernobyl. 'What's this?' I asked.

'Chernobyl,' he said in a frosty voice full of 'X's and 'Z's. 'They did not tell us. We have clouds over Sofia and we don't know what it is. We eat contaminated food – and they fly in clean food for the Communists. The Reds in Bulgaria are worse than in Russia.' He waved a finger at me, angry at first, but then he smiled and became apologetic. 'I am sorry. I get excited. It was four years ago, you know, four years this same month. It was the end of the Communist Party. We wait four years, but that was the end.'

'Good,' I said simply.

The man grinned and leaned forward. He lowered his voice. 'I tell you something: the Soviet Union paid billions of roubles in damages – to Sweden, to Germany, I don't know where. And how much did they give Bulgaria? Nothing. We are too insignificant to get compensation. That must change. We want to come back into the family of Europe.'

The centre of the main boulevard was jammed with entrepreneurs, some selling the oddest things: saucepan scourers, pipe-cleaners, needles and thread, single cigarettes, rubber face masks of the former Communist bosses; one man had a table with an eclectic gathering of figurines that included several apostles and Fred Flintstone.

Two new art galleries were in the process of opening and busy, bohemian types were positioning sculptures and hanging paintings that were free-flowing and abstract. The artists had been working in secret on their creations in hidden attics for decades and showing them was now more important than finding buyers.

We followed the smell of the bakery shop. Women were hurrying home with *baguettes* in linen bags. The Palace of Culture – briefly named the Ljudmila Zhivkova Cultural Centre, after the former dictator's deceased daughter – reared up over the park, a circular, black and white edifice like a giant sixties-style ear-ring. It had housed Party conferences, exhibitions, touring troupes of folk dancers, although, on 14 May, the main hall was booked for 'Bulgarian Rok', the nation's foremost heavy metal band. Like some Confucian axiom, as soon as Communism closes down, art galleries seem to open and rock bands appear. The girls slash 5 inches from the hems of their skirts and farmers roll into town selling cherries and strawberries from the backs of their wagons.

We had seen them on the side of the road on the drive from the border. It was only 30 miles to Sofia but, even that close to the capital, I had had the feeling of being in a very ancient land untouched by and unconcerned with the twentieth century. Throughout our journey from the Berlin Wall, it had seemed as if the last war had just come to an end. In Bulgaria, it was the War of Independence that sprang to mind.

Blossom had hung on the breeze like snow, a cliché, perhaps, but no less accurate. We had left the highway behind in Yugoslavia and the road had wound its way leisurely through the Balkan mountains. Fields were divided by bushes

sprinkled with pink flowers or, alternatively, picket fences, the wood unshaved
and unpainted. The meadows were awash in zdravetz, the wild geranium unique
to Bulgaria. The cottages were built in stone with thick walls, small windows
and low roofs. Peasants worked side by side in teams. Some waved and, when
we stopped, we were greeted with both friendliness and pride. The people were
poor but it was a well-fed, jolly, rural poverty, something primitive and more
acceptable, or at least understandable, than the poverty that haunts the streets in
cities everywhere. The roads were mere tracks, the traffic was all horse-powered
and the only intrusions from the contemporary world were us in our car and the
modern garages with their signs in English: HARD CURRENCY ONLY.

## Iris

I did not expect to be overwhelmed by Sofia. It was the rather shabby capital
of the Turkish province of Rumelia until the rebellion in 1877, scarcely more
than a town, with only fifteen thousand inhabitants and three thousand
houses. For reasons of Muslim bigotry, no Christian rooftop could rise higher
than a man on horseback, although the wily Bulgars overcame this edict by
sinking their Orthodox churches below ground level and making them almost
as grand as the numerous mosques. After the overthrow of the Turks, a new
plan for the city was designed, and the tangle of narrow streets and low
buildings became more like a Western city.

The history of Sofia, however, goes back many thousands of years, to the
time of the Thracians, when it was called Serdica and was mid-way on a busy
trade route between the Adriatic and the Black Sea. Waves of invaders
followed Alexander the Great: the Romans, Slavs and Turks, each leaving
their archaeological fingerprints.

First, we had to find a place to stay. We made our way to Lenin Square in
the heart of the city and stopped in front of the Sheraton Sofia Hotel Balkan, as
good a place to start as any. It was Clifford's turn to run in while I watched the
car. Two minutes later he ran out, a frown creasing his brow.

'Let me guess. No room at the inn.'

'Yes. Good thing you're not pregnant.' Instead of getting in the car he
opened the boot and rummaged through his duffel bag, taking out a tie and
jacket and putting them on as he walked around to the front.

'Did you try bribery?'

'Of course. But it didn't work. I have a hunch that in Bulgaria they respond
more to authority. I've got the address of another hotel. It's also fully booked,
but we'll go there and see if they have a cancellation.'

The Vitosha-New Otani had been designed by Japanese architects and was
set in a well landscaped garden near the outskirts of the city. Dozens of

flag-poles ringed the car-park. This time we both went to the reception desk.

'I'm Mr Thurlow,' Clifford said offhandedly. 'We have a reservation.' He flipped his passport on the counter.

The pretty young woman looked at it and then studied various lists in front of her. Finally, she said she was very sorry, but she had no record of a reservation for that name and unfortunately, they did not have any free rooms.

A look of controlled fury seized his features. 'I'm afraid that is impossible. My secretary made a reservation for me last week. I spoke to her on the telephone three days ago from Budapest and she said you had confirmed it. Please check again. I am a businessman, with many important people to see here in Sofia and I can't be bothered with this sort of inefficiency.'

The girl looked worried and disappeared through a door into a private office, emerging a few minutes later with an older man.

'Of course, Mr Thurlow,' he said jovially. 'Of course we have your reservation. The girl is new here. She only started two days ago. She did not know.' After a few more apologies and chuckles and great magnanimity on our part, we were shown into a corner room on a high floor with a sweeping view of Mount Vitosha, the city's private playground, summer and winter.

## Clifford

How clever it is to house the editorial offices of all the national newspapers in the same building. The Sofia Press Agency is situated at 113 Lenin Boulevard, which may sound like the centre of town but is, in fact, some miles away through long tracts of classical proletarian architecture, the suburbs endlessly repeating themselves, dreary and decaying.

We took a taxi and Iris waited outside to make sure we didn't lose it. The building, on eight floors, was dull, flat and unmarked except for a small sign in Cyrillic. Three cement steps led to a dark noisy lobby wreathed in cigarette smoke and busy with people with nothing to do. I was immediately accosted by a large man in uniform. 'Pass, pass, pass,' he screamed, a demand not an invitation.

'I'm sorry, I'm English,' I answered in English, showing the man a copy of the *Sofia News*.

He slashed it away with the back of his hand. 'Pass,' he shouted. Beads of sweat had broken out in the bald inlets beside the central greasy strip of his swept back hair. His face was reddening. 'Pass,' he shouted again.

Uniformed doormen, the lowliest peon in the Party hierarchy, were as rude as they were often powerless. Later I felt sorry for the man, but at the time I played out the drama with a certain arrogant and sceptical innocence. Several men in the crowded lobby had gathered around us and, by their expressions, I clearly had their support. Once more, I held up a copy of the *Sofia News*. 'Press,' I said.

'Pass,' he demanded.

A big man in a grey suit now stepped between us. 'Please, how can I help you?' he inquired.

I told him I was a journalist and that I had come to see a reporter by the name of Emilia Konstantinova. He thought about this for a moment. He then spoke gently to the functionary who, looking somewhat humbled, stood back and said in English: 'Six floor.'

'Thank you.'

The elevator was lit by a solitary red bulb, to save energy. The city museum, guarded by two regal and rather snooty lions, had no more than one light in ten working; and the Palace of Culture, with a great firmament of fixtures, had one shining star for every hundred black holes. The ride was painfully slow and, when my eyes had become accustomed to the lighting, I was able to study my lone companion. I was travelling with a stunningly attractive young woman in a neat, two-piece suit. We both got out at the sixth floor. The corridor was quiet and in semi-darkness. I asked her where I might find Emilia Konstantinova.

'Why do you want her?' she responded in perfect English.

'I am a journalist. I have been given her name by a friend in London.'

'Do you have any identification?'

I produced a press card, which she studied for several minutes.

'It is out of date,' she said.

'It's not so important.'

We were silent. We looked each other up and down. The woman was unlike any other woman I had so far seen in Sofia. Her clothes were of good quality and so were her shoes, rare in Eastern Europe. She was slender and poised with energetic features and bright eyes that finally met my own. She gave me a business card: her name was Ani Ivancheva and she was the economics correspondent for the *Sofia News*, a weekly opposition newspaper printed in ten languages and sent all over the world – a sign that the new Socialists believed in free speech and freedom of the press or, on the other hand, a ploy to create that illusion.

Ani Ivancheva went in search of her colleague and, not finding her, she promised to leave her my telephone number at the hotel. Before I left, I asked her why it had been so important to see my credentials before helping me. She seemed embarrassed by the question but quickly regained her composure.

'Six months ago, I could have been arrested just for talking to you,' she said. 'We have lived our whole lives with fear and doubt, a bit of both.'

'Are you still afraid?'

'She measured two inches of space between her fingers. 'A little, yes,' she said. She smiled. 'You are the first foreign reporter to come to our office. It is something we must get used to.'

'But there have been great changes in Bulgaria,' I said and Ani laughed.

'There have been small changes. They have opened the border and they have allowed us to form political parties. But the same people are in power. Todor Zhivkov has gone but the rest, the whole Socialist Democratic Party, it is just the same Communist Party.'

'Then they will be defeated at the elections?'

'I don't know. It will be very close. The Socialist Party has promised land reform. That does not affect the urban intellectuals, but the peasants will believe them. It is what they want. They have been waiting for forty years to get their land back.'

'Then you must make sure they read the *Sofia News*,' I said and a sad look entered her brown eyes.

'It is the intellectuals and the *émigrés* who read our paper. Not the peasants. We only preach to the converted,' she replied. 'And, another thing, we have problems with our paper supply, the same as before. In the past, any newspaper that was too liberal or too critical was closed down. They just said there was a shortage of paper. And if a particular journalist was too critical, the Black Raincoats came and took him.'

The KGB, the Stasi, the Securitate; in Bulgaria: the Black Raincoats. 'This is not Hungary or Czechoslovakia. The changes here are all on the surface. Underneath, nothing, nothing has changed.'

Bulgaria, more than its allies in the Warsaw Pact, had followed Stalin's blueprint for Communism with such faithful dedication that no Red Army troops were ever stationed within its borders. 'The painful realization for us was that the so-called dictatorship of the proletariat was nothing but a dictatorship *over* the proletariat,' Ani Invancheva said.

The Communist stranglehold had been such that dissent of any kind was swiftly crushed. As the Soviet Union had its labour camps, so did Bulgaria: eighty-six of them, many maintained in secrecy until recent months. 'Thousands of people disappeared into unmarked graves. They even fed prisoners to the pigs. The survivors from these camps are now coming forward and telling us what happened. It is unbelievable. We all feel a sense of shame and guilt. We are all Bulgarians.'

## *Iris*

After leaving the Sofia Press Agency, we asked the driver to take us to the Museum of History, a block-long neo-classical structure near Lenin Square.

While it cost 8 c. (5p) to enter, I would have rather paid more and had better lighting. A torch would have been useful to find our way up and down the dim corridors, especially on the upper floors. The information was all in Cyrillic and, though beyond our comprehension, it was a pleasure just to idle lazily among the exhibits. There were endless cases of antique peasant costumes with petticoats and overskirts, aprons, and intricately embroidered vests and jackets. Most impressive, however, was the Penagyurishte Treasure, a nine-piece set of gold dinnerware dating from the fourth to third centuries BC. Even the dismal lighting could not detract from the magnificent design and workmanship.

Out on the street once more, blinking in the sunlight, we contemplated the daily problem of where to have lunch. Our hotel was too far away so we walked north on Vitosha Boulevard. We found numerous coffee-houses that sold sweet cakes, a pre-war fashion that has survived the decades, and a few other establishments that resembled Salvation Army soup kitchens. Eventually we tried one, the cleanest on the block. We lined up with soiled wooden trays, pointing to the things we wanted, and pretending not to notice the curious stares of the other customers. We sat with some office workers at one of the communal tables, passive-looking men in baggy, shiny suits. The soup, a mixture of beans and vegetables, was not bad, and the *Kiselo mleko*, or yoghurt, we had for dessert, was excellent. Bulgaria is famous for its yoghurt and in fact, claims to have invented it.

Somewhat fortified, we took a stroll through TUB, the state central department store, which was scruffy and disappointing, and then made our way to the Sheraton, where an auction of paintings donated by dissident artists was being held. Lenin Square was crowded with people, cars, buses and men in the foreign exchange business. One, in particular, dressed in a bright-red track suit, followed us aggressively. 'Change money? Change money? I give the best rates,' he hissed. He had black hair and a dishonest smile.

'How much?' asked Clifford.

He was offering 20 leva to the dollar. The young man's rate was unusually high and we agreed to exchange $100 (£60) for 2,000 leva. He took a wad of bills from his pocket and counted out the correct number of notes, rolled them up and secured them tightly with an elastic band. All the time his dark eyes kept darting nervously around the square.

'We must be careful. The police, you know.' If he was worried about the police, I wondered why he wore such brightly coloured clothing. 'Show me your money. How do I know that you really have $100? Maybe your money is fake.'

Suddenly he was questioning our honesty! I should have known then that something was wrong.

'I have the money right here,' Clifford said, exasperated.

'Okay.' He handed Clifford the roll of bills, snatched the two $50 notes from his hand, and, the transaction completed, we immediately walked away in opposite directions.

Three steps later I heard Clifford groan. 'Oh, no! The bastard.' Under the top 20 leva note, the other ninety-nine were thin sheets of blank paper, meticulously cut to size. We were outraged and seized with a desire to shout 'stop that thief', but, of course, due to the delicate nature of the business, could not do so. I stepped up on to the running board of a parked van to scan the square but there was not even a hint of a red track suit to be seen. The man had vanished. In spite of our chagrin at being ripped off, we had to admit a grudging admiration for his skill. He was a magician. He had shown us the correct amount of money, and then, before our eyes, had made a substitution. Then he himself had disappeared. How? My gaze had never left his hands for a moment.

Clifford was much more upset than me. 'I've travelled around the world. I've changed money in all sorts of places with some extraordinarily slimy types,' he said. 'I just can't believe it's happened here, to me, in Bulgaria.'

'Look,' I told him. 'Just be glad it wasn't more, and chalk the rest up to experience.'

## Clifford

We entered the main reception hall at the Sheraton and were greeted by Svetlomir Kostadinov, the auctioneer and organizer of the first Artists for Democracy auction. Fifty or so Bulgarian painters, lithographers and sculptors had donated their work to raise funds for the Union of Democratic Forces, the umbrella group formed from numerous parties to fight the Socialists.

Viewing the work with the auctioneer, we circled the room behind a number of confident little groups of people all dressed in the carelessly smart attire you would expect to see in Soho or Old Bond Street. I was surprised to discover that most of them were Bulgarian. Our companions at lunch and the people in the city streets, even the magician in the red track suit, clearly furnished their wardrobes at TUB, Sofia's version of Moscow's GUM. But, like Ani Ivancheva, the artists and their admirers, anti-Communists, if not active dissidents, managed to present themselves as rather well-heeled Europeans. Was there a special shop in Sofia, just for them?

Svetlomir Kostadinov favoured me with a hearty laugh when I made the suggestion. 'No, no, it is not like that,' he explained. 'Many of the people here have some income abroad – the writers and painters. I work for Sotheby's. I am their Bulgarian representative.'

'So we can expect to see a lot of Bulgarian treasures leaving the country,' I said.

He smiled. 'Some, yes,' he told me. 'But that is quite normal. The work of the French Impressionists is all in Japan – and don't the English keep many valuable artefacts they removed from Greece and Egypt?'

'*Touché*,' I replied, and he laughed once again.

I changed the subject and asked him if he was pleased about what was happening in Bulgaria. 'It is so exciting we cannot sleep at night,' he replied, serious for a moment and then smiling again. We shook hands and Svetlomir hurried off in short fast steps, dapper and, I now realized, oddly English in a tweed jacket and a sober blue tie.

By this time, Iris, armed with a list of the items going up for auction, had marked three pieces with a tick and a sum in leva. 'We must buy something,' she said with a worried look on her face and rushed off to register her name.

There were no reserves. Bids were made in sealed envelopes and the bidders were expected to be generous. My genial friend Svetlomir conducted the proceedings in Bulgarian and English and, two hours later, we paid $300 (£180) for the cause of democracy and left with two paintings.

Sofia reveals itself slowly, much like the people. They seem wary and none too friendly at first, but this belies a quick wit, a sense of irony and a feeling that when you do make a friend you have a friend for life.

Bulgarian names take their roots and endings from all around the Balkans – Kostadinov, Konstantinova, Dimitar, Nikolaev, Stamboliiski – and among the people there are body types with faces you might expect to find in fishing boats on the Aegean and in the bazaars of Istanbul. The music, food and peasant costumes have crossed the borders for so many centuries it is impossible to know where anything began and who borrowed exactly what from whom. The similarities are countless, but so too are the differences. Bulgarians are less morbid than the Turks and laugh more than the Greeks. They do not have the volatile Latin nature of the Romanians, their northern neighbour, and they try not to take themselves too seriously, unlike the peoples to the south and west in Yugoslavia.

There is something in the taste of the air and the colour of the sky that is unique, something intangible yet unforgettably Bulgarian. The paving stones in central Sofia are yellow. The city contains the most grotesque collection of buildings in Stalin Gothic outside the Soviet Union and suburbs that make you reel from a nightmarish sense of *déjà vu*. On the surface, everything is as modern and lacklustre as a styrofoam hamburger box but, look closer, and there is a mosque, an old wall, a synagogue, a monkey on a leash and a man with a one-stringed violin.

During excavations for a new subway, builders unearthed the walls of Roman houses and the flagstones of a Roman road. They were carefully restored and included in the pedestrian tunnel that exits in Lenin Square. It doubled construction costs but the city councillors readily agreed to fork out the money to preserve a piece of ancient Serdica. In Bulgaria the government bosses had a secret pride in their national heritage and had no desire to submerge it in the Party mythology. Like the rest of the population, the Communists were incurably enamoured of their own country. 'When Bulgarians talk about their attachment to their land, the talk may sound exaggerated and overly emotional to a foreigner,' Stefane Groueff tells us in *Crown of Thorns,* his biography of King Boris III. 'Yes, of course they love it, but who doesn't love his homeland? For Bulgarians, however, the attachment has a different meaning. The feeling has such intensity that it can only be compared to the state of being in love – an obsessive, romantic, exhilarating, possessive feeling, a source of pride and jealousy, of continuous inspiration and reassurance.'

We walked down the Roman road, carrying our purchases, and emerged as a violinist and his small entourage were approaching. The snap of my camera shutter was answered by the rattle of coins in a pewter pot. The monkey screeched and the musician's assistant grinned at me with silver teeth. '*Bella, bella,*' I said and she ran her hand up and down over her face, frowned, as if to say she doubted my word, and then repeated what I had said. '*Bella, bella.*' She rattled her pot again. I dropped all my change into it and the trio continued their circuit of the square.

I could see Lenin in the distance, peering over a metal fence. The crane still stood in place behind the statue, threatening by its very lack of motion. That part of the square, an annexe off to one side, was always empty but every day someone left some flowers, as if in mourning for the past and a future quickly changing, to most, for the better. Demonstrations in Sofia continued through the year until Thursday, 29 November, when the besieged quasi-Socialist premier resigned and parliament formed a cross-party coalition. Communism finally, unequivocally, had lost its grip.

## Iris

We met Emilia Konstantinova in the hotel bar. 'I'll be reading a newspaper so you can recognize me,' she had said. It was hardly necessary as she was the only woman in the room. She stood to greet us, an attractive, rather well-dressed woman in her early thirties, her pretty face sparkling below a halo of black curls.

'I have a very big problem,' she announced. 'I do not speak English very well. I only start learning six months ago.'

'But we have seen your articles, written in English,' I said. Just that afternoon I had read about the atrocities committed in the labour camps during the past four decades. It had been under her by-line.

'I write in Bulgarian. Everything is translated.'

'Well,' I said. 'Now you will be able to practise.' Practise she did, and for the next six hours, over drinks and dinner, she had an intensive English lesson and we had an insider's view of life in Sofia.

I liked her immediately. She was a political journalist and although she had never left Bulgaria, she had an extensive knowledge of European and world affairs. She also managed to find humour in the absurdities of life in present-day Bulgaria.

'Since November,' she told us, 'Bulgarians are free to travel outside the country, but the catch is we do not have any money for this.' She herself earned a pittance. 'Even the maids working in this hotel make more money than I do. But I love the freedom and I love my work.' Her book explaining the events that had led up to the resignation of Todor Zhivkov on 10 November, 1989, after twenty-five years as Bulgaria's Communist strongman, had just been published.

She lived with her parents and her four-year-old son. She and her husband, a television newscaster, had separated after the November uprising because he had joined the Communist Party in order to secure his position and she was a passionate member of the democratic opposition. 'You have a word.'

'Hypocrisy,' I suggested.

'That is it. I could not stand the hypocrisy any longer,' she said. She then told us that many marriages were breaking up over political differences now that people were free to express their opinions.

The next morning, promptly at ten, Emilia was back at the hotel to be our guide on a tour around the city. She took us first to the most expensive residential areas to see 'where the rich live.' We drove down tree-lined streets and glimpsed villas tucked away in shady gardens, solid structures built before the war.

'Did people have to be a member of the Party to be rich?' I asked.

'Yes. With the exception of a few artists.'

Then she steered us to the poor sections of the city, where endless rows of grey concrete apartment blocks stretched out as far as the eye could see, lines of washing strung across practically every tiny balcony.

'Here, the people are very nervous,' she said. 'The apartments are small, crowded, everything is broken. This is where I live. I hate it.'

I admired her even more. It seemed so unlikely that such a clever, elegant woman could emerge from such an environment. I was prompted to ask a question, 'How do you manage to have such pretty clothes? I haven't seen anything as nice for sale in the shops.'

'I am fortunate. A friend in France sends me old magazines and sometimes cloth. My mother is the best dressmaker in Sofia and copies them for me.'

She had been in the hospital two years earlier with pneumonia and said it had been the worst experience of her life. She had shared a room with nine other women, 'and the meals were so bad my mother and husband had to bring me food every day or I would have died.'

Her mother took care of her child so she did not have to put him in a school during the day while she worked. The nursery-school classes were overcrowded. 'Sometimes forty children to one teacher, and they are always catching colds and illnesses from the other children.'

I was curious to know about the status of women in Bulgaria and if they had equal rights with men. Her heart-shaped face became indignant. 'It is not good for women. We have big problems with men. In Bulgaria, the attitude is that men should work while women stay home to care for their family and house. In reality, the men make so little money the women are forced to work outside the home also, and still care for their children and husband. The men do not help. They are very macho. The women work very hard.'

I had to smile. 'It is still like that in the United States, too. Maybe a little better, but not much.'

Next, Emilia took us to the Alexander Nevski Church, built in 1912 as a memorial to the 200,000 Russian soldiers who died in the liberation of Bulgaria. The neo-Byzantine building was imposing from the outside and inside wafts of spicy incense drifted over the high frescoes and ornately-carved altar. There was poverty in the streets but plenty of gold decorating the church interior. I much preferred the spartan simplicity of the little Church of St Sophia opposite, which dates back to the sixth century. Traces of two even older churches were found during recent restorations.

We then made our way to a small square where artists and craftsmen displayed their creations. 'We call this The Arrested Square,' Emilia said, and she broke into laughter. She explained that in October, several hundred people, including many students, had gathered there to protest against pollution. They had been savagely attacked by the police. Many had been injured and had had to be taken to hospital. The following day, the square had been thoroughly cleaned and policemen, spaced 2 feet apart, had stood guard around the entire perimeter. 'Look,' someone had shouted. 'The fools have arrested the square!' and the name had remained ever since. 'That was when the revolution began – that day in October,' she added. 'It was the last time the police acted with brutality and were allowed to get away with it.'

On our way back to the car we passed the Georgi Dimitrov Mausoleum and decided to go in, much to Emilia's dismay. 'We had to come here as children, once a year, like going to a religious ceremony. I hated it,' she said.

'Now you must view it with the dispassion of a journalist,' Clifford told her.

'Of course. But it is hard. We have suffered so much.'

After spending the war years in Russia, Georgi Dimitrov had led the Communists to power and in 1946 had become the Party's first General Secretary. He died three years later, in his beloved Moscow, and the Mausoleum, much like the tomb of Lenin, was erected in his honour. We had to check our bags at the entrance, which I did with great reluctance and only after Emilia assured me that it would be safe. 'We have many problems but not so many robbers,' she said. It took only a few minutes to take a glimpse of the embalmed body of the revolutionary and we exited in time to see the hourly changing of the guard, a ceremony performed with the same solemnity as that of the guards outside Buckingham Palace.

In Bulgaria, you must know people to get anything done. Contacts are important,' Emilia whispered, as we were shown to a table in a rustic restaurant on top of Mount Vitosha. We had driven up the mountain to have lunch before leaving for Plovdiv, our next destination.

The head waiter had gravely informed us that he was fully booked, even though we had been able to see many empty tables behind him. Emilia had taken him to one side and they had spoken in private for several minutes. When they had finished, he had smiled in our direction. He had discovered that he did have room, after all. I was eager to know exactly what she had said.

'I told him where I worked. My editor is a good client here. In Bulgaria, it is always necessary to do things this way.'

Later, Clifford asked her if she worked with Ani Ivancheva, who had made a big impression on him.

'No.' Her nose wrinkled and I sensed that there was some rivalry between them. 'Her grandfather was a Communist. So was her father. She has had a privileged life. Her family had a house in the country and she went to school in Switzerland. Now, she has switched to the democratic camp. I don't trust her.'

We said goodbye to Emilia outside our hotel. We told her that she now had two friends in London and New York and invited her to visit us.

'If the Communists win on 10 June, I may have to leave,' she laughed, but I knew she was not joking. Since November, Emilia had written many articles against the Communists, including a major exposé on the eighty-six labour camps around the country. If the same people gained control again, her name would be on the hit list of the Black Raincoats. We hugged once more and she climbed into her Trabant. It started on the fourth try and she drove off leaving a trail of blue smoke behind her.

## Clifford

In Plovdiv there is an amphitheatre built by the Romans in the second century AD. The curved bowl of the auditorium faces a row of marble columns that, apart from a few repairs, have withstood the test of time. The amphitheatre is just below the peak of a steep hill and, with the tall, graceful columns as a backdrop, the view sweeps over a valley to a range of rolling hills that were now slowly darkening in the distance. It had been a long drive from Sofia and the evening cool was invigorating.

The view of the hills that the Roman theatre-goers would have seen was now interrupted by lines of crude apartment blocks, the most common and repetitious memorial to forty years of Marxism. We had looked at them earlier, passing in the car, buildings that were, without exception, dull, brutish, crumbling slabs of squalor, blackened by pollution; anonymous institutional boxes pierced by small windows like prison cell windows, they were joined by flights of grey unlit stairways where dirt and danger were forever lurking. The people who lived in these buildings, often three generations of the same family in two or three small rooms, should have been the cockroaches they were often called by the party élite. But they are not. Far from it.

It was 6.30 in the evening after an unusually hot day and, while we climbed the hill from the city centre, we heard a piece of music that, while familiar, was continually being cut off, as if a madman were lifting the needle from a record and then replacing it, over and over again. When we reached the amphitheatre, we found a full orchestra rehearsing the opera *Pagliacci* with a company of almost a hundred singers and a conductor who was a perfectionist.

A few stars had appeared above us. We sat behind the orchestra and watched the conductor and choreographer plan their sequences. The conductor was tall and thin with sensitive features and pale intelligent eyes. He looked like a man who had spent twenty years in a labour camp and had left with his integrity intact. The choreographer was a young woman, all in black, who shouted her instructions through an antiquated megaphone. The players in the orchestra and the members of the cast were all dressed in the drab shoddy way that was standard, but their faces were filled with enthusiasm and, I would say, even happiness. Most of the instruments were old, pre-war I imagined, and I wondered how much deprivation and hunger had been necessary to save the money for those violins and French horns that were new. The average wage in Bulgaria was $100 (£60) a month – less for a journalist or a doctor than for a hotel maid, Emilia Konstantinova had explained. A maid carried the added burden of trust. 'They work for only three or four hours a day and they all run small businesses in soap and shampoo, in towels, even sheets and blankets,' she had told us.

The sun had gone down and it was only the cold creeping into the worn marble that finally drove us away. We had remained at the rehearsal for nearly two hours and I left with the feeling that the people performing Italian opera for their own pleasure, after a day's work, in spite of all social restrictions and deprivations, was in some way an act of defiance, of human will and dignity over the politics of repression. One constantly wanted to ask why they had waited so long to rebel and had to remember the Hungarian uprising in 1956 and the Prague Spring of 1968. They had been answered with Soviet tanks and blood on the streets. The system had survived through the force of fear and it was only Mikhail Gorbachev who was changing all that. In Bulgaria, the same as every country we had visited, he was universally popular. It was hardly surprising he survived the attempted coup that lasted just four days in August 1991.

We continued our walk through the winding hills of the old town, where the merchants had cleverly overcome the problem of owning only a small ground area by constructing overhanging tiers on each floor of their houses, the top floors almost touching across the narrow streets. They were beautifully embellished with designs cribbed from architectural ideas being tried in other parts of Europe in the eighteenth and early nineteenth centuries, a style that became known as Bulgarian Nationalist Revival.

These houses had become the homes of Party officials and were, naturally enough, well maintained. In one, through the open door and behind a walled flower garden, we saw a family at dinner being served by a uniformed maid. Outside most of the houses there were new cars parked on the ancient cobbles. As the path descended, the houses grew smaller, the cars older, until both disappeared into the wide boulevard of the main shopping centre, another architectural kaleidoscope patterned with Islamic turrets, mosques like little jewels in a bracelet alongside churches from numerous periods, dry fountains and dusty palm trees as high as the buildings. There were no actual beggars in the streets, although the benches were all occupied by humble-looking souls selling a few pathetic items: a half-dozen balloons, four torch batteries, single unfiltered cigarettes. Plovdiv was a poor city.

We had a barely edible pizza in an outdoor café and a language dispute with a gigantic, javelin-throwing waitress; my fault, not hers. I kept asking for two beers and pointing at the stuff on the other tables. She kept telling me that, yes, they did sell beer, but they had run out. We were joined by two skinny girl students who did the translating and the four of us sat down together.

I asked them if they were excited about the election and they both shrugged. 'No, not really,' said one. 'We are still too young to vote.'

'But don't you want to see democracy in Bulgaria?'

'I suppose so.'

Her friend continued. 'My father says the new politicians will be the same as the old. They are only in it for what they can get out of it themselves,' she said.

'But democracy will still be better than Communism,' Iris said.

'Maybe.'

I was a little taken aback by the exchange. After witnessing all the passion and energy in Sofia, it was strange to find such apathy in the nation's second city. We had seen remarkably few posters in the streets and, at the top of the hill, those who had the cash were clearly in no hurry to hide the fact that a maid in their classless society was employed to serve dinner. Emilia, Svetlomir Kostadinov and the others I had spoken to all had the same fear: the democrats were sure to win all the seats in Sofia but, outside the capital, people were still afraid of the Communists.

We said farewell to our two companions and set out for the pension on the far side of the Maritsa River. The street lights were turned off to save energy, although the red Socialist Party flag above Party headquarters was lit from below by a strong beam that made the flag look like a flame in the dark sky. The towers and the domes of mosques gave the city a distinctly oriental air and the smell of spicy food drifting from open windows brought back memories of Istanbul and Cairo. Away from the centre, the streets were deserted except for the occasional wraith that appeared from the shadows and quickly vanished, the tap of footsteps moving away like a fading heartbeat. A few grim characters approached us from doorways whispering their mantra: 'Change money?' – as if we were wearing a neon sign that shouted 'foreigner'. Changing money on the black market was problem enough in the daylight.

## Iris

A wedge of morning sun like a slice of orange was lighting the tiled rooftops of the houses as we drove out of Plovdiv towards the Valley of the Roses. We had loaded the bags into the car in darkness. I clutched a list of names that I had painstakingly printed out in Cyrillic, the triangles and backward 'N's spelling Klisura, Sopot, Karlovo, Kalofer and Kazanlŭk, the towns and villages along the way.

The photographs in the glossy brochure I had picked up in Sofia showed pretty young women in elaborately embroidered peasant dresses, with coronets of roses in their hair, roses twined around their wrists and behind their ears, girls holding wicker baskets filled with rose petals, all against a background of rose bushes. The reality was quite different. The roses are cultivated in fields much like vineyards that stretch for miles on each side of the valley road, the Balkan range rising slowly in the north, and the hills of Sredna Gora in the south. Groups of heavy-set peasant women, dressed not in brightly-coloured clothing, but in more practical blacks and browns, stooped over in the back-breaking labour of picking the petals. In May and early June they begin each morning at dawn when the flowers open, and work until eight, when the hot rays of the sun start to burn off too much of the precious oil.

It takes from three to six tons of rose petals to make one-quart of rose oil or oil of attar, which, ounce for ounce, makes it more valuable than gold. It is used in the making of perfume, liqueurs, sweetmeats, jam, medicine and Turkish delight. The production of attar of roses began in the 1830s under the Turks and is the oldest industry in Bulgaria.

We pulled off the road beside a field where numerous women were hard at work stripping the flowers with nimble fingers. At first they looked startled and suspicious.

'Good morning, *dobro outro*,' I called, smiling, '*Dobro outro.*' I hoped my pronunciation was clear. I took out my camera and started taking pictures. They relaxed and a few smiled back at me. One woman, her head wrapped in a brown scarf, even waved and held up a half-filled basket of rose petals.

Further on, we passed another group of women, their field work finished for the day, resting in the shade of the roadside trees and eating breakfast. The scene was straight out of a painting by Bruegel.

## Clifford

After discovering an appalling lack of interest in the coming election in Plovdiv it was refreshing to see a more lively effort being made in Veliko Tŭrnovo. A car was going through town with a loudspeaker and a message from the Union of Democratic Forces; there were handbills and posters, the most common being a map of Bulgaria showing the Communist Party headquarters in the capital and skulls where each of the labour camps had been, negative advertizing which was later deemed a failure. I took a handbill and stared down at the unreadable script.

'Democracy or death,' said a man in English; he was short and bandy in leather boots and looked as if he had just climbed down from a horse. 'You are German?' he asked.

'No, English.'

'Then I was right,' he said and laughed. 'We must laugh. It is laughing that makes us Bulgarians.'

'Are the people going to vote for the Democrats?' I asked him.

He scratched his chin thoughtfully. 'Who knows?' he said. 'They tell the Socialists they vote for them and tell us they vote for us. They are afraid to make decisions for themselves.'

He continued on his way, rolling down the hill on his bowed legs like a landbound mariner, and we continued exploring what the Bulgarian writer Ivan Vasov thought of as the most amazing, most unbelievable city he had ever seen: 'at Veliko Tŭrnovo, I think I am looking at a vision, at an illusion to the eyes.' It was a wanderer's paradise, a touch of Venice with a sprinkling of Athens, even a dab of Canterbury. It had medieval buildings sharing walls with Roman remains, Revival bridges, churches in creamy rich colours and mosques with onion domes and slender towers. Iron balconies, thin and elongated, were shaded with vine arbours; geraniums leaned out from window-boxes like nosy neighbours and peered along white stone tracks the colour of burnished marble.

Fountains picking out glints of colour gave the hot afternoon a feeling that somewhere there was an oasis of cool. I watched a horse, panting in a cloud of steam, dip its head into a water trough and spray the water over its back. There were few cars and the streets were too narrow for the huge Bulgarian trucks we had passed on the road from the Valley of the Roses. Artists and craftsmen have made Veliko Tŭrnovo their home for more than a thousand years and many still do, occupying wooden studios balanced on top of each other like an enormous house of cards that has been caught in a mud slide and then thrown up again, haphazard but aesthetically pleasing.

I had noticed something special about Veliko Tŭrnovo the moment we had driven into it: the sky was clear blue without its usual veil of pollution and there were no giant factories shouldering in among the old sites. It has been constructed in a deep, narrow valley within a loop in the River Yantra, which snakes back on itself in such an extravagant way that the city appears to be on an island. The houses and ancient fortifications tumble down the steep slopes from every direction.

In the museum, stumbled on, rather than sought out, a brochure in English told us the city had held an important place in the hearts of Bulgarians since 1185, a memorable period throughout the whole of Europe. The winter never came that year. Trees were in full blossom in January; flowers covered the hills and the citizens saw this as a message from God. Led by two boyar noblemen, the brothers Assen and Peter, the people marched out of the Church of St Dimiter and Salonika in the old town determined to shrug off the yolk of Byzantine rule, which they achieved after two years of war. The king was restored as the head of Bulgaria. The city became the capital and remained so for the next two centuries. During this time, the hills became fortresses; palaces were built, art and literature flourished.

In 1393, the city came under attack and, after a bloody battle that lasted for three months, it fell once more to the Ottoman warriors and remained a Turkish dominion for the next five hundred years.

Throughout this time, Veliko Tŭrnovo remained the centre of Bulgarian culture and the desire for freedom kept alive under the Turks must have been passed on through the generations to the people who live there today. They had loathed being a vassal of foreign rulers and, as I sensed from the staff in the museum – three women in aprons and headscarfs – they had never been happy with the subtle bondage of Communism.

They ran round behind us, pointing out all the little details that made Bulgaria unique and, to them, the centre of the universe. Communication was close to zero. Two of them spoke a little German but my own command of the language was too weak for the complexities of history. I was carrying our electronic translator for the first time in weeks. I tapped in words in English and, as words of German came singing out, they looked at the machine with all the wonder the Red Indians must have shown the white man with his Winchester rifles. I gave it to them and they gave it back to me. We in the West take the state of material well-being as a birthright, like the air we breathe, but to these three women the object was far too valuable to give away. It was too great a gift.

'For the museum,' I said. 'For everyone.'

They thanked me profusely in Bulgarian, the oldest with tears in her eyes, and it was only later that I realized the translator was next to useless without a command of at least English, German, French or Spanish.

The road from Veliko Tŭrnovo falls in long graceful curves to the wide Bulgarian plain. This is vineyard country, green and lush as it stretches east and ends abruptly on the silver beaches of the coast. Since crossing the English Channel from Dover to Calais, we had not had a glimpse of the sea and, suddenly, I missed that intangible sense of liberation wide open spaces inspire and Marxism alone tried to eradicate. Closed borders was always an insane and suspicious policy.

Poverty in our streets is the result of greed, corruption, a lack of care and changes in the political as well as the family structure. Poverty in Eastern Europe, stemming from the same sources, has the added fuel of inertia, rampant nepotism, disorganization, bad management, hopeless distribution networks, a lack of motivation and few rewards for industry or brilliance. Present-day capitalism in many Western democracies allows too many people to slip through the cracks. Communism, from what we had seen, failed on every level, miserably and utterly. As Allen Ginsberg said on May Day in Prague and Vaclav Havel and other fledging politicians have been saying since they took office, what is required is a middle way, encouragement to wealth creating free enterprise, but not at the cost of human suffering.

What I was unable to understand was why the bright young members of the nomenclature, a word always spat out like a vile oath by those not a part of it, why these people did not see how thoroughly their system was failing and revise it. To go wrong and not change course, it is said, can clearly be defined as going wrong. A governing body that rectifies its mistakes and produces something better would surely have won the support of the populace, even election to office. I can only imagine that the fear, real or imagined, the Soviet Union engendered in the West was a mere shadow of the absolute terror it inspired in the East.

Perhaps it was solely the rural peasants who retained a measure of freedom. They certainly remained poor. The villages in eastern Bulgaria were virtually the same as they must have been a hundred years ago, each one a concentration of modest cottages around a stone church placed always on a low hill, like a small fortress, with slit windows and buttressed walls. Before the Turks, the Mongols, Huns and Romans had all marched their armies over the plains, making building for defence more a matter of instinct than policy. Villages still without running water were often blessed with electricity and bristled with television antennas, the only change clearly noticeable.

All work in the fields was being carried out with primitive tools: rakes, hoes and scythes with wooden shafts; horse-ploughs and horse-drawn harvesters. In the capital, some women had been elegant, even fashionable. Now, moving towards the sea, we were closer to Istanbul than Sofia and the girls were wearing black tunics with red and gold embroidered bodices, their hair wrapped in scarfs Muslim style. The men wore colourful waistcoats, bushy moustaches and knee boots, the same as their great-grandfathers, some keeping faith to those boots with awkward upturned pointed toes. Shepherds stood in the meadows, their arms locked around long slender crooks, guiding the sheep with a melodious series of clucks and whistles. Some had dogs, but not many.

I was driving slowly. I wanted to see the countryside, unlike the people who lived in those parts and appeared to nurture the sole ambition of reaching their destination in record time. Having suffered forty years of totalitarian government, Bulgarians are prepared to die rather than sit on the tail of a slow-moving vehicle. Trucks that appeared as flecks in the rear view mirror hurtled down on me like meteorites and shot by without concern for oncoming traffic. The road running from Sofia to the Black Sea was like a racing track and local drivers had learned to use the fields, thankfully unfenced, as an extension to the highway.

There were few private cars and fewer still in the rural areas. We did see other foreign vehicles but, without exception, they carried West German registration plates and always gave me the distinct impression they were motoring east on business. I had expected to meet up with others like ourselves, travelling for the sake of travelling, but if curious visitors were flying into capitals, they were not crossing the land borders – at least, we never saw any and we never once met anyone making the same journey. In a shrinking world where few small sections have been left untouched, it was a rare bonus to have this neglected patch of Europe severed by the Iron Curtain virtually to ourselves.

We were there at a unique time, when endings and new beginnings were overlapping. Our reward was the dancing bear. It was market day in the village of Kotel. Carts of a simple design, centuries old, pulled by melancholic donkeys with the soulful eyes of saints in icons, had converged on an open piece of land next to a large modern garage, a meeting place of truckers, gypsies and traders on the black economy. Some stood behind rough stalls, while others wandered by, kicking up the dust and holding up their goods like surrender flags. Two men had set up stands selling cassette tapes opposite each other and both played balalaika music at such a pitch it sounded like a cat fight and made communication impossible and redundant. A man with arms laden with tattoos, a single gold ear-ring and hair greased flat over his collar like a circus performer trailed along behind me making offers for my shirt, jeans and shoes, and it was a relief to vanish into the magnetic jangle of the duelling stringed instruments and ignore him. There were blue jeans for sale but they were not like my blue jeans. Even in Bulgaria, the *conoscienti* knew the difference.

We ate lamb kebabs laced with *kiselo mleko* and drank hot lemonade that was three-parts sugar to one-part dangerous chemicals. Girls of nine carrying sobbing infants of nine months and pursuing the traditional gypsy craft of begging joined us in procession but small donations were to no avail. They wanted dollars or Deutschmarks; lira, francs, sterling and the peseta were not in their vocabulary.

Then we saw the bear. A cart rolled into the centre of the market and the animal reared up on its hind legs and prepared to dance. It was on a long fine chain and moved in the ungainly waltz the distorted music deserved. The bear was black, nearly as tall as a man and lashed out with its forepaws at anyone who invaded its dancing space. Some of the gypsy boys moved close enough to lose an eye and moved back at the last second, playing dare, proving themselves men while their sisters still bawled for baksheesh. I could see by the look in Iris's brown eyes that she was repelled and excited. We had left Europe behind. Kotel was the invisible gateway to a land before Communism. The noise, strange music, customs, the smell of dust and spicy food, the dancing bear, all were exotic and intoxicating.

The girls other than the gypsies were dressed in long black skirts and peasant blouses. They wore heavy silver necklaces and ear-rings, hand-carved in the traditional way, the very things one hopes to find and take home. But these heirlooms were not for sale. The jewellery that was being sold was made of base metal, pressed out on a machine. The people were also selling eggs wrapped in straw and live chickens in wooden cages. There were displays of plastic combs and children's toys in violent colours, nylon shirts, and misshapen sweaters, too hot for the season.

We bought a bag of cherries and as I was parting with 4 leva, a man leaned over, took the two notes and gave one of them back to me. 'They double the price for foreigners. Even me,' he laughed. 'And I was born here.'

Emil drove a Daf truck from Ankara to various capitals all over Europe. He wore a neat moustache and a three-day designer beard. 'I take leather things to Italy and I bring different leather things back from Italy. It is economics,' he said.

'Your English is good,' I remarked.

'I live five years in Australia, with my brother. It is too far,' he said.

I offered him some cherries and he held up a defensive palm as a non-smoker would being offered a cigarette. He then lit up.

'I am Turkish, not Bulgarian. But I was born in this country,' Emil said. 'You know, it was the Turks who began the revolution. They made the Turks change their names – they had to have Bulgarian names. Then, they grew to hate it. They are Muslims, religious people. You cannot be a Muslim and a Communist. It is like oil and water.'

I asked him what the future for the Turks was in Bulgaria now that democracy was being installed. He drew on his cigarette and took a deep breath. 'The same as in Germany,' he answered.

## Iris

Burgas was awful. It scared me. The second largest port on the Black Sea, it has oil refineries and industrial complexes pumping out poisons that darken the sky. It took us about forty minutes to slowly manoeuvre around the city following the signs that pointed south. Much of the road was under construction, so there was plenty of dust and fumes from trucks to inhale as well as the pollution. Then, everything changed. All the traffic turned one way and we another. We headed along the coast on an empty road towards Turkey, sun-burnished waves all the way to the horizon on our left, lush woodland stretching out on our right.

The weather had become extremely hot. We were on our way to Sozopol, at the suggestion of Emilia Konstantinova, and arrived in the late afternoon. It was a truly magnificent village, neither Eastern nor Western, but totally original. It sits on a tiny cape, shaped like a crooked thumb and finger. Although it had Greek settlers in the seventh century BC and Roman and Turkish visitors after that, nothing of its historical past remains. What it does have are numerous National Revival houses, dating from the eighteenth and nineteenth centuries, similar but smaller than the hill-top houses in Plovdiv. The ground floor of each is built of stone and the second, overhanging storey is made of dark wood. Little balconies, shuttered windows and red-tiled rooftops complete their exteriors. They are immensely appealing and crowd around the edge of the narrow peninsula, the oldest part of town, and the few tiny streets that link the two coasts. The construction laws are strict and all new building must be in harmony with the old. Artists and writers the world over choose to live in beautiful, inexpensive places; in Bulgaria they came to Sozopol.

The town was deserted. We passed a low white building with BALKAN-TOURIST written in big letters on the outside. We had been in Bulgaria long enough to know that they controlled tourism in the country and the only way we would find a room would be with their help. We parked and climbed the stairs to a tiny office on the second floor. Inside, nine women, dressed like country and western singers, sat tightly squeezed behind four desks.

'Does anyone speak English? Italian? Spanish? French? German?' Clifford asked, giving them our entire repertoire and exaggerating a little on the last two.

Nine pairs of eyes stared at us. Finally, one girl admitted to knowing a little English. Clifford explained that we wanted a room for a few days.

'It is very difficult. It is not the season,' she said.

'A nice room. With bath,' I added with determination.

They proceeded to talk noisily among themselves for about ten minutes. We could only hope that our request was the subject under discussion. Finally, the English student, looking very serious, produced a map of the town.

'You are here,' she said, without preamble, making a red 'X' on one of the streets. 'You go there.' Another 'X'. 'There is a room. You look. But you must return here to pay.' We thanked her and left.

The address was 51 Odessa Street. We drove slowly and counted off the numbers on two blocks of modern, grey houses with little gardens in front, pleasant enough but hardly the pretty Revival houses on the peninsula.

'Not too bad,' I said hopefully. They were simple but looked neat and clean. We slowed to a stop. Just ahead of us a heap of rubble half-blocked the road. Behind it, in the garden of a house, were the corpses of several battered cars that were being cannibalized by two men in filthy overalls. It was number 51. We were going to pass the house by but a woman, plump and smiling, was waiting at the gate. We had to go in. We parked and picked our way through the rusting bits of metal that protruded from the piles of junk.

Inside, we followed her up to a tiny attic room. 'This is awful,' I said to Clifford, knowing that the woman could not understand. 'I'd rather go back to Burgas and sleep inside an oil refinery.'

We thanked her, still smiling, as we made our getaway. 'I did not like it very much,' I said as tactfully as I could, back at the office. 'Do you have something better?'

They went into another nine-part conference. Eventually, a decision was reached. The English-speaking woman focused on us. 'We have one place you can stay. It is like a hotel, but it is not a hotel. You will have a room and a bath. It is near here. You will pay them directly. Not us. It is called,' she paused to take a deep breath, 'Spartakus.'

We entered the Spartakus – the hotel that was not a hotel – with great curiosity. It was a large building on the outskirts of town and was part of a complex; it had a stark, no-frills atmosphere. As we went through the usual check-in procedure at the front desk, I noticed that the men and women going through the swinging doors were all young and had extremely impressive physiques. Most of them wore T-shirts and shorts or tracksuits. All had running shoes on their feet.

'What's going on?' I whispered to Clifford. 'Have we stumbled into a breeding ground for perfect human specimens?' In the lobby a huge mural depicting people involved in different sports, with the five interlocking rings of the Olympic Games underneath, gave us the first clue. Arrows pointing to a swimming pool and gymnasium confirmed that we had landed in a training centre for athletes.

## Clifford

On the road south between Sozopol and Primorsko there was a long, high fence that was falling down. Behind the fence, there was a gypsy camp. It was not made up of ornate, colourful caravans but of shanty huts made from pressed out oil drums and sheets of asbestos. We had seen men filling oil drums with water from a roadside tap and this was where they had been heading, the loads carried on carts pulled by small donkeys.

I stopped to photograph the encampment, transgressing some unspoken though palpable code, and almost paid the penalty for it. Three drooling mastiffs, as proportionately large as the donkeys were diminutive, came charging towards me and I wasn't sure whether to run or remain stationary. The moment of indecision came fortuitously to an end with the appearance of a man who called the dogs off. He kicked one of them and all three retreated, snarling bitterly.

The man beckoned, pointing at me and then at the ground in front of where he stood. Reluctantly, I joined him. He took my camera and held it up as if to take my photograph. He then gave it back to me. I understood the point.

I was now at the entrance to the encampment. It was larger than I had first thought and, though it had a feeling of being deserted, numerous naked and near-naked children began to materialize. Then some older women and another man appeared. The young people worked as day labourers. We had seen numerous groups of them on construction sites along the coast, the girls always busy, carrying bricks, mixing cement, the young men idly standing by and watching. Like the Mexican fruit pickers in California, they earn little, pay no taxes and have no social benefits.

My host was wearing traditional gypsy attire: a waistcoat over a puff-sleeved shirt, baggy pants and a sort of small turban. He had a white moustache, a bomb site of stumpy brown teeth and a large gold ear-ring in one ear. He looked like a harijan, the caste of untouchables in India: the same finely-carved features and dark skin, and clothes that were remarkably similar, anthropological proof that the gypsies migrated from India in the early years of Christianity and fanned out all over Europe.

Most of the others in the camp wore cheap, worn-out modern clothing. The exception was an elderly woman who I assumed was the chief's wife. Her clothes were bright and richly embroidered – a long, heavy skirt, a blouse and a man's waistcoat. Her small feet were in brown leather boots and her hair was covered by a thick scarf. Around her neck she wore a collection of silver necklaces and her heavy silver ear-rings had exaggerated the holes in her ears. The chief grunted out some orders to her and she went to fetch Iris, who had been watching the scene from the car. The children remained silent, motion-less as statues against the backdrop of broken car parts and useless abandoned objects. The smell was dreadful. With no water, the camp certainly had no other facilities either.

We moved into the centre of the site and stood around a giant cable spool which served as a table. The old woman produced an ancient, filthy pack of Tarot cards and, though we had not a word of communication between us, as she spread the cards in their patterns of symbolic mandalas, making gestures and animated expressions, we acted as if we understood everything and hoped we did.

One thing was clear: she rubbed two fingers together to indicate that we would get married. I thought this was rather intuitive on her part, as a more obvious guess would have been that we already were.

'Children?' Iris asked, pointing at the little urchins who had stopped being statues to move closer. The gypsy turned over a card. It was the four of swords.

'*Ne*,' she replied, nodding to indicate no. She tapped a grubby finger on another card, a stone tower that was toppling over, and then glanced towards the horizon: I imagined we were too busy seeing the world to start a family!

I crossed her palm with a $10 bill and went to the car to get some packets of biscuits for the children. I still had the democracy leaflet from Veliko Tǔrnovo, and I gave it to the old man. He shrugged, turned it over and gave it back to me. He was unable to read.

'*Domocracia*,' I said.

He thought about that for a few moments. He said the word democracy and drew his finger across his throat. Then he said Communism, and repeated the action. His dark eyes were sparkling and his lips were a straight line. He walked with us back to the car, the three large dogs trailing along behind us, and watched as we climbed in and set off on the return journey to Sozopol. I drove slowly and neither of us spoke. The sky was clear blue and the sun's fierce light made the sea as white and smooth as a glass of milk.

After seeing the gypsy camp, the village seemed positively luxurious. The Revival houses were polished by the sunlight and the shutters had all been freshly painted. It reminded me of certain hill villages in Andalusia. It was Saturday. The tiny stores were open and housewives were shopping for the weekend. We queued for a ration of *hylab* – bread. We bought cheese, tomatoes, a cucumber, yoghurt; then some melon seeds and peanuts that came in cones torn from an old newspaper. Each time we made a purchase we said *molya* and *blagodarya*, please and thank-you, and it is amazing how far a few words said in another's tongue can take you. We were made to feel welcome.

Sozopol is a special place and not at all like the other villages on the Black Sea. Todor Zhivkov once asked Stalin if he considered it a good idea to develop the coast and Stalin's nod of approval was *carte blanche* for the string of ugly, high-rise hotels that were thrown up with little thought in the 1960s and 1970s. Sozopol has not been developed or modernized. It has always been there. It was the port of Apollonia, a Greek settlement, six hundred years before Christ and remained an important trading centre until AD 72, when it was sacked by the Romans. The Greeks during a period of particular prosperity erected a marble statue of the Sun God Apollo and it can still be seen – in a museum in Rome. All that remains on the site today are a few stone footings.

Apollonia, like ancient Troy, vanished into the history books and Sozopol grew from a fishing community to a small town with cobbled streets and tiny squares. Avenues of cypresses run down to the sea and artists were sitting in the shade with their easels painting the fishing boats and ignoring the naval hardware that lies beyond in the outer harbour. The naval base was surrounded by a mesh enclosure decorated with signs saying 'No Photography' in numerous languages.

When the Germans began to take holidays on the Black Sea so many of them stripped off their clothing that the local Party bureaucrats were obliged to find a compromise. What they did was to fence off the furthest corner of all the beaches and mark them off for 'Naturists'. We left the nudists in their compound on the outer fringes of Sozopol and made our way towards the inner harbour. Fishermen wearing berets and smoking hooked pipes were mending their nets and a line of fishing boats moved restlessly on their moorings. No boats were out, a warning to the observant. The day had been hot and clear, perfect for swimming. Now, at the very moment we sat down on the main beach, storm clouds appeared like an invading army from Turkey and Russia and joined over the horizon. The sea turned grey and serrated like dragon skin. Large drops of rain began to fall, thudding into the sand. The waves came roaring dramatically up the beach and we ran for shelter.

## Iris

I awoke to the sound of rain; our weekend in the sun was not turning out as we had planned. Rather than spend the day watching the weight-lifters flex their muscles, we decided to pack and move on.

We retraced our path out of Sozopol and drove in a northerly direction, carefully picking our way around Burgas and the refineries, until we again had a view of the sea on our right. It occurred to me that we had passed the point of no return. From now on, even though we still had to drive through Romania, each mile would bring us closer to London, our departure point, and the end of the journey.

In the distance, through the rain and swipes of the windscreen wipers, I could see what looked like a huge battleship, anchored just offshore. As we drove closer, I realized it was a tiny peninsula, saved from being an island by a strip of sandbar. I checked the map.

'This must be Nesebar. Let's stop,' I said, and Clifford, ever obliging, turned off the main road.

Nesebar is one of the oldest villages in Bulgaria, with a history similar to Sozopol. The difference is that Nesebar, on its 65 acres of land, is filled with the remains of ancient churches and buildings, in various stages of preservation. The earliest date from the fifth and sixth centuries. Hugging the romantic little streets around the churches was another collection of Revival style houses. The village looked old, wise and sombre.

It had finally stopped raining. It did not take long to walk from one side of town to the other. We saw a small crowd of people in front of a church, clustered around a bride and groom and went over to inspect the scene. The bride, tiny and dark, wore a long white wedding gown with a veil and layers of white ruffled net on the skirt. The groom, in a pale grey suit, managed to look both ill at ease and pleased with himself. It was obvious that they were poor people – perhaps the groom was a farmer or a fisherman – but this was their wedding day and they were determined to follow tradition.

Everyone seemed to be waiting for something to happen. Then we heard the sound of music, drawing closer, and suddenly five musicians appeared around the corner. They were playing a Bulgarian wedding march on two accordions, a clarinet, a long drum that was beaten at both ends in double tempo and a peculiar wind instrument that resembled a bagpipe. The newly-weds followed them through the streets and the rest of the wedding party fell in behind. Every few minutes they stopped and the people joined hands and danced, executing intricate steps I was unable to follow.

I nudged Clifford. 'I just realized no one is taking pictures. These people probably can't afford a camera.' Clifford sprung into action and took two rolls of film. Later, from England, we sent them the photographs.

We followed the dancers until they stopped in front of a restaurant. 'Ah,' I said, 'the wedding lunch.' By this time we had become part of the group. After everyone had gone in, a young man motioned for us to join the party. '*Deutsch*?' he asked.

'No. American and English,' I replied. We were always being mistaken for Germans, and blamed the error on Bulgaria's lack of contact with the outside world.

Inside, the air was already dense with cigarette smoke. Some of the guests were starting to get drunk. One man, his green shirt sliding up and out from his trousers, was drinking what looked like vodka straight from the bottle. There was a lot of loud, happy conversation. A woman with a gentle face under a flowered babushka, possibly the bride's mother, passed a plate containing slices of cake. I took a piece and she grinned at me. Her two front teeth were missing.

'My name is Stefane,' said our benefactor. 'I speak Russian very good. I speak English no good. I wish other way round.' The people we had spoken to in the restaurant in Sozopol had told us exactly the same thing. Stefane smiled apologetically and offered us drinks.

'Thank you,' I said, taking one. I also had my eye on a plate of little round cupcakes, sprinkled with pink and green sugar.

'My sister, she get married,' he said, stating the obvious.

'You speak English very well,' Clifford shouted above the din. 'Where did you learn?'

'In school. I am engineer in Burgas. Is necessary read English textbooks sometimes.'

Stefane must have been the local success story. The people were very poor and uneducated. Most of the women wore cotton dresses with aprons. The bride and groom circled the room, shaking hands and kissing people. The quintet was playing louder and faster and soon hands reached for ours and we were part of long lines stepping nimbly to the music.

There was no lunch – it would probably have been too expensive – only drinks and cakes. Soon everyone left to follow the bride, groom and musicians to the gates of the town where a car, covered with ribbons and flowers, waited to drive them away, Stefane at the wheel.

I felt very elated by the experience, which had lasted no more than an hour. I was also feeling dizzy. 'I'd like to know what was in that drink?' I asked Clifford, who just smiled and did not reply.

We continued our drive north along the coast. I left my window open to feel the air on my face. The clouds had broken and shafts of sunlight highlighted the brilliant colours of the flowers beside the road: lilac, lavender, red poppy, endless varieties of yellow and pink roses that grew wild on dark green bushes.

Outside Varna, the major port city of Bulgaria since the days of the Roman Empire, I saw a shanty town that clung to a steep hillside like some absurd parody of Veliko Tŭrnovo. We stopped to look and within seconds a swarm of small, ragged boys appeared at my open window, talking excitedly. My first instinct was to be slightly wary, but then I realized they were just curious to see what we looked like and touch the car. They all had bright, animated faces and large dark eyes. I wanted to give them something but our packets of sweets were stowed away in the boot so I took two 20 leva notes from my wallet, held them out, and in perfect sign language explained that they were to be divided equally. One boy jumped up, snatched the notes from my hand, and turned to run back up the hill. His companions gave chase, and, to my dismay, fell on him with swinging fists until the whole pack dissolved into a squealing heap of tumbling arms and legs. I was horrified. My pleas for peace went unheeded.

'Don't worry,' Clifford laughed. 'They're too small to inflict much damage on each other.'

## Clifford

We drove the last 9 miles to Druzba through the wooded foothills of the Balkan range over a terrain that was almost tropical. Like the weather, the road improved, curving among old stone houses with neat gardens and cars in the driveways.

There was no gypsy squalor in Druzba. There were outdoor cafés, bicycles for hire and arcades filled with handicrafts. The beach was clean and dotted with blue and yellow umbrellas that looked like giant mushrooms from the cliff tops above. Lifeguards were perched on high towers every few hundred metres although, being May, most of the swimmers were in the thermally heated swimming pools. The hotels were of the highest standard we had come across in Bulgaria and in the Duty Free shops hard currency dollars and D-marks could buy an odd variety of imported goods: Nescafé, breakfast cereals, chewing gum, Italian sweaters, American jeans, English jam, Lux soap and Tampax – commonplace articles laid out with all the pomp of the crown jewels.

We walked along a tree-lined path towards a magnificent white building and, as we approached the entrance, an electric fence slid silently into place, barring our way.

A fat woman in an apron came out to inspect us and, smiling quixotically like a lunatic, which often worked, I made as if to pass. Her querulous but benign expression became that of an angered mud wrestler and she held up her fists as if to challenge me to three rounds.

'This place must be for the Black Raincoats,' Iris said, tugging my arm.

'I know, that's why I'm trying to get in,' I replied.

The big woman was waving a stubby finger and abusing me with short little words that sounded like a hacking cough. I continued to grin, staying in character, and tried unsuccessfully to get a better view of the white building hidden in the undergrowth.

'*Viva* Stalin,' I finally called, backing away.

'You child!' said Iris, and we made our way into the centre of Druzba. I was beginning to like the small town. It was odd.

We were anxious to find out what was happening in Romania, it being 20 May, election day, but there were no newspapers among the other Western goodies in the Duty Free shop. It came as no surprise. There had been no foreign newspapers in the capital, either. As we were leaving, Cyril Tibbett introduced himself. 'English, aren't you, same as me,' he said. 'You won't get any papers in this place. Scared of them, they are.'

Cyril was a dapper Yorkshireman in his seventies and had been a regular visitor to Bulgaria for fifteen years. 'For the rheumatism,' he explained. 'Does me a treat. Always come in May. It's dead cheap. There're a lot of widows here in May . . .'

There were numerous thermal pools and mud baths along the coast and the hotels catered for elderly people on package deal holidays, mainly from Britain and West Germany. 'It costs £300 all in, flight, grub, the lot,' Cyril told us. 'They don't like you having any of their money. You get vouchers for everything and if you want to buy anything extra, you have to pay in American money.' Cyril found this very strange. 'This country's got itself in a right mess,' he went on. 'The people who run the hotels take liberties, but the ordinary staff are a decent lot. Just like us, really.'

I told him everything might change after the election in June and he had no idea there was one. 'Not here,' he said. 'They don't have them in this part of the world.'

We sat and had some glasses of *sok* – fruit juice that came in vivid colours and, assuming Cyril had no Bulgarian money, I paid the bill.

A limited choice of morning papers lay in fans on the various low tables in reception at the Grand Hotel Varna the following day: *Pravda*, with Lenin's head in profile in the top left corner; *l'Humanité*, the French Communist Party paper; *l'Unita*, the Italian Communist Party paper; and *Soviet Union*, the illustrated monthly printed in twenty-two languages, with a cover photograph showing a breast-feeding Madonna and the headline, 'Society is Indebted to Women'. All were out-of-date, like the perceptions of *Soviet Union*.

I spoke to the receptionist, a pretty, gamine type in a grey suit, who was sitting behind a desk. I asked her if she spoke English. She smiled; of course she did.

'What happened in the elections in Romania yesterday?'

Her smile vanished. 'In Romania?' I repeated.

'I don't know.'

'You don't know?' I insisted. I felt Iris's sharp poke in the ribs.

'I don't know anything about that sort of thing.' She hurried away.

We treated the car to a clean at a mechanical car-wash, the first I had seen since West Berlin, and left dripping and gleaming to negotiate the serpentine coastline that uncoils itself at Zlatni Pjasaci (Golden Sands), a resort town with eighty hotels thrown down as if by an overtired child bored with his building blocks. Sun-beds in military ranks carpeted the beach. Female attendants in uniform (aprons and long socks) raked the sand. The smell of hot-dogs and fried onions overpowered the sea air.

We moved on to Balchik, a small cautious town unsure whether to develop or adopt the rustic approach. It is on the most northerly strip of the coast in the territory ceded by Romania and contains the summer-house built for the English Queen Marie, wife of Romania's King Ferdinand. The house is famous for its terraced garden, but the countless varieties of shrubs and trees collected from all over the world have been neglected for so long the gardens had the melancholic air of an empty theatre. I sat on the Queen's favourite bench and, staring out to sea, as she had often done, it was easy to imagine her thoughts and feelings of nostalgia. When we left, we found a man admiring the Range Rover and he had sufficient English for a conversation. I asked him about the election in Romania and on a piece of paper he wrote: '83 per cent'.

'Ionescu,' he told us and shrugged. I looked suitably bereaved. He then tapped the side of his head. 'Communism . . . it makes us all mad,' he said.

We shook hands for some reason and I drove back to the hotel where again I asked at the reception desk for news of the election. There was a man and a different woman.

'The prognosis is that Mr Iliescu has won with sixty per cent of the vote, but the voting will not be completed until Friday,' the woman said without a breath of hesitation.

'Is this good for Romania?'

Silence. They were unsure what to say and I had a feeling people simply did not ask questions.

'It is difficult to know,' the woman finally answered. She had an open face with strong features and eyes that were dark and defiant.

'What is going to happen in Bulgaria next month?' I pressed.

Again they remained silent for several seconds. The man then spoke in Bulgarian and left for his office. When he had gone, the woman translated. 'He thinks the Socialists will win with a five per cent margin,' she said, a forecast that turned out to be uncannily accurate.

'What do you think?' I asked.

She leaned forward. 'I will vote for the Democrats,' she whispered, and then a puzzled frown entered her face. 'But it is very hard for us. Now, there are about seventy different parties that have registered . . .'

Unlike the shrubberies laid out for Queen Marie, the gardens around the hotel were as tidy and regimented as the sun-beds at Zlatni Pjasaci. Tall poplars and cypresses were surrounded by honeysuckle bushes, beds of poppies and lupins. The garden appeared to be part of one large park dotted with neat stone buildings, many overlooking the sea. But this was not the case. Each hotel or pension, or private house, had an allotted plot that was self-contained within unbreachable frontiers. The narrow pathways simply came to an end at high, delicately concealed walls or metal fences. The beach was unfenced but the stairways carved into the cliffs were either barred by tall gates or guarded by men in faded, scruffy uniforms. Getting lost was impossible. There was always someone at hand wordlessly to point you back the way you had come.

In the garden, surrounded by flowers, we saw a stone hammer and sickle – in green. 'Caring Communists,' Iris suggested.

We had been asking a lot of questions in the hotel and continued to do so. I ordered a German beer – not covered by our vouchers – and the waiter informed me that, though this luxury would be expensive to him, it would not be for me. He was half-Russian, half-Bulgarian, he told us, and had worked in

East Germany and Cuba. He was tall and willowy with rock star looks and a spiky, post-modernist hairstyle.

'Except for the Romanians, we are the poorest country in Europe. Albania is not even in Europe. It is out of this world,' he said, showing us the universe beyond the ceiling.

'Now you can change all that, with the Democratic Forces,' I said.

'I think not. They have no leaders. The Socialist Party brought us democracy in November. We must give them a chance. We have lost forty-five years.'

As he had assumed I was rich, buying an imported beer, I asked him if he considered all the hotel guests rich. He thought carefully. 'Most of the English are poor people. The Germans, they are not so poor.'

I had made the same observation.

The mezzanine floor of the hotel was half-blocked by leather sofas and within this barricaded, private section a live floor show had been provided to entertain the smartest group of people I had seen in Eastern Europe. In the hotel car-park that day, I had noticed a number of luxury cars, including an American Cadillac.

I asked various members of the hotel staff who the guests were. Customs officers, we were told; a private party.

'The Communist Party?' No reply.

The guests sat at tables overflowing with food and drink, the outer ring reserved for what appeared to be a separate convention of broad, big men wearing wide ties that hung loosely from bull necks, and jackets filled to the brim like rice sacks. Were these the Black Raincoats without their black raincoats, I wondered? Were they bodyguards? Customs officers with bodyguards?

From outside the ring of sofas, we watched the show. It was sleazy: girl singers with raucous voices, cowboy boots and solid thighs; a bone-thin contortionist who was amazing and bare-breasted, tiny but bare; some dancers in gossamer veils who draped themselves seductively over the guests, fat men mostly who sucked cigars with self-satisfied expressions, although there was a sprinkling of painted women and a table of Africans who knew a very good tailor.

By 10.30 we were bored with our speculations. We entered the elevator and, as the doors closed, a man with a wide tie stepped in with us. He stepped out with us on the sixth floor.

'Mr Thurlow.' He paused, but not long enough for me to speak. 'No more questions,' he said, and gave me our two passports. They had been left at the reception desk. Iris stiffened. We watched the man get back into the elevator and watched the numbers drop to the ground floor. We checked out early the following morning.

## Iris

I was far from unhappy to wave goodbye to the Grand Hotel Varna. It had been intriguing to see how the top one per cent had lived during the last forty-five years, but the threatening tone of the man in the elevator on our last evening had been, to say the least, unsettling. Clifford had laughed it off, but I noticed he checked three times to make sure our door was locked before we went to sleep. I spent a restless night and we had breakfast earlier than usual. By nine o'clock we were on the road to Ruse.

We drove inland through rolling hills, passing numerous collective farms, dotted with toiling farm workers. Near Shumen, where we had to veer north to the Romanian border, I had read there was a wondrous spot called Madara, filled with mountain caves that had been inhabited from prehistoric to medieval times. The focal point of the area is the Horseman of Madara, which was chiselled into the side of a cliff in the eighth century. It depicts one of the earliest Bulgarian kings, Tervel, astride his horse, spearing a lion with his lance. We left the highway running through the valley and joined a narrow track that wound into the hills.

Turning off the main road is like turning back in time. Immediately, horse drawn carts replaced the cars, shepherds coaxed their flocks of sheep across the road to different pastures, gypsy caravans moved at the speed of a tired donkey.

The farms gave way to forests as we climbed higher. The road finally came to an end in a tiny clearing where a few cars and a battered bus were parked. We spent an hour wandering through a maze of paths, peeking into dark caves, but could not find the famous Horseman. We struggled up a steep path that ended abruptly at the base of a sheer wall of stone. We were starting to feel a little frustrated when a group of schoolchildren arrived with their teacher.

'Hello. Do you know where the Horseman is?' I asked her.

She pointed to the cliff behind me, and then I saw it. I had been expecting Mount Rushmore, and instead, it was more like a frieze on an Etruscan tomb. Thirteen hundred years of wind and rain had taken their toll and the outline of the life-sized equestrian, carved into the flat rock, was barely visible.

Much more interesting were the teacher and her class. The children, who looked to be around ten years of age, were obviously not used to meeting foreigners, judging from the way they stared at us. Their teacher, like a good professional, turned the occasion into a learning experience. She asked us where we were from and translated for her pupils. We were expressing ourselves in sign language and a few words of German. I drew a rough sketch of the United States on a sheet of paper and put an 'X' to mark New York.

She explained that the children were Russian, on a school trip to Bulgaria. Several of the little boys and girls had badges pinned on their sweaters and shirts. I looked closer. No, they were not symbols of the Russian Youth Movement, but cameos of – Michael Jackson! Clifford started giving an impression of a moon walk, and the children laughed and clapped their hands. Several of the boys attempted to do break-dancing until their teacher told them to stop, and pointed out that they were getting dirt on their clothes.

One shy little girl, with brown pigtails and big green eyes, indicated that she had something very important to tell me. The teacher told her to come forward. From what I was able to gather, she had an aunt who lived in Brooklyn. This momentous news safely delivered, she covered her face with her hands and burst into nervous giggles.

They were all carrying their lunch in paper bags and sat down, under the omnipresent King Tervel, frozen forever in his struggle with the lion. They insisted that we join them and offered us pieces of bread and some sausage. Clifford went back to the car and returned with our lunch, hastily assembled that morning in the hotel dining room. He also brought two packets of milk chocolate digestive biscuits, which were greeted like manna from Heaven. Chocolate biscuits were obviously a rare luxury and I was glad we had refreshed our sweet stocks and cigarette supply for Romania.

The children were enchanting and their young teacher friendly and serene. In spite of the lack of a common language, we found other ways to communicate. They sang songs for us and then we joined them in a game similar to Drop the Handkerchief. We stood and held hands in a circle, while someone ran around the outside and deposited a scarf behind an unsuspecting person, who had to pick it up and give chase.

Soon, however, it was time to go. Clifford lined us up for a group photograph and we exchanged addresses.

## Clifford

I finished the film taking some shots of peasants working in the fields. They were not unhappy or angry. They seemed pleased, even proud, unaware of the immense gulf that separates their lives from our own.

In Ruse we checked into the Riga Hotel, one of those grey, Stalinesque buildings that had the one great advantage of standing on the banks of the Danube. Our room on the fifteenth floor with damp patches and iron beds looked out across the broad stretch of river and, beyond, our final port of call: Romania. Iris was coming. I always knew she would.

# Romania

## Iris

The Friendship Bridge spans the Danube and is one of the main border crossings between Bulgaria and Romania. It has two levels: one for a railway, the other a road. We drove through the dusty streets of Ruse and my heart sank as we approached the river bank. All I could see were long lines of trucks, mostly from Bulgaria and Turkey, with some Greek plates. There were hardly any passenger cars.

We were waved to a special gate, and two Bulgarian border guards came over to look through the window, with friendly smiles and greetings. I had liked Bulgaria enormously. I did not want to leave. I certainly did not want to go to Romania. Even from this side of the bridge it looked foreboding and dark.

We had been unable to spend all of our leva, and as it was technically illegal to take it out of the country, and worthless if you did, Clifford had gone to the exchange office to get back what he could in hard currency. We had used the black market, but we also had receipts from legitimate exchanges, and he felt confident he could talk them into giving him back some Deutschmarks. I waited in the car, looking at a map of Romania. A voice interrupted my thoughts.

'Hello. How are you doing?'

I looked up, startled, into a pair of bright blue eyes set in a handsome, craggy face.

'I saw your license and US sticker and just came over to speak a little English.'

He was a truck driver from Manchester, England, and pointed proudly to his 'rig', a gigantic blue and white truck that stood out from all the others because it was clean and looked freshly painted. I had not had a conversation with an English-speaking person, apart from Clifford, for weeks and was surprised at how happy I was to talk to him. 'Where do you live?' 'Where are you going?' 'How long have you been travelling?' All the questions foreigners in strange lands ask each other were quickly dealt with. He was driving back to England through Romania and had done the same route many times over the years.

'Do you ever have difficulty finding petrol?' I asked, voicing one of my many fears.

His answer of 'No, because I carry my own supply with me,' did not make me feel better. 'Never let your tank get too low,' he cautioned.

For a moment I felt like begging him to take me with him. His big truck looked so safe and full of petrol . . . . The Customs official handed him back his papers and we said goodbye, shaking hands warmly, and wished each other 'good luck'. A few minutes later Clifford returned.

'Guess what? They actually gave me back 200 Deutschmarks. It took some doing, but in the end they caved in to my persistence.' He was very pleased with himself.

The Friendship Bridge boasts two lanes, one of which was solidly blocked by trucks, bumper to bumper, crossing into Romania as we were. They stood at a complete standstill. Strangely, no traffic approached from the other direction, so Clifford pulled out and passed the whole lot of them, while I searched frantically for a blue and white truck.

The bridge looked like it could have used a little friendship in the form of a repair crew. It was over a mile long and not in good condition. It even had pot-holes. Behind us a couple of Trabants took advantage of our trail-blazing. Mercifully, we did not encounter any on-coming vehicles and, suddenly, we were in Romania.

Two young border guards appeared and held up their hands for us to stop. Each looked about seventeen years old. They were flushed and laughing. The brown uniforms they wore must have violated every point of the dress code: their shirts and jackets were unbuttoned; their hats sat askew on their heads; their boots were caked with mud. They laughed and jostled each other and finally one of them said, 'We have big problem. You must help.'

'Yes?' said Clifford.

'We need cigarettes.'

Even though I had heard that the border guards in Romania pestered new arrivals for cigarettes, it was still a shock to see them appear, as if on cue, and ask. It was also a bit frightening, because although they looked like schoolboys they had rifles slung over their shoulders and the authority to make things uncomfortable if their demands were refused. Without a word, I reached into my handbag and handed them each a package of Kent. They thanked me, apologized for the delay and waved us on. Further down the road we had to stop at a barrier and go through the official passport and Customs control.

This time, the man who approached was older and more serious. He did not ask for cigarettes, but for our passports and visas, which he studied carefully. Another officer in a different uniform indicated that he wanted to look into the boot. Clifford was happy to oblige but less happy when he demanded that everything be removed and put on the ground.

'What are they looking for?' I whispered.

'I don't think they know themselves.'

I got out of the car to help. I had heard stories of women being stripped and body-searched. If they suggested that, I would return immediately to lovely Bulgaria.

The Customs officer, short and stocky in a jacket that strained across his massive shoulders, pointed to my black duffle-bag and asked me to open it. He would pick mine! I always hate it when officials at borders or airports search my bags, poking their none too clean hands into my neatly folded clothes. But I had learned long ago never to argue. I unzipped the bag and stood back. He slowly pressed his fingers into each of the four corners and lifted up some of the items on top. Satisfied that it was not filled with whatever it was that he was looking for, he stood up, and I closed it.

Then his interest shifted to the car. He sat behind the steering wheel and opened the storage compartment between the front seats. I guessed that he did not see many foreigners driving into the country. Most visitors to Romania are businessmen, who fly in and out of the major cities and never venture into the countryside. He walked around the car several times, even peering underneath. After several more minutes, he turned his attention to a truck that had stopped behind us. We took this to mean that the search was over. We put everything back in the car, our passports were duly stamped and returned to us and we left.

'What was that all about?' I wanted to know.

'Probably nothing. Old habits take a long time to die.'

There is only one good highway in Romania. It runs 70 miles north-west from Bucharest to Pitesti, the centre of the petro-chemical industry. Elsewhere, there are only roads that are in various states of disrepair. We passed through several villages on the 40-mile drive to the capital.

Romania is not like anywhere else in Europe. I could see that immediately. The word 'poverty' took on a new dimension in this country. It made Poland and Bulgaria seem positively rich by comparison. Even the few trees beside the road looked half-dead. The peasants were shabbier, and when we stopped and said the word 'Bucharest' to some of them, just to make sure that we were going in the right direction, they looked fearful, pointed, and hurried on – afraid to answer, and afraid not to. Before Ceauşescu was killed, it had been necessary to report every conversation with a foreigner, no matter how small, to the police. Although he had been dead five months, the people were still confused and apprehensive about any contact. The road was wide enough, but dusty, and most of the sparse traffic was wagons, pulled by tired-looking horses, and trucks.

Up ahead we saw a sign by the side of the road. An arrow pointed straight upward and over it was written 'Bucuresti'.

'Stop the car. I want to take a picture.'

Clifford pulled over and I got out, shivering a little as my feet touched the ground. I sensed an evil atmosphere all around me, a legacy from the Ceauşescu regime. Like millions of others, I had seen the tragic pictures on television of the orphanages, read the horror stories about the lack of any form of birth control, and seen the tragic results that this had for tens of thousands of babies, as well as their mothers and families. The suffering and deprivation of the people had known no end. I had read about the brutality of the secret police, the deceit of the countless informers, the severe shortages, the robot-like secret guards who killed without any sense of moral wrongdoing. The people I had seen so far had a desperate, cagey look about them, the look an animal gets when it is locked up.

Then there were the gypsies. I had started the trip thinking they were a romantic and colourful tribe of people, but no more. I had seen the squalor of the camps they lived in, the dirt and poverty. What I felt about them now was pity and wariness, because people who always remain on the bottom have nothing to lose and are capable of extreme criminal acts.

I was dreading the trip through Romania. I hated the idea of spending ten days in the country. The only way I could face it was by taking it one day at a time.

Clifford had been able to talk me into going to Romania against my better judgement. He had said that it was the climax of our journey, and I could not pull out. I did not think too much could happen in Bucharest; it was the rest of the country that worried me. I hoped the two of us, alone, would not be a target, as my sister had once predicted.

I snapped my picture and climbed back in the car. Closer to Bucharest we began to see huge tracts of apartment blocks stretching out on either side of the road, notable because they were only half-finished, and there was no sign of any work in progress. Weeds were growing through the piles of bricks and dirt that surrounded them. A few cranes, beginning to rust, stood motionless against the sky. The scene was desolate and eerie and did nothing for my mood. We realized that we had arrived at the outskirts of the city, and followed the tram lines to the centre.

## Clifford

The election may have been over but demonstrators still filled University Square. Some were on hunger strike – and had been for twenty-two days. They lived in a squatter camp of blue and orange mountain tents, their banner the Romanian flag with the Communist symbol torn from the centre. Four ambulances were standing by. Different speakers, young and old, men and women, were climbing the steps to a tower-like stage to take a turn at the microphone. One had the feeling that decades and whole lifetimes of anger and frustration were the theme of their messages. There was much clapping and cheering.

'Tomorrow at three there will be a bigger demonstration,' a student wearing an official-looking armband told us, thrusting a handbill through the car window as we eased our way through the crowd spreading across the street and came to a halt at the Hotel Intercontinental.

The car-park was filled with diplomatic vehicles and trucks sprayed with the names of television stations from all over Europe. Two armed guards watched over them. 'At least the car should be safe,' said Iris, her tone lacking the irony intended. She was not happy to be in Romania.

Press photographers like a strange army, their uniform a multi-pocketed, sleeveless jacket crammed full with lenses and film, were spilling out of the hotel with reporters wearing name tags and television crews with cannon-sized cameras and yards of leads that wriggled down the broad steps like black eels. Small boys were selling books of political cartoons for $5. Gypsy children in rags clawed at our clothes. We paid a dollar to have the windscreen smeared with a dirty sponge and the half-naked boy who had performed this labour joined our entourage pleading for a packet of Kent cigarettes. A handsome Arab stepped out of the black Mercedes parked in front of us and offered to change money.

'Later, maybe,' I said.

'I will be waiting.'

A platoon of porters appeared, like toy soldiers in maroon and gold braid, and argued over the luggage. Iris had a tug-of-war with an elderly man with stylish white hair who was trying to relieve her of the green bag with its burden of precious papers. They fought in Italian, strident but good-natured. A man with one leg and a hopeless smile lurched towards us on crutches and I gave him a loose dollar from my shirt pocket. The gypsies had been crying, their little hands held together in prayer and, glimpsing the flash of green, they began chanting morbid evocations and wailed even louder.

'One packet Kent, *Monsieur*, one packet Kent,' yelled the windscreen-cleaner.

'Ignore them. They are the waste of humanity,' said the head porter, and he clipped one of the boys across the ear with the back of his hand.

It made no difference. They followed us up the hotel steps and only shrunk away before the doorman, an ex-wrestler by the look of him, pyramid-shaped, and omnipresent during the five days we spent in Bucharest. There were eight doors along the front of the hotel but only one was ever open. Guests, which meant just about all foreigners, entered freely but prostitutes and petty crooks only passed through after exchanging a Masonic handshake with the big doorman.

The lobby inside conjured up memories of Olivia Manning's *The Balkan Trilogy*. It was as full as a railway station at rush hour. Dark men sat with small cups of Turkish coffee behind newspapers. Elegant women in evening dress wandered by as if in search of a cocktail party. Journalists were shouldering their way through with impatient expressions. I heard one of them complain that he had been waiting two hours for a line to London. His companion, a beautiful American woman all in black, confided in a fatigued tone loud enough for the world to hear that she was a 'moral Fascist', which I hastily scribbled in my note book. Everyone appeared to be waiting for something to happen – for riot police to arrive and clear the square, for Hungarian troops to march across the border, for embittered workers to storm the capital; some waited for a forged passport, a contact, a secret document; the girls in evening dress for a customer to take them up to the air-conditioned rooms above.

I changed 50 Marks with the cashier. He gave me almost 600 lei and then informed me that I would get six times as much on the black market. He nodded towards the dark men behind their newspapers and, as I turned, they were all looking in my direction. They acknowledged the introduction and continued reading.

There were no English or American newspapers on sale, the same as in Sofia, but the newsmen more than made up for it. The reporter anxious to get a free line was now screaming at the top of his voice and the dark-suited reception clerk acted suitably apologetic with shrugs so extravagant he could have been exercising his shoulder muscles. I asked another reporter what was happening. 'Bloody chaos,' he answered.

He was leaning over the counter, his story in one hand, his free arm around the waist of a girl whose yellow dress was slashed down to her navel. 'There's more pussy here than in Bangkok,' he said.

It seemed as if little had changed in Bucharest since the war, although my only authority for making the claim is to quote Olivia Manning's tale about the Romanian walking with his German friend down Calea Victoriei and naming the price of every woman they meet. 'Good heavens,' says the German, 'are there no honest women here?' 'Certainly,' replies the Romanian, 'but very expensive!'

Five porters carried our four pieces of luggage to the room. I tipped them all in lei and the white-haired man brought a tear into his eye as he folded it away. 'You have a dollar or two?' he said. 'My daughter is in need of an operation . . .'

'My wife has cancer,' said one of his companions. He held the 50 lei note in his hand like a child showing his father a dead bird.

'No, no more dollars, no Marks. Next time,' I said sternly. It is always difficult to know what to do when you give someone a tip and they demand more. You feel annoyed, then mean. You pay up – and then feel annoyed again.

The porters shuffled out, heartbroken.

'God,' said Iris. She threw herself down on the bed.

The room was modern, comfortable and American. It was on the fourth floor and had a wide balcony that perched above the square. A forest of wind-torn banners like the flags of a defeated army hung limp over tent city. The speaker on the tiny stage was an elderly woman with a frail voice that issued from her thin body like air being let from a balloon, gasping then screeching. She was waving her small fist at the crowd, young people for the most part, enjoying the sunshine. Across the square were four long banners inscribed with neat, two-foot letters. They read:

Remember May 1989. Puppets on a String: Tiananmen

*Zona Libera de Neo-communism a Romaniei*

Welcome to Golonia

*Golans sans Frontiers*

*Golan* is the Romanian word for hooligan, the insult evoked constantly by the executed dictator Nicolae Ceauşescu for all those who opposed him. It had been used during the previous thirty days by Ion Iliescu, the new president and head of the National Salvation Front, to describe the protestors in the square, an echo from the past that did not bode well for the future.

Iliescu, a former Communist, had taken the Front to victory in the nation's first election in more than fifty years on 20 May, three days before our arrival in Bucharest. The Front had won more than two-thirds of the seats in Parliament, while Iliescu was elected president with a staggering 85 per cent of the vote. The people had queued at the ballot boxes for up to seven hours and, clearly, most had ignored the opposition claims that the Front was just the old Communist Party in disguise. The Front itself claimed that it stood for social democracy 'of the Swedish variety' and a free market economy, something that was going to be harder to achieve here than elsewhere in Eastern Europe. Romania had made few experiments in economic reform; Stalinist planning prevailed. And privatization was going to be difficult, however slowly it was taken. There is no money in Romania for local buy-outs, nor is there much that foreign investors are likely to be interested in buying.

Iliescu was being accused of stealing the revolution, vote-rigging and intimidation. The protest was being voiced because it could be voiced. Stopping the protestors with armed police would be too reminiscent of

Ceauşescu, a dilemma Iliescu was to solve a month later when coal-miners armed with pick-axe handles left their pits in 'a mood of national solidarity' and, after being transported to the capital, finally cleared the square of *golans*.

I knew that day, leaning out from the balcony, that it was only a matter of time before it happened. The people were too happy; too liberated. It was a *fiesta*. They wore the letter 'G' painted on their foreheads, or badges saying *golan*, like the red hearts stuck on the chests of men stood before the firing squad in the Mexican revolution.

Iris joined me. 'What's going on?' she asked.

'It's a rock concert,' I replied.

She laughed. I was glad she had come. It was not frightening, not to me. But, for all the clapping and cheering, it was a sad little gathering. Twenty million people live in Romania and a thousand or so young people dressed in wretched clothes were sharing the passing joy of calling the president bad names.

## *Iris*

The Hotel Intercontinental was definitely the centre of the action in Bucharest. Just getting from the car-park, through the lobby, into the elevator, to our floor was like running an obstacle course. I could not count the times we were asked for cigarettes, money, to buy something. The balcony of our room literally hung over University Square, scene of non-stop demonstrations.

'This is like having two front row seats to the best show in town,' I remarked.

'You mean the only show in town,' Clifford replied.

He was behaving like a child on Christmas Eve. The banners, crowds, loudspeakers, the small tent town on the side of the square below us had made him act like a junior reporter hot on the trail of a story. He loved the chaos, the buzz of excitement, the hint of danger. He wanted to go immediately down to the street to mingle, but I insisted on having something to eat first. It was mid-afternoon and I was starving. Clifford did not want to waste time sitting in the dining-room so we compromised and went to the bar just off the main lobby.

Inside, it was very dark, and my eyes did not become accustomed to the dim light for several minutes. We found two chairs at a corner table. Overhead, a television set was showing a gymnastics display with the sound turned off. No one paid any attention.

The bar was packed with thirsty newsmen. Everyone was drinking beer from litre-sized steins that a waiter kept filling from an ornate pump. Two others delivered them around the room as fast as they could. The sun outside over tent city was stoking up to over eighty degrees but the air-conditioned bar was cool and dark.

We ordered cheese sandwiches and beer and, while we waited, studied the tables around us. At one, the largest and noisiest, I saw the American brunette we had seen earlier in the lobby, holding court at a table full of men. She was speaking in a low voice. They leaned forward attentively, straining to hear her every word, looking like a nest full of newly-hatched birds waiting for their mother. Every few minutes they exploded with laughter and then leaned back for more.

Our cheese sandwiches arrived and they were toasted and excellent. Outside in the street, people queued for hours to buy food. Many people were starving, but the Intercontinental was an oasis of luxury.

We were sharing a table with a team of journalists from Denmark. 'Why are there so many media people still here?' I asked one. 'The election is over.'

'We wait for something to happen,' he replied in a sing-song voice.

'In the square?'

'Yes. There is going to be a bloodbath, I think,' he said cheerfully, his pale-green eyes shining.

At this his companion, a photographer, unconsciously patted the two cameras hanging around his neck.

## Clifford

The big doorman was pawing one of the working girls. We edged our way around them and thirty beggars surrounded us pleading and crying. '*Madame, s'il vous plait, Madame,*' wailed the children, clinging to our legs and arms. '*S'il vous plait.*' It was like walking through quicksand.

'Come here,' the Arab money-changer demanded, pointing at his car.

'*S'il vous plait.*'

The booksellers were approaching. Then came a man with a refined accent who needed a set of batteries, 'for my research,' he said.

'What shall we do?' Iris called.

'Hang on to your bag,' I replied.

I took all the lei I had in my shirt pocket and tossed it into the air. There was a mad scramble and we fled into the mill of people pushing forward towards the stage. The speaker now was a man with a pony-tail. He was waving his fist.

'. . . a nation asleep creates monsters,' said a student, handing me some literature. 'He is quoting Goya.'

I was impressed by how well most of the people we met spoke English and said so. 'We learned because they did not think to stop us,' the student said simply.

The two mimeographed sheets he had given me were in English. The printing was poor. Along the top was the title: The Independent Group for Democracy. I asked our new friend more questions and, rather than answering, he led us mysteriously through the moving throng to the rear entrance to tent city. We were introduced to Razvan Savulescu. As he was about to speak, there was a great cheer from the crowd.

'. . . a land of free men,' said Razvan, translating. He shrugged, a Latin gesture. He was wearing a dirty checked shirt and a sad dirty tie. We sat around a camp table at the entrance to one of the tents. Behind us, on the ground, were a sleeping bag, a primus stove and some plastic cups.

The Independent Group for Democracy did not begin life as a group. They were the individuals who stormed the television station during the December revolution – medical students, intellectuals, professors. 'We kept seeing the same faces so we banded together and formed the group.' Razvan was the press spokesman.

He was anxious to answer our questions. 'We want the world to know what is happening here. The revolution has been stolen.' His group did not seek political power. It thought of itself as the conscience of the nation, a watchdog with demands for human rights, freedom of the press and freedom of expression. I wanted to know why so many people had voted for Ion Iliescu.

'Because the election was run with misinformation in a climate of fear and violence,' he answered mechanically. 'The people are victims but also accomplices.'

'Is Iliescu a good man?'

'He is an ambitious man. He ran his election campaign on lies. You cannot build a new Romania on lies. He has made many promises, but he is an integral part of the nomenclature.'

Razvan said most of the former Securitate officers were now camouflaged in the army and police. 'They are still there,' he added darkly. 'They are there to do the bidding of the power clique.'

We fell silent. It was very hot. The sun was baking my skull and I began to feel dizzy. The crowd was growing like a tide, lapping against the rope that separated tent city from the square. Various people came up to the table with questions. A man, his head humbly bowed, took a photograph from a beaten up leather wallet and showed it to us. He ran his fingers around the brim of his hat. He was a country man and wore the odd halves of two ancient suits. He was searching for his son, missing since December. No one had seen him. More than ten thousand people were missing.

'The Securitate hid people in mass graves. We are still finding them,' Razvan said.

The colour had drained from Iris's face.

'It is a war we are fighting,' he explained. There was a gleam in his eyes. 'The election was just a battle we lost. We fight on. If we die or disappear, there will be others to take our places. We fought with the army. They had guns and we had no guns. We said "Come and join us", – and they did join us.'

He paused for a moment. He was gripping the side of the flimsy camping table. There was something savage about his expression. 'It was the happiest hour of my life,' he said. 'I lost my fear. I became a free man. I regained my dignity.'

Razvan straightened his filthy tie and then went into lengthy detail about the group's need for financial support. We made a donation and, exiting through the far side of tent city, the Arab was waiting for us.

He had moved his smart car. He leaned through the window, opened the glove compartment and we stared into a deep cave full of 100 lei notes in tight rolls. He took one of them out, removed the elastic band and played the grimy blue notes through his long fingers.

'They give six. I give ten.' The Arab was tall, dark and exotically good-looking.

I studied the notes. They were real all right. After getting stung so thoroughly in Sofia, I was wary. But less wary than tempted. There were about 20 lei to the dollar. The Arab was offering 200. 'First, you give me the money. Then she will give you $100.' I pointed at Iris. She was still ghostly pale. But patient.

'$200,' the Arab demanded.

'One.'

'One hundred and fifty.'

'One.'

'Please.'

It reminded me of being in an Arab bazaar. No object is priced; barter is innate to the deal.

'Maybe another day,' I said.

He seemed satisfied with this, flicked deftly through the roll and peeled off a wad of two hundred notes. The paper was as fine as old book pages and extraordinarily dirty. I did not count the money. Iris gave the man a solitary bill. We were in the open, for all the world to see.

We had the equivalent of a thousand dollars. But there was nothing to buy. We had not stumbled upon any rare porcelain or stray first editions of Joyce on our travels and Bucharest was to be no exception. We searched for an English–Romanian dictionary without success. There were none in French, Italian or German but we did find a Danish–Romanian version, long rows of them in every place we looked. In one of the bookshops there was an English section containing just two weighty tomes: the Australian Agricultural

Review 1953, volumes one and two. Above, the French section was barren.

Ceauşescu, apart from being a madman, had been an avid scribbler and copies of his many titles, bound in imported calf, had filled the bookshops until his demise. Now most of the shelves were bare and bare shelves in bookshops had more of a melancholy air than the empty food halls. There was no smell of leather bindings, forgotten bookmarks, no curious jottings in faded blue ink, nothing to inspire the belief that dissidents had met among the ancient philosophers to plot against the regime. Intellectuals, writers and painters had made little protest under Ceauşescu. Unlike the other Eastern Bloc countries, there had been no opposition groups prepared to go to prison for their beliefs and thus no organized alternative to the National Salvation Front. There had been some notable exceptions but, as the American consular official in Budapest had told us, the Romanians were not courageous people.

The lines outside grocery stores, mere saplings elsewhere in Eastern Europe, were sturdy, three and four abreast trunks of humanity that blocked the pavements everywhere there was something worth buying. Inside, the people moved through the unlit rows of near empty shelves like phantoms, then emerged into the daylight, clutching their purchases to their breast.

An elderly woman, tall and strangely chic in a turban and rags, kissed me on both cheeks and wandered on, not walking, but dancing to silent music in long flowing steps.

I bought a hat to keep the sun from the top of my head. It cost me 65 lei and I gave the change to one of our followers. The man pointed at the peppered brickwork next to where we were standing. 'Securitate,' he whispered and hurried away. Two very small hands were dragging at my shirt. '*Madame, s'il vous plait.*' The beggars hovered around us like flies. There were beggars everywhere: in shop doorways, under desolate trees, stretched out on benches. They crossed the road to join our caravan. '*Madame, s'il vous plait,*' cried the children in chorus and, when you gave them 100 lei ($5 (£3) at the bank rate), they screamed for more.

As we approached the National Gallery, a boy soldier with a Kalashnikov assault rifle ordered us to give the building a wider berth by walking in the street, which we did without discussion. The public buildings were being guarded – like the car-park at the Intercontinental – to prevent a repeat of the violence that had destroyed the History Museum to the Socialist Republic. In the museum, there had been 'two permanent exhibitions' displaying 'Evidence of the love, high esteem and deep value enjoyed by President Nicolae Ceauşescu and by Comrade Elena Ceauşescu from the people of Romania . . . and from the world.' The display had included the ribbons and medal of knighthood bestowed on Ceauşescu by the Queen, lost forever in the flames.

'Change money?' Two young Arabs blocked our path.

'*Madame, s'il vous plait.*'

We escaped into a gloomy café and a waiter in a once white jacket chased our retinue away with a broom. He managed to catch one of the smaller children a good blow across the back of the legs and grinned triumphantly. They were violent people. It was something I had seen suppressed in the features of Razvan Savulescu, in the doorman at the hotel, in the porter who had cuffed one of the gypsy boys, in the gypsies who tormented us with their dire, dreadful poverty.

In the heart of Bucharest, there is a mausoleum containing the remains of Vlad Tepes, the prince who defended Walachia against Turkish expansion into the Carpathians in the fifteenth century. He had the decapitated heads of the slain placed on poles around his camp, while his greatest pleasure was dining in the midst of a howling, weeping circle of enemies impaled on oak staves, an amusement that earned him the title Vlad the Impaler, and inspired Bram Stoker's *Dracula*.

Where truth ends and the myth takes over is uncertain, but the legendary brutality of Prince Vlad is typical of the nation's turbulent history. The area which is now modern Romania was first inhabited by Thracian tribes conquered by the Romans in the first century. Waves of warring Goths, Huns, Avars, Slavs, Bulgars and Hungarians roamed across the fertile territory from the fourth to the tenth centuries, but the original people survived in isolated communities with the language bequeathed to them by the Romans largely intact. Converted to the Orthodox faith, the Romanians are the only Latin people not under the wing of the Catholic Church.

Through the Middle Ages, the states of Walachia and Moldavia were constantly at war. They were finally united in 1862 under the single name Romania. Neighbouring Transylvania, where the majority of the population were Romanians under Hungarian rule, came into the kingdom under King Carol I in 1918, with the defeat of Austro-Hungary in the First World War.

The people had been abused and savaged during centuries of foreign rule and responded like savages whenever they were in a position of power. Ceauşescu was the country's own invention, its own monster. He was universally despised but also respected, as a beaten dog respects its master. The dictator employed a large army for protection and to protect himself from his protectors he created Brigade Five, a force of 1,500 men and women whose sole job was to guard the Ceauşescu clan. This private army, the cream of the Securitate, was said to be made up of people who were barely human, more sadistic than the SS élite that guarded Hitler. Many were orphans who had been taken as children and reared to be totally loyal to the family. The orphaned children not taken lived in notorious institutions like medieval prisons. The rest, perhaps the lucky ones, were the beggars who shadowed our every step on the streets of Bucharest.

## Iris

Communism and dirt seemed to go hand in hand in Romania. Pavements were not kept clean. Piles of rubble were allowed to become a permanent part of the landscape. It was still possible occasionally to see, behind the crumbling façades, in spite of the careless insertion of bleak modern blocks, why Bucharest had once been called the Paris of Eastern Europe. The wide boulevards that cut through the city and the occasional architectural gem were testimony to a former elegance.

When people travel with open minds and a sincere curiosity to learn about the region they are visiting, it is remarkable how easy and pleasant it is to meet strangers and have thought-provoking and informative conversations. Unlike the peasants in the countryside, we found that the students and intellectuals in the city were eager to talk to us about their nation and its problems. One such encounter occurred on a street corner.

We had spent hours walking around the downtown area and had realized that our map was hopelessly out of date. We were standing at an intersection trying to decide which way to go when a tall, slightly stooped young man offered his help, which we gratefully accepted. His name was Stefan Cordescu. He was a professor of mathematics at the university and deeply troubled by what was happening in his country.

His theory was that the Russians wanted the Communists to win the elections in Romania and Bulgaria to ensure their continued access to the Dardanelles. Lies were systematically spread throughout the country. The peasants were told that if they did not vote for the National Salvation Front, the *boyars*, or old nobility, would return and buy all the land. The factory workers were told that the capitalists would buy the factories and that they would all be out of jobs. None of it made any sense, but, still, it frightened them.

Stefan Cordescu was proud to tell us that he was one of the 'hooligans' in the square. 'We must keep the flame alive,' he said. 'When the people wake up, we will be there. We are worse off now than before, because now there is the appearance of democracy, but no real democracy. The same people are still in charge.' He picked nervously at his thin beard as he talked.

'What Romania needs is investment from the West,' I suggested.

'This will be very difficult. Iliescu has said that nothing will be privatized except for small businesses, such as hairdressers and taxi-drivers. No one can have a company that employs more than ten people. The climate is not good for foreign investment. You know,' he continued, 'Iliescu's father was one of the original founders of Communism in Romania in 1941. He ingested Communism with his mother's milk.'

We exchanged names and addresses. 'If you ever come to New York . . .' I said.

'Or London,' added Clifford.

His smile was melancholy. 'For me, I do not think it will ever happen.' He kissed my hand in the formal farewell of an older man. 'Please do not let the West forget about us,' were his last words.

Using Stefan's directions, we made our way back to the hotel. We passed several makeshift shrines on the way, marking the spots where people had been slain during the uprising. Each had a small cross, usually with a photograph of the deceased. All had burning candles and bunches of fresh flowers had been strewn on the pavement. I noticed that most of the victims were exceptionally young, scarcely out of their teens. It was sorrowful evidence of the recent horror in the streets. I clutched Clifford's arm. At one shrine a woman dressed in the black of mourning kneeled as if in prayer. Her eyes were closed and tears wet her cheeks. I glimpsed a picture of a smiling young man with a mop of dark hair who looked like he had just graduated from high school. I knew she must be a mother grieving for her son.

That evening, we dined in the hotel. Afterwards, by unspoken agreement, we wandered out into the square, as if pulled by a magnetic force. The austerity programme meant that all street lights in the country were turned off at ten in the evening to conserve energy, which made it hazardous to walk around on one's own. University Square, however, was brightly lit by several strong floodlights and more clamorous than ever.

I marvelled at the energy and enthusiasm of the demonstrators. They never let the tempo slow down for a minute. The crowd had swollen to many thousands, who stood or sat on what little grass there was and listened to the speeches, interspersed with live folk music. A singer, reminiscent of a young Joan Baez, strummed a guitar and sang several songs, including 'We Shall Overcome' in Romanian. Babies and little children clung to their parents. Young people in groups listened attentively, with rapturous faces. Old people drifted through with bewildered expressions. As Clifford had said, it was the only show in town.

After a while we went back to our room. The loudspeakers blared on into the night. There might have been a period between four and seven in the morning when things were slightly quieter. Even though I am a light sleeper, the noise did not bother me, maybe because I sympathized so much with their cause. I fell asleep as soon as my head touched the pillow.

## Clifford

The sun rose in a haze over the city, lighting the domes of the churches and the motionless cranes like the rigging of phantom galleons in the shifting darkness. Romanian flags hung exhausted above the rooftops. The candle flames around the memorials to the dead painted shadows on the city of mountain tents. I could just make out the sign '*Golans sans Frontiers*' as it moved almost imperceptibly in the dawn silence. The ambulances were still standing by. The young people on hunger strike had passed their twenty-second night.

We had breakfast sent to our room – coffee, *croissants*, fresh orange juice – and thought about the people in tent city who would have no breakfast at all. It is a wretched experience to be in a place where some people are starving, while we and others choose dishes from a range of menus. The hotel was like a medieval citadel in the midst of a wasteland. The people camped below our balcony were rising for the day, brushing off the dust and preparing new speeches that would go unheeded within our fortress walls. The gypsy children would be creeping across the car-park to gather just beyond the reach of the doorman.

We negotiated the front steps. You cannot give to everyone and you hate yourself because perhaps you can. Then there are the rumours: the children are sent out by rich gypsy patriarchs; the young mothers prick their babies with safety pins to make them cry – and maybe it is true, but what if it is? And what if it isn't? It is a constant dilemma.

In Asia, South America, in Africa, throughout the Third World, there is poverty, disease, hardship. It is no worse in Romania but it seems worse. It is unexpected. The Romanians have the same ethnic roots and religion as the people of Western Europe. East Berlin is the fork in the road and Bucharest is the furthest point of Communism's disastrous mismanagement. All that is bad in Eastern Europe is accentuated in Romania; anything remotely good does not exist.

The speeches we had heard from room 404 at the Intercontinental had gone on late into the night. They were impassioned, histrionic, punctuated with words we could understand: Democracy, No Communism, Freedom, Liberty. They chanted 'Victory, Victory, Victory'. But the battle was already over. 'The revolution has been stolen,' we had been told again and again, and it was hard to believe the revolutionaries clinging on with their slogans and folk songs were going to make a jot of difference in the plans of Mr Iliescu and his cabinet drawn almost entirely from compatriots in the nomenclature.

Even the journalists had lost interest in the demonstration. They were waiting for the violence that would end it. I had sat in the bar briefly the previous evening taking down notes. 'Who are you with?' an English voice had asked. 'No one. I'm writing a book,' I had replied. 'I need to record my impressions before I forget them.' He had finished his beer. 'It's easier for me, I only write facts. I can make them up.'

We were both privileged to be there in Bucharest at that moment, while the road through Europe was merging. Or not merging. Europe was changing but its metamorphosis had come to an end on the shores of the Danube and across the high peaks of the Carpathians. Adventurous entrepreneurs were beetling over the fallen walls of the Iron Curtain. They were in Warsaw and Prague and Budapest; they filled the towns and cities of East Germany; some were nervously entering Sofia. But there were no businessmen in Bucharest. The only trade I saw was in black market lei and the oldest profession in the world. There had been optimism everywhere. But not in Romania; and not a lot in Bulgaria. 'Don't forget us,' Stefan Cordescu had said. 'Don't forget us,' Emilia Konstantinova had said.

I had a feeling they would be forgotten. The shifting elements of power in Eastern Europe were simply moves in a game as complex and as subtle as chess. Romania and Bulgaria were pawns to be sacrificed in strategies that may have been understood by the grand masters in Washington and Moscow, in Tokyo and Bonn, but which were incomprehensible to the young boys with their immature beards and the girls singing for liberty in University Square. Such is the politics of expedience; compromise before conscience. The people of Romania had given up half a century of development and it was a safe bet that a few more years and a few more lives would be wasted before any real changes were made.

## Iris

If Romania had been a rich country, with its citizens prosperous and happy, then perhaps Ceauşescu could have been excused for wanting to turn a large chunk of Bucharest into a sort of Washington, D.C., and for building a White House that was, in fact, about one hundred times bigger. As it was, the contrast between the impoverishment of Bucharest and the opulence of his plan only emphasized that the late dictator was indeed mad.

We had left the hotel right after breakfast, fighting our way through the forest of small arms that waited for every guest who exited through the one, swinging door, shedding blue bank notes like confetti as we hurried towards a waiting taxi.

'The People's Palace, please,' I said in English, and without a word the driver started the engine and eased into the traffic.

The newly-planted trees were in bloom along the Avenue of the Victory of Socialism, which softened the view of the neo-classical People's Palace, immense beyond imagination, that straddled the top end of the wide boulevard. By now I had mastered the double talk that was the backbone of Communism. The more the rhetoric stressed being 'for the people', the less likely it was to be true. Certainly Ceauşescu never intended the colossal structure that loomed before us to be accessible to anyone other than his family, their faithful underlings and the occasional illustrious guest.

The palace, almost half a mile wide and eleven storeys high at its central core, gleamed with a dazzling whiteness in the brilliant morning sunshine. Outer construction appeared to be completed, as it was for the buildings that flanked the palace, at a respectful distance, and which were designed as administrative offices. Several long recessed balconies formed part of the façade, and it was from here that Ceauşescu had dreamed of addressing the adoring masses that he hoped would fill the huge square that stretched out beneath him and spill over into the 2½-mile long Avenue of the Victory of Socialism that led, in a straight line, to the Palace.

The Avenue is bordered on each side with modern apartment buildings, eight floors high, all finished in the same pale stone material and of post-modernist design. They are not ugly, but need the patina of age and the benefit of landscaping to relieve their harsh newness. Down the middle of the Avenue thirty mosaic tiled fountains, that had yet to taste their first drop of water, were spaced at intervals.

I had read in a newspaper article that when Gorbachev had been shown the project by Ceauşescu, he had gasped in disbelief. It must have made him realize, as nothing else could, the madness and excess that Communism fostered, and perhaps was a factor in his later change of policy towards Eastern Europe.

The further away from the Palace we went, the less completed were the stages of construction. Near the end of the boulevard, a good 2 miles away, cranes still loomed over holes in the ground, and at the extreme point, existing buildings were frozen in a semi-demolished state.

What I found most astonishing of all was that the entire area, almost the size of Central Park or a London borough, was deserted, a modern ghost town. Not one workman laid a tile, not one shop sold a loaf of bread to a housewife, not one person walked on the street. There were not even any sightseers. Our taxi was the only car that cruised on the vast thoroughfare. It was as if everyone hoped that by ignoring this enormous miscalculation, it might disappear. No such luck. The new administration is saddled with it. Whether to complete it, leave it or demolish it will keep many a politician awake at night for some time to come.

If he had decided to build his dream city on a tract of vacant land, it might have been slightly less preposterous, but Ceauşescu destroyed whole areas of

Bucharest that were filled with ancient churches, historic buildings and characteristic streets. It is true that some of the neighbourhoods had been damaged by an earthquake in 1978, but they should have been lovingly repaired and restored, not obliterated by the dictator to make way for a monument to his ego.

We asked the taxi-driver what he thought of it all. He lacked the English to explain; he simply shook his head from side to side and tapped his forehead with two fingers.

Still reeling from the sheer magnitude of Ceaușescu's folly, we asked the driver to let us out at the Old Princely Court, the ancient heart of the city and now a museum. It had been a thriving commercial centre in the sixteenth century, but was now a ruin with a maze of cellars and corridors, mostly off-limits to the visitor. We took a peek into the mausoleum of Vlad the Impaler, a hero of sorts to Romanians, but found it dingy and disappointing.

All the action in the area seemed to be taking place next door at a small church, the Curtea Veche. I dragged Clifford up the steps and through the door, in spite of his aversion to churches. A strange scene greeted our eyes. Dozens of women of all ages stood or kneeled in front of elaborately carved silver icons scattered around the interior, whispering prayers, asking for favours. Some had their eyes closed, others wept. Flickering candles provided the only illumination, and cast an eerie glow over the spectacle. The stern faces of the saints stared back impassively from their frames.

During all this outpouring of piety and devotion, it was business as usual, as two old men conscientiously swept the floor, occasionally asking a woman in trance-like prayer to move her feet.

'Let's go,' Clifford said, not surprisingly.

We stopped to buy a postcard from a stall inside the door and dropped a donation, generous by Romanian standards, into a box. As we were walking down the steps, a thin, white-haired woman, bent with age, called after us. She held out her hand to reveal two little paper packages, the ends twisted to contain a cube of bread and a few grains of salt. Clifford recognized it immediately as an offering and blessing for a safe journey. '*Bon voyage*,' she said, and her face was more gentle and kind than any of the saints in the chapel.

I thanked her and carefully put the two tiny packets in my handbag, in a special compartment with my most valuable documents. In a few days we would be leaving Bucharest for the remainder of our travels through Romania, and then the long trip home. I am not superstitious, but I was definitely not going to let anything happen to those two small gifts.

We could hear University Square before we actually saw it. Loudspeakers continued to boom out the message of the revolution at the crowd. We picked our way through the hundreds of onlookers. It was the quietest time of the day. Later on in the evening the assembly would swell to thousands.

'Look!' I cried. 'We know that man.'

'It's Stefan, the mathematics teacher,' said Clifford.

He was standing by the side of the platform, his long frame stooped over a pretty young woman holding a baby on her hip.

'Hello, hooligan,' I called.

He looked pleased to see us. 'Ah! My American–English friends,' he said, and introduced us to his wife and baby daughter. 'They come to bring me food and news of my family.'

His wife, Sonia, did not speak English as well as her husband, but the spirit of revolution and change burned just as fiercely in her brown eyes. She was on her way to leave the baby, a solemn-looking ten month old by the name of Katya, with her mother before she went to her job as secretary at the university. Stefan tenderly kissed them both goodbye.

We told him we had been to see the People's Palace and a look of great pain crossed his face.

'Would you like to see something else interesting in Romania?' he asked.

'Yes, of course,' I replied. 'That's what we are here for.'

'Tomorrow I must go to my grandparents' village. Would you like to come?'

'Very much.'

'There is a train . . .'

'No. We will drive you. I insist,' interrupted Clifford.

We arranged to met at our hotel at nine o'clock the following morning.

## Clifford

He was waiting as arranged at the bottom of the steps. Being Romanian, Stefan Cordescu was unable to enter the hotel lobby without first bribing the doorman.

Our entourage quickly gathered and I led the gang screaming and wailing across the car-park that bordered tent city. The *golans* were painting the letter 'G' fresh on their foreheads. The people starving for democracy had passed their twenty-third night.

Iris carried a bag with some bread, cheese and fruit, the remnants of breakfast that would serve as lunch; we had become old hands at long days in the countryside.

The armed guard watched our slow progress from under the brim of his pudding basin tin helmet, a style so similar to those worn by German storm-troopers in the last war, design seemed more likely than coincidence.

The boy soldier – they were always boys – had cruel, impassive eyes.

The gypsy children and booksellers climbed over the car like chimpanzees. They clung to the wheels and doors. A thirteen-year-old mother with an infant plugged to her tiny breast pulled a button from my shirt and I gave her 200 lei before the rest of the shirt was ripped from my back. The girl had the dark brown skin of an Indian untouchable and a gold tooth among the white.

We bundled into the car and I threw a handful of blue notes from the window. The beggars fought for the money like footballers for the ball and we pulled into a twelve-car traffic jam caused by the diversion around University Square. Stefan admired the numerous clocks and dials that studded the dashboard and, as I did my best to answer his complicated enquiries, I could almost hear the information filing into place in his mathematician mind. It is true, as the French anthropologist Michel Peissel learned from his work among the Mayas, a man's intelligence is best judged by the questions he asks. Once his quest for knowledge had been satisfied, the young professor sat back and, pressing the electric switch at his side, watched the window rise and fall, shaking his head as if each time it was a new experience.

The city centre was mobbed with people aimlessly wandering the streets as if in search of another revolution although, if one was to trust the election returns, two-thirds of them should have been contented. Stefan kept pointing out shop windows with bullet holes perforating the glass. 'In the first few days the police killed hundreds of people,' he said. 'Then they changed sides and the Securitate started killing them. None of us really knew what was happening.'

The assortment of rusting Skodas, Polskis and Ladas all but disappeared as the downtown avenues narrowed and, with the daylight seeming to fade from the sky, we were suddenly deep in a cement channel between files of apartment blocks that gave the impression of being alternatively half-finished or recently abandoned. They reminded me of photographs I had seen of the tenements in pre-war Glasgow. I told Stefan this. 'They are late Romanian,' he said with a sardonic smile. He was nervously tugging at his thin scholarly beard and his dark eyes had the intense look of a thoughtful child. 'The apartment homes are not built with doors and windows,' he then explained. 'The people must put them in themselves. If they have no money, they make do with plastic sheets, or nothing.'

He threw up his hands in an apologetic gesture, something we had encountered often among the intellectuals in Eastern Europe. Iris wanted to know what the apartments were like inside. 'Small,' Stefan answered simply. 'There are usually two small rooms and no bathroom. There is a washroom and toilet on each floor which the people share.'

He became quiet and stared out of the side window. The blocks of housing fell in size. A few mansions, homes of the *boyars* before the war, rose out of the desolation like distant memories and marked the frontier that opened on to the countryside and another century. We passed through hamlets with tumbledown cottages the size of garden sheds. Beehives painted in primary colours stood at the sides of fields where shapeless women were bent over primitive hoes weeding around corn stalks that marched in lines as far as the horizon. Romania had been the bread basket of the Balkans. The soil was rich and dark; the weather kindly. Yet rationing had long been a way of life. Virtually everything grown in the country was exported to pay off the National Debt caused by the drop in oil prices in the 1970s. It was one of Ceauşescu's passionate obsessions.

'We are allowed 400 grams of meat a month and a quarter of a chicken,' Stefan said. There were no consumer products in the stores (although many luxury items were available on the black market); the street lights were turned off; even water was rationed: twice a week cold, once a week hot and for four days in seven the communal toilets were blocked. 'In the ancient city of Knossos in Crete, the citizens had better plumbing than we have today in Bucharest.'

Why the people did not rise up in revolt much sooner remained for me a puzzle I was unable to solve because I could only see it through the eyes of my own development and education in Western society. What we take for granted – food, shelter, clothing, a free press, free enterprise, foreign travel – were beyond the reach of most Romanians. Their sole concern was survival and people trying to survive have little time for revolution. It may be a paradox but, far from consumerism being the preserve of the West, it was essentially the driving force of Communism: the reward to the party faithful; the hope of the have-nots. It is only when people have acquired all the things they want that they can reject them. It is then that the mind may turn to politics, justice, philosophy. In the Communist world, particularly in Romania, the people needed all their energy to labour at the treadmill of everyday survival and, in such a situation, all interest in external matters dwindles to non-existence. Independent thought, if it exists at all, is seen by the majority as being unrealistic, self-indulgent and totally alien to common concerns. In Romania, it was also very dangerous considering the extreme vigour with which any form of dissent was persecuted by the regime.

The fact that there were no creditable dissident groups in Romania was hardly surprising. 'We were completely demoralized. We had no fight in us and, if we did feel frustrated, there was no one to share these feelings with,' said Stefan. 'One in every three people was a police informer. We lived in constant fear. We were incapable of creating the conditions that are necessary for the overthrow of a dictatorship.'

Stefan told us a story about Stalin who one day entered a meeting of the Politburo with a live chicken that he roughly proceeded to pluck before his startled comrades. When he had finished, he placed the terrified bird on the floor at his feet. It did not flee. On the contrary, the chicken clung to his trouser leg as if for protection. 'That,' said Stalin, 'is how we must treat the Russian people.'

Ceauşescu, so Stefan believed, modelled himself on Stalin. If you can convince yourself you are right and you can convince others that you are right, the more you will feel obliged into bullying the rest into this belief. 'You must know Shakespeare,' Stefan continued. 'Once you make a man king it is only a matter of time before he thinks he has divine rights.' He paused and a smile crossed his slender features. 'That is why even if the people were unsure what they did want, they were sure what they did not want – the return of King Michael.'

The smile instantly vanished and his fine, ascetic face became haunted and drawn. I had sensed a certain pent up violence among Romanians but, like the old woman with her gift of bread and salt at the Curtea Veche, in Stefan Cordescu I found the very opposite. He was gentle, forgiving, intelligent to the point of wisdom, a man destined it seemed to be crushed beneath the wheel of the Romanian revolution.

We pulled into the first open petrol station two hours from Bucharest. Iris's sigh of relief was audible. The bill in lei, at the official exchange rate, came to more than $40 (£24). I gave the attendant a $10 bill and 400 lei. 'Merci, Monsieur,' he said, tucking the American bill in the back of his leather money bag.

The law required me to pay for fuel with benzine coupons paid for in foreign currency. I had not bothered to buy any. 'Communism,' wrote Vaclav Havel, 'makes everyone dishonest.'

Throughout the journey to Vladiceascu, Stefan had been reluctant to answer questions about the village. 'Wait and see,' he kept saying. I understood why when we turned off the broken highway on to a muddy track and finally came to a halt at our destination.

We were in the middle of a grotesque graveyard filled with giant graves. In the distance, blurred by the afternoon haze, some peasants were picking over the mounds like body-snatchers. They glanced up, stared for a moment at the car and then continued digging. The stumps of crippled trees appeared from the earth like gnarled fingers and I imagined that below the ground there were lost troglodytes trying to reach the surface. A bicycle wheel was leaning against a crumbling length of stone wall topped by a brave and rootless plant with tiny blooms the colour of bougainvillaea. I noticed a kitchen sink half-full of brackish rainwater; the china head from an ancient doll, the glass eyes glinting maliciously; a door frame without a door and a view over a surreal landscape so ideal for the lens of a movie camera one suspected the intrusion of Luis Buñuel.

'This is where I was born,' said Stefan. He shrugged and then pointed towards the two old people. 'They are my grandparents.'

Vladiceascu had been a village of eighty dwellings. The previous year, shortly before the fall of the Ceauşescus, a government commissioner had appeared with 'systemization' orders, which the terrified peasants had signed without protest. Within a few days, a convoy of earth-diggers had arrived. Deep holes were dug in the gardens where the people kept their secret supply of vegetables and bulldozers pushed the houses into the holes. The excavated earth was heaped on top, just like a grave.

The village was erased from the map: the houses, the small church, the tombstones, the old stone walls, the store, the barns, the past. Buses were provided and, with their pots and carpet bags, the people were moved into the unfinished apartments we had seen that morning, grey pigeon holes where the Securitate had untold eyes and ears.

During the demolition, Ceauşescu would sometimes arrive in person and ask in feigned surprise why the houses were being destroyed. 'The peasants want them pulled down,' the director in charge would reply. 'They understood the country's need for systemization.'

'The President would drive away with his army of body guards *and the people would wave.*' Stefan threw up his hands. 'This is a primitive society,' he said. 'The people admire tyrants. They do not understand democracy.'

We got out of the car and went to meet Stefan's grandparents, two squat, weather-lined peasants who looked very relieved when they discovered we were not officials. They had some bread and pickled cucumbers. We had our bag of breakfast leftovers. It was late in the afternoon and the hot sun had lost its sting when we sat down together in the rubble to have a picnic. 'Everything is still here,' the old man said enthusiastically; Stefan translated. 'We will have our house back up again by Christmas, God willing.'

'God willing,' repeated the old woman.

## Iris

It was almost midnight by the time we arrived back in Bucharest. The city was pitch-dark and deserted, the same as it must have been during the Second World War. Forty-five years later, the Romanians were still fighting a war.

Stefan seemed relieved when we offered to drive him to his apartment. It occurred to me that it might have been risky for him to be out alone walking the unlit streets.

Clifford turned left, right and left again, following Stefan's directions. I had no idea where we were, but suddenly he said 'Stop. This is it.' We got out of the car. I grabbed a torch from the glove compartment but Stefan said no, it was not necessary. Then I was certain that he felt himself to be in some danger. He took my hand. I held Clifford's arm, and the three of us snaked our way up several flights of stairs.

Sonia opened the door to his four sharp knocks. She was happy to see him and quickly pulled us all inside. The apartment was just as he had described: two tiny rooms side by side, a small window at the end of one, while the other had a minute balcony, where clothes were washed and hung to dry.

'I would like to offer you tea,' said Sonia, 'but today we had no water.'

I could see almost the whole apartment from where I stood. We were in the living room. Along one wall there were rough shelves made from bricks and odd pieces of wood, which held a surprising number of books, old, scruffy and lovingly preserved. I saw titles in French and English as well as Romanian. At the far end a single bed, where they both must have slept, was covered with a multi-coloured afghan. That left just enough room for a chair and a folding card table. On top of the table stood a vintage typewriter. An electric cord dangled a dim light bulb from the ceiling. A paper lantern, in pale pink, had been fitted over the top, and gave the room a rosy, fireside glow.

I peeked into the tiny room next door and saw Katya sound asleep in her bed, which had once been a large, deep bureau drawer. Two brass handles still adorned the side. Neatly stacked cooking utensils and dishes on more shelves made me realize that the room doubled as a kitchen during the day. Everything was orderly and spotlessly clean.

I felt like adopting the whole family and taking them to New York. Katya could go in a year or so to the International Play Group nursery school; Sonia would soon perfect her English; Stefan could easily find a job teaching mathematics. . . . I gave them my address and telephone number for the second time, and insisted that Stefan write his down clearly in my book. At the very least I would keep in touch and send them clothes for the baby and anything else they needed.

Stefan laughed and added the telephone number of the university office where Sonia worked. He told us that only two per cent of the people in Romania had telephones. 'I am lucky because Sonia takes messages for me.' He winked at her and it reinforced my feeling that Stefan played a much more important role in the anti-Iliescu movement than I had initially imagined.

Meanwhile, he had packed a small bag and I realized that he did not intend to spend the night at home, but would return with us to University Square.

'My place is there for the time being,' he explained. 'Sonia understands.' She nodded gravely. 'Anyway, you could never find your way back without me.'

## Clifford

On Thursday, the members of the Independent Group for Democracy banged drums and waved the shredding battle flags. They were injecting new energy into the protest to rival an official conference where a professor and other 'experts' were to speak on the secret cliques within the army and Securitate that had long been plotting against Ceauşescu, and that had enabled the National Salvation Front to seize power 'for the people'. On a table in the hotel lobby, in front of the man-high stacks of Kent and other brands of American cigarettes, there were leaflets in various languages advertising the event.

There was little interest. Outside, the television trucks were being loaded with spools of cables and silver camera boxes. The election had been over for almost a week. The shooting had stopped. The *Observer* correspondent who had stayed on told me he was going straight to Spain. He would return when there was something gutsy to report on: an assassination, a dramatic suicide, death in Piata Universitatii.

Thursday night: a distant clock in the old city chimed the hour of ten. The square was lit by thousands of candles. A parade was moving in slow, silent procession around tent city. It was very pretty. I took some photographs. The speeches that came later promised continued struggle but it occurred to me as I listened that it was less a demonstration than a wake for the glimmer of hope that had briefly shone in the Romanian darkness but had again been extinguished. We watched from the balcony like characters in a Jean Genet play while the world around us got on with the business of anarchy and chaos.

We watched long into the night. We watched Friday night and Saturday night.

During the morning hours, the television crews steadily vacated the car-park and made room for more Arab money-changers with their black Mercedes cars. What were they doing in Romania? Who were they working for? Why always Arabs? I never discovered the answer to these questions.

There is never a right time to leave although, as the five porters in their story book livery placed our four pieces of luggage into the car, I wondered if we were leaving at the wrong time. It was Sunday morning. There was a stillness in the air. It seemed as if something was going to happen. The sky was clear in a shade of blue that is not quite blue in Romania or anywhere in Eastern Europe.

I gave each of the porters a dollar. I gave the one-legged man a dollar. I bought two identical books of cartoons from the booksellers and I gave all the beggars a dollar. They screamed for more. '*Madame, s'il vous plait. . . .*' Iris carried lunch in a plastic bag. Her green canvas bag was slung bandit-style across her chest. We had grown closer in Bucharest. It had changed her. It had changed us both.

A stray boy smeared a rag over the windscreen. I gave him a dollar. I smiled at the two armed guards. One of them was erotically polishing the barrel of his Kalashnikov. Both ignored us. I tooted the horn for no reason at all and stepped on the accelerator.

The dozen or so hunger-strikers had gone twenty-six days without food. The ambulances were still in position.

There were numerous gangs of policeman standing listlessly along Boulevard Gral Magheru. Trucks with soldiers hanging over the sides swerved with excessive speed as they negotiated Piata Roman. We turned on to Calea Victoriei where Queen Marie, the English queen, the grand-daughter of Queen Victoria, had promenaded under the trees with her court of admirers. It was rumoured that a cavalry lieutenant had been her lover.

My limbs ached. I felt fatigued. The anti-Communist, anti-Iliescu protest had gone on throughout the night and at daybreak the faithful had still been there. Stefan Cordescu was among them but, though we searched for him from our balcony, we never saw him again. I had heard the song 'Don't Worry, Be Happy' several times as I had lain awake and I had heard it again at seven in the morning when room service had appeared with hot coffee.

The sign 'Remember May 1989. Puppets on a String: Tiananmen' came into my mind as I was leaving the city. The words were enigmatic and yet ominous. They were in English, most of the signs had been in English, and only now did I realize why: they were solely for the television cameras, for the viewers in their cosy living rooms at home on the other side of Europe and far away across the Atlantic. That was the purpose of the demonstrators' constant vigil, to tell the world: Don't forget us. The Revolution had been stolen. It was a palace coup. The king is dead. Long Live the King.

I was sad to be leaving and yet another part of me was relieved. Had the authorities come to clear the square, I am sure I would have been there with the *golans*, fighting for democracy. I would have offered up my skull for the police batons. I might have been the unfortunate foreigner whose name clouded the tragedy of what the protest was really about. I studied the policemen and callow soldiers, just boys with the cockiness and confidence that comes from wearing a uniform.

The wretchedness of downtown Bucharest grew smaller in the rear view mirror. I filled up with petrol and paid with dollars. The road beyond Calea

Victoriei turned into a tree-lined avenue with rose bushes that made islands in the central strip of grass. We passed grand villas where the coloured flags of many nations marked the homes and embassies of the diplomatic corps. Labourers in orange vests cleared the litter and gypsy-women in bright ragged clothes swept piles of dust from place to place, their task like that of the seven sisters in Greek mythology who murdered their seven husbands on their wedding night and were condemned to an eternity of ferrying water in jugs perforated in such a way that they were dry by the time they reached their destination.

Romania is a morality play from Greek drama, a tragedy, naturally. It clings by its fingertips to the edge of Europe, a step-son that may or may not belong, unsure whether to be oriental or Latin; Romans below Orthodox cupolas, smaller than Hungarians, dark like the Turks, more South American than European, the people are flamboyant and violently aggressive: in Bacău, in Moldavia, an activist for the National Peasants' Party was beaten to death by a group of Iliescu supporters who then cut out the man's eyes and tongue. The new prime minister, Petre Roman, a life-time friend of Iliescu, has said: 'From democracy to dictatorship, sometimes you need a day. From a dictatorship to democracy, the way is very much longer.' It is unclear whether this is a prediction or a pledge and that is the essence of Romania: mystery and misunderstanding.

The wide boulevard drew us through a different Bucharest: the Bucharest Nicolae Ceauşescu wanted new arrivals to see when they were driven in from the airport, 'the second largest in Eastern Europe after Moscow'. The dictator liked to do things in a big way. He had a whopping great airport and virtually no air traffic; a palace with seven thousand rooms and never did an overseas delegation spend the night below its roof; a square that could hold the adoring multitudes from a small city and not even a stray dog marked its limp trees. It was all wind for the sails that carried the lie that was Romanian Communism.

We were heading north to Brasov and passed through the town of Ploiesti, described in the country's own tourist literature as being 'of no great interest except to people in the oil industry'.

Tongues of orange flame leapt from hundreds of black metal chimneys. Crumbling ghettos lined the streets and, beyond, cooling towers with feminine waists were belching smoke in rainbow colours into the sky. There was a narrow square in the centre of the town, but no bright umbrellas and nowhere to have coffee. The people were grim, ashen, unsmiling.

We motored on through the valleys of Prahova and Timis, the industrial tableland gently rising until the smog was sufficiently diluted for us to see the snow-capped Carpathians, so pure and majestic in the distance I could understand why primitive men considered them holy. The villages run quickly one into the next, each settled on small hills with green meadows flanking the surrounding valleys. The houses were of an alpine style with touches of Switzerland and the Pyrenees and an end result that was totally Romanian. The façades were painted in pastel colours, the headstones and window frames were white and there was something oriental in the turn of the gables. Polished-wood shutters opened on to narrow windows and tall brick chimneys mingled with the television aerials on the roofs. The solitary television station, the heart of the revolution, showed a lot of gymnastics and promised to screen live debates from Parliament once it opened.

The churches, castles in miniature, had sturdy walls and, in contrast, incredibly detailed ornamentation below lofty spires and golden domes that looked like little fires in the sky as they appeared far off beyond the curve in the road.

We stopped at Predeal and, as we were studying the church from outside the low stone wall, the door-keeper appeared with a bunch of keys on an iron ring and insisted on taking us on a conducted tour. The woman spoke a few words of French and, with these few words, she told us it was the most beautiful church in Romania in a voice that was so convincing I believed she was right. It was certainly neat and clean. Wooden saints filled arch-shaped niches; the icons glowed above candles placed in rising tiers by the faithful. The door-keeper smoked non-stop, flicking the ash into her palm and crossing herself after lighting a new cigarette from the butt of the last. She was wearing a great number of skirts and aprons. Her round face nestled in the midst of a headscarf. I gave her 300 lei for the church and two tiny tears welled into her eyes. 'Merci, Monsieur, merci,' she said and I was moved to see her meagre joy.

She waved as we pulled away. The road became steeper. Green hills, thick with trees, turned blue across the horizon. The mountains were venerable and intimidating. I could imagine brutal streaks of winter lightning tearing the sky to shreds, low hanging mist, the cries of wolves, the dusty flap of bats' wings. We had passed out of Walachia into Transylvania. This was *Dracula* country.

The wind had joined us, disturbing the birds and tossing strands of hay from the bullock carts that snailed their way through hills embroidered with orchards. I saw a man in a long black coat riding a chestnut stallion. 'It's Count Dracula,' I said. Iris politely smiled. We had talked very little on the journey.

The villages slipped by, all identical except for the place names fading on wooden signboards. From the distance, everything appeared picturesque and in good order but, close-up, the paint was peeling, the wooden gables rotting, the road broken, the people awfully poor. There was less misery than we had seen in the capital; life in the country was backward more than deprived, preserved in formaldehyde, suspended like the bottled apricots you see in huge glass jars on the shelves in every Comturist shop. It was another age; another century: the clothes, the farm tools, the covered wagons, the bullock carts like dinosaurs, the man on horseback, even the expressions worn by the people in Transylvania seemed otherworldly, uncertain more than unfriendly. Almost no cars passed us or approached us. The Sherwood-green Range Rover could have been a spaceship and we travellers from far across the universe.

## Iris

I had left Bucharest with a feeling of regret. It was not that I wanted to stay longer; quite the contrary, I was eager to move on, but I felt sadness for the people and problems we were leaving behind.

The five days in the capital had been intense. I would never forget the struggle in University Square that went on night and day, or the people who came to us for help because we were foreigners, like the woman who had tugged at my arm one afternoon on the street. Frail, my own age and dressed in black, she had shown me a card with a man's passport-sized picture on it. I had not understood what she wanted. I still don't. I had assumed the man was her husband. Was he missing? Had we seen him? She had tried, unsuccessfully, to explain. Then she had shown me a letter from the United States State Department, dated August 1988. Three sentences thanked a Mr Nicholae for pointing out the dilemma of Romanians who could not get visas to the United States, and said that they were looking into it. But I had still not known how I could help the woman.

'Maybe she needs money,' Clifford had suggested.

I had offered her five 100 lei notes. She had shaken her head. '*Nu, nu,*' she had said hopelessly. We had both been frustrated by the lack of understanding. She had wandered on, clutching her file of papers and letters to her chest.

Then there was the little gypsy girl, about five or six, who had come into the pastry shop on the Calea Victoriei one afternoon when we had been having tea. She had been wearing a long ragged skirt that skimmed the tops of her dirty bare feet and a filthy T-shirt that came to her knees. Her dark hair had been unwashed and uncombed. Silently she had gone to each table and stared mutely at the diners until a waiter had spied her. He had yelled and chased her outside, but not before she had burst into tears. I had rushed after her into the street to give her some money, but she had already disappeared.

The scenery, now that we were approaching the foothills of the Carpathians on the way to Brasov, was stunning. Huge vistas of green meadows, hills and forests stretched as far as my eyes could see. It was a treat after Bucharest.

The traffic was light. Among the gypsy caravans and horse-drawn carts, I noticed several makeshift buses that carried field-workers from one collective farm to another. They had 'Autotransport' written on their sides. I wondered what official had allowed such an ugly, uncomfortable form of vehicle to be conceived and constructed. It looked as if a wooden freight car had been nailed on to the back of a flatbed truck. A few slits had been cut near the top for air, but the passengers could not see outside. At first I thought they were designed to transport animals, but I saw one stop at a crossroads and a group of farm-hands got out.

We were in the vicinity of Bran Castle, once the home, they say, of the ubiquitous Prince Vlad, and decided to make a detour to see it. I had imagined that the castle would be tucked away in the mountains and have a menacing appearance. Instead, it was in the middle of a delightful village and could not have been more appealing. It was the kind of fortress that anyone could happily call 'home', not too big, with rooms on a human scale and small gabled windows that looked out on an enchanting garden.

There was a car-park at the gate circled by a large number of stands selling the whole repertoire of Romanian handicrafts and souvenirs: carved wooden objects, including trays, walking sticks and vases, all with pictures of Bran Castle painted on them; heavy, rough woollen sweaters, in earth colours, hand-knitted by peasant women; embroidered blouses; woven tablecloths and crocheted doilies – someone should tell them that no one uses these things any more. Our car was the only one in that vast space and all the vendors looked hopefully at us when we got out.

There were four people in the ticket office. One spoke a little English and was summoned to the front to deal with us. For the second time since arriving in Romania I saw postcards on sale. Miraculously, they also had stamps and a post-box. Such a sensible correlation of related objects took us by surprise.

The fourteenth-century castle reminded me of the châteaux in the Loire Valley. Inside, a few decrepit shields, helmets and a variety of tools were displayed in glass cases. The furniture was neo-baroque, of the nineteenth century. What was interesting was the architecture, although it had been restored several times over the centuries, and the history illustrated by numerous drawings that adorned the walls.

Four giant earthenware jugs were lying on their sides in the garden. Had they held Vlad's grain? His wine? His victims? I sat on a carved stone bench. Had Vlad's bottom helped to smooth the seat? Had his hands felt the curved arm rests, as mine did at that moment? The garden was so quiet and peaceful we decided to stay and eat our picnic lunch.

Of all the things I had packed for the trip, elastic bands and plastic bags had become the most indispensable. As it was almost impossible to find anywhere that served lunch (sandwiches were unknown), and as the breakfast buffet in the hotels offered an excessive amount of food – cold sliced ham, salami, hard-boiled eggs, cheese and pickles – we had married the two phenomena by bringing a plastic bag to the table and filling it with all the things we felt we would like to eat at lunch. Everything was then tightly secured with a rubber band.

On our way to Bran, we had pulled off the road to study the map. A man had suddenly materialized from an orchard and had smiled at me through the window. I had lowered it and he had handed me a bag of ripe, plump cherries. He had been very old and most of his teeth were missing, but he had spoken eloquently and passionately. I had understood only the occasional words: '*nationalism*', 'Romania' and 'America'. I had been very touched. He reminded me of Stefan's grandfather, who had radiated the same kind of goodness and dignity. We polished off our lunch with his bag of fruit.

We entered Brasov late in the afternoon and made our way to the Carpati Hotel. Prudently, we had telephoned before leaving Bucharest. Although it was listed in luxury category, the room we were given was abysmal, even by Romanian standards. Several things were unacceptable the main complaint being that the bathroom floor was an inch deep in water from a leaking toilet. After a few minutes of complaining on the telephone, two grumbling old men appeared in scruffy uniforms to move us to what must have been the presidential suite. In addition to a cavernous bedroom and triple-sized bathroom, we had an entrance hall and cloakroom, a dining-room with a table set for ten, a living room filled with stiff, formal furniture and two large balconies. Within ten minutes we had managed to spread our clothes, books and maps over all of it.

Brasov, formerly called Stalin (1950–61), is a medieval town that nestles in a valley, so that each narrow street ends in a spectacular sweep of lush greenery. The cobbles are black stone shot through with veins of white that sparkle in the sun like precious ore. A blue-painted town hall has a tower with four clocks, all stopped at different times, so that eight times a day one is momentarily correct.

The houses crowd each other in tight packs around the old-world central square and slide off into the side streets, leaning at odd angles like drunken clergymen. I adored the architecture, a mixture of Gothic, Renaissance and baroque, with an added touch of Transylvanian fantasy. Nearby, the famous Black Church was covered in a cobweb of scaffolding while the ravages of four centuries were being repaired. Three hundred years earlier, an invading army of Austrians had torched the church, and although the flames were extinguished, the smoke-blackened walls were never cleaned, giving the church its name. Brasov had happily escaped any urban renewal and was attractive and surprisingly clean. I guessed that the further away things were from the Ceauşescu clan, the better.

We bought the evening paper, sat in a pavement café under a striped awning, ordered cherry juice and tried to translate the headlines. Our efforts caught the eye of a tall university student wearing large, owl-like glasses, who looked more American than most Americans. She offered to translate the articles on the front page for us. They were generally scathing about Communism but optimistic about Ion Iliescu. There was something on economic reform; private companies were to be permitted to employ twenty people rather than ten. No one would be allowed to invest in more than one company. We asked her if she liked this plan.

'Yes. I think it is very good. We do not want to lose the gains we have made with Socialism.'

'Gains?' I asked, trying to hide my surprise.

'We do not have your drugs and gangsters. There is no Aids in Romania.'

I had read reliable statistics to the contrary. There was Aids; thousands of children were dying from it. Theft and murder were common. There was rampant alcoholism and a high rate of suicide. The figures were simply not made public.

I wanted to know what she thought of Campaneau and Ratiu, the two main opposition leaders. Her eyes moved obliquely across my face. 'They are foreigners,' she answered matter-of-factly.

Earlier in the afternoon we had noticed a Chinese restaurant in the main square and we returned at sundown to investigate. A Chinese restaurant? In Romania? It seemed absurd. Yet, there was the doorman, resplendent in a slightly too large and heavily gold-braided uniform, who greeted and ushered us into a mammoth dining room, painted appropriately in red and topaz yellow. Chinese scrolls decorated the wall. About twenty round tables, covered with pristine white cloths, had bouquets of fresh flowers in blue and white porcelain vases on red brocade-covered lazy Susans. Overall, the effect was more pleasing than in most of the Chinese restaurants scattered along Lexington Avenue.

'Tell me,' I asked the waiter, 'whose idea was it to start a Chinese restaurant?'

He looked blank.

'Do you have a Chinese cook?' I pursued. 'A Chinese owner?' I had decided to be daring.

'No. No Chinese involved. All Romanian,' he replied.

As he walked away he called over his shoulder, 'Only Chinese owner,' leaving us more confused than ever.

The choice of food was limited but rather good, and it certainly made a change from French fries, the new staple diet everywhere in Eastern Europe.

After dinner we hurried back to the hotel through streets as dark as London during the Blitz. Had they turned the *belle époque* street lights on, it would have made no difference. All appeared to be broken and stood in the shadows like gaunt trees.

## Clifford

Outside Brasov's elegant main square, the shanty town of nameless factories are a cold reminder that the medieval city founded in 1211 by the Teutonic Knights was more important in 1990 as a centre for the production of aircraft, oil-drilling equipment and tractors which I assumed were for export only. I saw them there, shoulder to shoulder in a wire compound like a caged army of orange rodents, but I never saw them in the fields.

Farming in Transylvania was labour intensive. Men and women wearing the same Chinese coolie hats moved across the landscape like a sundial shadow, each dark form bent double as they worked around the crops that are grown in lines that are ruler straight and run parallel over the hills until they vanish from sight.

I stopped in Vista de Sus for no other reason than that the village was deserted. A pair of geese waddled proudly by leading a family of graceless goslings. A stream ran down the centre of the dusty street. There was no litter, no motor cars, no advertising. Insects hummed lazily in the air. Way off in the distance, there was snow on the mountain-tops and the sun, directly overhead, added a shine to the three silver domes that crowned the small church. The porch was wide and under its awning, protected from the weather, there was a mural of lost saints searching for the way ahead in the clouds into which each of them was peering. The silence was pure and invigorating. Not even a dog barked. In the villages close to where the Ceaușescus had their country houses, dogs were not permitted to bark. Church bells never chimed. The dictator needed quiet for his writing.

Behind the church, through a low iron gate, the gravestones marched down the hillside like white dominoes, all identical, an equality in death. There were flowers in old glass jars, pansies and peonies; butterflies in pairs like yellow bows hovered around us. There were some offerings of bread and some dreadful-looking pieces of fruit, just as I had seen in temples in Asia. Even the saints in their haloes of light were remarkably similar to Tibetan *tankas*. It made me aware that it was here, in the Carpathian foothills, that East and West joined hands. The mountains are a wide semi-circle of embracing arms. It was easy to visualize a minaret above the church and the muezzin calling the faithful to prayer, and just as easy to imagine an Anglican curate saying prayers over one of the graves. I read the dates on the inscriptions.

The day was warm. I bent down and ran the soil through my hands. You know a country best when you have felt its earth below your fingernails. Already Bucharest seemed so far away.

As we were leaving the graveyard, the still was broken by the lumbering sound of a hayrick pulled by a pair of black buffaloes yoked in a wooden harness. It was piled precipitously high with freshly-scythed grass. The driver wore a grim frown below his wide-brimmed felt hat and, as he turned his head to continue his observations, it seemed almost certain that his expression must have been the same as that worn by Iberian sailors when they first sighted the shores of the New World. Even the hayrick moved like a Spanish galleon. I tried a smile and the man's face remained a portrait of immobility.

The road looped through the rolling foothills, the way marked by lofty willows, their overhanging branches making an arch just tall enough for high vehicles to pass under. There was so little traffic, the occasional presence of a sixteen-wheeler truck came always as a surprise as it thundered by in its own private dust storm.

We pulled to a halt for the herds of sheep being moved up to higher pastures, where they would remain until autumn. Shepherds with long crooks and cotton capes were urging them on, whistling esoteric messages, their dogs soundlessly rounding up the stragglers. They crossed the road before us like a great cloud that seemed to last forever. Beehives stood in fields, the drones dashing off in swarms to collect pollen and dashing back by some miracle to the right hive. A violent rainstorm that lasted no more than ten minutes put a glow over the landscape. We walked in the wet fields. The colours were vibrant, fresh from a painting box, the distant mountains like a barricade around the picture book world Iris remembered from her childhood and Patrick Leigh Fermor recalled so lovingly in *Between the Woods and the Water*, the account of his incredible journey across Europe on foot in 1933. 'Transylvania had been a familiar name as long as I could remember,' he wrote. 'It was the very essence and symbol of remote, leafy, half-mythical strangeness; and, on the spot, it seemed remoter still, and more fraught with charms.'

I felt so in tune with this observation as we ambled through the rain-dampened grass, I began to envy Fermor when the sheep finally passed and it was time to move on. In a motor car, you are cut off from the world about you. You cover more ground but you actually see less. Fermor, as a boy of eighteen, had taken almost a year to walk from the Hook of Holland to Constantinople. We were racing through Eastern Europe in eight weeks, in fear, in some way, of missing something that, by the very nature of the unknown, is elusive and abstract. History, or so it seemed, was being made on a daily basis and we needed our daily fix.

Such were my thoughts as I glanced up and saw a rainbow stretching across the sky. I felt, during those few minutes, at one with the remote, half-mythical strangeness of Transylvania, a feeling that was to come back to me just forty-eight hours later with melancholic irony. That Monday morning on our journey to Kolozsvar (Cluj-Napoca), we had no way of knowing that deep beneath us the plates of moving rock that form the earth's core were on course for a fatal collision.

Agribiciu has the distinction of possessing three churches for its fifty pretty houses, stone dwellings with uniquely-crafted roof-tops and pastel façades the austerity measures had been unable to obliterate. They had been built to last and to look elegant and both aims had been achieved.

We reached the Little Somes, a small, shallow stream, true to its name. On the near bank, two women were washing clothes, rinsing them in the flow before beating them with a wooden paddle. It was a remarkable, primeval sight. We had seen dirt, poverty, deprivation. We had seen suffering in Romania on a scale that shocked us deeply and left us feeling empty and impotent. But there is nothing in the world more backward than women doing the family wash on the riverbank.

As soon as we crossed the Little Somes, the silver domes and fading whisper of the Orient surrendered its influence before the raised lances of steeples, spires and soaring towers that patterned the landscape of a more familiar Europe. The Gothic churches were sober affairs where man and his maker met without frippery or excess; the walled farmhouses were severe; the barns more solid. We had entered the rich farmlands colonized by roaming tribes of Saxons who had begun their long migration from the Rhine in the Middle Ages. They had reached Romania more than three centuries ago. They built towns on the ancient sites abandoned by the Dacians and, having adopted Luther's teachings when the Reformation reached the Carpathians, even their language had weathered the passage of time. The villages were tidy, solemn and lacking nothing but a few barrels of whitewash. The women wore long, black dresses that dusted the ground and white scarfs that, covering their heads and cheeks, gave them the serene appearance of holy sisters. The men stood firm in sturdy boots and wide hats with a feather decorating the hatband. When I slowed in the narrow lanes of their villages and tried a smile they were inclined to look me squarely in the eye and smile back. They had red faces and broad shoulders. They were beer-drinking men who liked plenty of butter on their bread and pork sausages for breakfast. They had been cut off from the Fatherland for generations beyond memory and yet, apart from the clothes, they were incredibly similar to the West Germans we had seen at Easter wandering aimlessly through East Berlin eating ice-cream.

We followed a very old car that moved slowly beneath the weight of numerous trunks piled so high on the roof it made me think of a snail carrying its home on its back. Suddenly, and inevitably, a box tied with string came flying at us and I had to swerve into a ditch to miss it. Iris screamed and we came to a halt.

The driver stopped and came running back, a profusion of apology, his German so swift and heavily accented I understood not a word. The rest of the family arrived – Mama, round and rosy, all in black, and three grown-up children, two boys and a remarkably pretty girl with a thick flaxen plait that reached the base of her spine. She was wearing a traditional Bavarian dress like those worn by the barmaids in Munich beer halls.

'*Danke, danke, danke,*' they sang in a Gilbert and Sullivan chorus.

'Eighteen years we wait. Eighteen years,' Papa said carefully. He was inordinately happy. The other members of the family were merrily smiling and stood around us like people waiting for a party to start.

'Are you going on holiday?' I asked in phrase-book German.

'No, no, no. We go to Germany. Eighteen years we wait for papers. We are going home.'

The two young men took the box and they all hurried back to the car. I reversed out of the ditch and called good luck as we passed.

'Go with God,' they shouted in reply. 'Go with God . . . Go with God . . . Go with God . . .', the words followed us like an echo as the road climbed up through the hills and plunged down into another Transylvania.

The afternoon was hot. The blue sky was fading to grey like the sea at twilight. The windscreen began to smear with small black explosions I at first thought were insects. It was soot. The washers cleaned the marks away and left two arches. The sky grew darker. It began to feel as if we were driving into a tunnel.

The broken road took us through Valea Lunga, a grubby town of humble clutter. Beyond, the landscape had the charred, sombre look of the Black Church of Brasov. There was an impenetrable cloud slung across the valley like a cloak over the shoulders of the steeply rising hills. The earth in the fields was black. The bark peeling from the avenue of withering poplars was black. The grass was black.

We were approaching Copsa Mică and, as we reached the outskirts, I noticed that the houses were black: the stone, the roofs, the window frames, the windows. The road and crumbling pavements were black, and so was the church, and the gravestones, so black the names of the dead were unreadable.

In the centre of the town, blasting out a continuous stream of toxic waste, stand the vast, grimy satanic mills that process chemicals, sulphuric acid, lead and zinc and produce, among other things, the core ingredients necessary for the construction of nuclear reactors.

The factories were originally built with the aid of British and Japanese companies. The Ceaușescu regime's expansion programme in the mid-1970s did away with many safety requirements and pollution controls. The new production levels demanded were unreasonably high and wages were cut if quotas were not met. Copsa Mică had been a farming community. The green hills where sheep had roamed turned black. The cloud of fumes became permanent. In 1978 twelve cases of industrial poisoning had been reported. In the months before the general election, in a climate of openness, the town's doctor, Sandra Bocan, revealed that six hundred workers a year suffer from the sickness known as saturnism – chronic lead poisoning causing stomach pains, headaches, vomiting and, in time, a slow and painful death. Under the former Communist government, the factory clinic was permitted to report only two cases a week, since the hospital budget did not allow for more. In reality, the whole town is ill. Spring flowers bravely growing on the wayside are coated in flecks of carbon. White sheets on a washing line turn grey before they are dry, which gives a good idea of what is happening inside the lungs of the town's 7,500 people. 'Everyone is receiving medical treatment,' said Dr Bocan in her report to the Red Cross.

No pollution in the world is as bad as that in Copsa Mică. No words are adequate to describe it. No photograph quite captures the dismal gloom of the sky, the misshapen dark leaves on the dying trees, the dirt deeply ground into the people's hands and faces. In the factories the men have always worked and still work without protection: no masks, no special suits, no gloves. They labour in barbarous conditions to earn money to feed their families who are slowly being poisoned. There was a strike during those heady weeks of freedom that followed the fall of Ceaușescu but the men were soon back at their jobs. Death by breathing the filthy air seemed favourable to death by starvation. In Romania there are no easy answers. The strike, like the election, changed nothing. The black cloud of waste is permanent, a shadow that throws the valley into stark silhouette, even in the afternoon sunshine. An indelible stain has tattooed the town and, like a fungus, it is spreading towards Valea Lunga one way and Medias the other. Skywards, it must be boring its own black hole in the ozone.

'It's unbelievable,' whispered Iris.

Her words were no exaggeration. Even the word pollution is inapt to describe the tragedy. Perhaps holocaust is more appropriate. The people have been made into half-people, bent and black and ill in dirty black clothes and living in wretched black cottages. Life in Copsa Mică is a parody of life; a parody of a town: it is even burdened with its onomatopoeia – Copsa Mică sounds murky and polluted.

If Ion Iliescu is going to be the caring president he promised when he led the National Salvation Front to victory, the first thing he should do is to close down the chemical factories at Copsa Mică and find some alternative work and an alternative place for the people to live.

## Iris

We had parked in the main street of Copsa Mică and gone off in different directions to take photographs; Clifford towards the industrial complex, and I, the streets and people. I went back to the car to change the film in my camera and became aware of a little boy, who looked like he had just emerged from a coal mine, studying me, and the car, from soot-rimmed eyes. I smiled. He smiled, and continued staring. I reached into the bag of treats we always carried and gave him a pack of chewing gum. He said thank you very much in Romanian and ran off at great speed across the road and around the corner of a building.

Two minutes later he came racing back, followed by a pack of his friends, thin, grimy copies of himself.

'*Mi collega*,' he said by way of introduction.

I had just passed out the last of the chewing gum when there was a knock on the other side of the car. A stout woman was pointing to a tiny girl clinging to her hand, and demanding something for her, too. I still had several packs of sweets and chocolate bars so I gave one to her. Then there were more children, more hands, a few young men who asked for cigarettes. Within a few moments I had given away my entire supply of gifts.

They wanted more. The smiles had left their faces.

I took the plastic bag, now empty, stuck it outside the window, turned it upside down and shook it.

'Empty. No more. *Finito. Termine.*'

They understood. The stout woman took the bag from my hand, folded it, and solemnly marched off.

I started the car and drove up the street to meet Clifford. Within seconds I was surrounded again by a group of boys. The word must have gone around that a crazy woman was handing out free sweets and cigarettes. They started climbing over the car. They were on the hood, the roof. Little arms reached in through the windows. One managed to grab a corner of my jacket, lying over the seat, and pulled it out.

'Hey. Give that back,' I shouted, and snatched it from his hands. He smiled sheepishly, surprised at his own daring. I saw Clifford in the distance, walking slowly back to the car, still taking pictures. I gave the horn three sharp blasts to make him hurry. The boys scattered.

Clifford got into the driver's seat and we continued our journey, passing a few miles later through Medias, one of the ugliest towns I have ever seen. The main street looked like a battlefield, filled with holes, rubble and pools of water. It might have been like that for years, and how long it would remain so was anyone's guess. On our left, an industrial sprawl, black and unsightly, pressed up against the pavement. On our right were the shops, and the people walking in front of them looked dazed. It must have been a beautiful valley once.

Just outside Medias we began to pass small groups of peasants who needed lifts to the next village. We saw one old woman standing alone; short, fat, a worn handkerchief around her head, she had thick legs with bulging veins and her face was a criss-cross of lines. We stopped. She seemed startled, but bravely climbed up into the back seat where she and her big brown plastic bag settled in. She was going to Tîrnăveni, about 15 miles away.

I got out my phrase book and practiced my pronunciation. She laughed and repeated the words properly. She had fine, intelligent eyes, and seemed to be enjoying the adventure. I turned away for a moment and, when I looked back again, I saw that she was making the sign of the cross, continually touching her forehead and breast, and whispering a prayer over and over. The laughter had left her face and she looked pale and worried. Then I understood. She was feeling car-sick.

'*Mal?*' I asked, rubbing my stomach.

'*Da,*' she nodded, looking miserable.

Clifford speeded up and I kept my eyes glued to the old woman's face. We were only a couple of miles from her destination and I hoped she would make it. She did. We were all relieved.

We let her off at the outskirts of the town, as she asked. Before she left she offered me some coins, the custom in Romania, because rides are usually given by other local people. Unlike the day before with the cherries, I refused to accept. She grabbed my hand and kissed it in a final farewell.

A few hours later we arrived in the ancient city of Kolozsvar (Cluj-Napoca). Here, the resistance continued. The main square, Piata Liberatii, was a smaller version of University Square in Bucharest. It was used as a base by the students and intellectuals who had helped to overthrow Ceauşescu and who were not in favour of his successor. In front of the imposing St Michael's Church, a solid fifteenth-century Gothic structure, and the large equestrian statue of the Hungarian king, Matthias Corvinus, was a memorial to the protesters who had lost their lives in the demonstrations of December 1989. A street leading to the square, formerly called Boulevard Lenin, had a new name painted on a fresh sign – Str. 20 December – the day Ceauşescu was overthrown.

## Clifford

There were storks in the fields, picking at worms, so graceful in the air they seem awkward on the ground with knee joints that work in reverse to our own. The peasants were bent over the crops, oblivious to the rain. Children made victory signs and waved for us to stop. We kept moving. They wanted chocolate bars but the treats had gone. Even the bag had been left behind in Copsa Mică. The town's grime was turning yellow on the paintwork and the car looked as if it had been driven through a bog. A 15-foot statue of Lenin stared quizzically like a blind Oedipus over some slum development with a name we missed.

We had left the rural heartland of Transylvania where the churches like jousting penants identify the different settlements: Romanian, Hungarian, German and Austrian, the gypsies without churches, and each distinct in language, dress, customs. Quasi-democracy had opened a Pandora's box of nationalist feuds and hatreds: the Romanians and Hungarians were trying to kill each other. The Germans and Austrians were going home. In three hundred years, the two communities had avoided integration within Romania and had even remained separate from each other, preserving something Communism tried to destroy and only made stronger.

We crossed and recrossed the River Mures and, finally, the downward flow led us over a wide bridge to Alba Iulia, once the capital of Roman Dacia. In more recent times, at the Museum of the Union in 1918, it was here that the agreement joining Transylvania with Romania was officially signed. Romania's second modern king, the short and famously modest Ferdinand, the nephew of Carol I, was crowned with Marie of England at the dark, overbearing Orthodox Church, which, though baroque in appearance, was built during the 1920s. The church stands in the centre of a formal park patterned with stone paths, where squads of young soldiers were alternatively frog-marching like Nazis, or drilling with a song GI style, the contrast illustrating the country's lack of cohesion and direction. The soldiers looked like farm boys and probably were; and I wondered if anyone had ever told them that the only time the Romanian People's Army had been called into action in the past forty-five years had been against the Romanian people.

The rain penetrated our coats. There was a woman with two ragged children begging outside the church. We gave them some money and drove on.

Plastic awnings, swaying in the wind, were tied loosely to trees. Some peasant women, taking the first tentative steps on the path of free enterprise, were selling honey, cheese, cherries and pies of an old-fashioned design. We did not stop, though later we would regret it, as at the time I was more concerned with the petrol needle hovering over the danger zone. The garages in Kolozsvar and Alba Iulia had both been closed and it came as a relief as we approached Deva and saw a file of more than a hundred cars trailing back towards the town.

I slowed to a halt. One of the attendants caught my eye and what then took place was one of those fortunate and bothersome experiences that frequently befall the hard currency traveller. The man stopped the line and motioned me to the empty space at the pump.

'*Complet?*' he asked. I nodded. '*Zece dollares?*' I nodded once more.

As we were being served, two modern cars with Romanian plates pulled in and went straight to the head of the line immediately behind us. The men who got out were young, looked prosperous and wore sporty bright sweatshirts that had not been bought in Romania; Cannes or California was more likely. They had the nonchalant confidence of policemen – Securitate, if our friends in Bucharest had been right, still functioning, the same as ever. They casually studied the Range Rover. One of them said something but I turned away. The men waiting in the line of cars may have been afraid of them but I had no reason to be. Power through fear rises in a pyramid, each layer terrified of those above. We were outside the pyramid, protected by our foreignness. I paid $10 (£6) for the petrol and drove on into Deva. We counted 120 cars; a three hour line.

No one complained that we had barged the queue. No one expressed any surprise. It was expected, an ingredient in the messy, dishonest soup that remained the Romanian staff of life. In the ten years before Ceauşescu's fall, the US Government had covertly bought advanced Soviet technology from Romania through the dictator's two brothers, both senior members of the administration. The US paid $40 million (£24 million), twenty per cent of it going into a numbered Swiss bank account. 'They were corrupt to the core,' a White House official told Benjamin Weiser of the *Washington Post*; the Ceauşescus were not betraying their Russian allies out of any secret affection for US policy or ideology. 'It was just greed, pure and simple personal greed.'

Greed had filtered through every level of society, from the Ceauşescus at the top, to the border guards demanding cigarettes, to the doorman at the Intercontinental extracting bribes, to the man pumping fuel wanting dollars. We had journeyed through a land peopled by brigands and beggars; a land where women give their children away, babies with Aids are neglected and prostitutes with hopeless smiles fill the hotel bars; a land where the shady, devious, perverted specimens of humanity seem to outnumber the Stefan Cordescus and old men with bags of cherries; a land of great beauty, great contrasts; a land where corruption has long been as normal as drawing breath in the foul noxious air.

It was still raining, a grey, misty, steady rain that veiled the landscape and made us both quiet and reflective.

## Iris

Modern Deva must have looked good on the drawing board and even better on the scale model that architects love to make. Identical miniature apartment blocks with tiny balconies would have faced each other across inch-wide streets. Lilliputian plastic people with a few trees and cars would have kept everything in scale. An occasional building of a different shape would have HOTEL or OFFICE printed on it, and everyone would have said how delightful the whole concept was. Then it was built and became Deva, without heart or soul, filled with monotonous structures that had not aged well. It had but one saving grace: it had been built beside the remains of a thirteenth-century citadel.

We found the building that said HOTEL and carried our bags through the driving rain into the dark lobby. Everything smelled damp, as if it had been raining forever.

A woman sat behind the reception desk, as animated as a tailor's dummy. Yes, they had a room; by the number of keys hanging on a board behind the desk, they had a lot of free rooms. Ours was on the fourth floor and, it goes without saying, the elevator was out of order. We struggled up a stairwell lit by the faint glow of a distant skylight, trying not to trip on the folds of carpet, which were not tacked down and kept sliding beneath our feet. The room, when we found it, was minuscule and spartan.

We were hungry, but the restaurant on the ground floor was closed. The tailor's dummy found the energy to explain that there was no food. There was another hotel in town; we should try there. '*Unde este?*' I asked, and she waved her arms towards the door. We found the other hotel by trial and error but they had stopped serving lunch, and we were told to come back in the evening. It had been a big mistake not to stop and buy some of those delicious pies we had seen for sale beside the road earlier in the day.

We decided to drive a few miles out of town to visit Hunedoara, said to be the most beautiful castle in Romania and little known outside the country. Unfortunately, it is completely surrounded by a vast and seemingly endless sprawl of factories and steel mills.

The road to the castle wound through a maze of grimy concrete buildings, connected overhead by a web of cable cars carrying iron ore and connected along the ground by wide pipes that should have been buried. Next to these ugly plants, the yards overflowed with towering pyramids of red slag and old railway lines choked with the rusting shells of rolling stock. Everywhere we looked we saw smoke-stacks, silhouetted against an orange sky, belching an amazing variety of coloured smoke into the atmosphere. Each breath smelled of burning waste and chemicals. Industrial complexes exist in every Western country but in Romania, and throughout Eastern Europe, there were no controls. No one cared about pollution. And what is pollution other than greed? It was a sad and sorry sight and my heart went out to the workers and their families living in the rows of apartment blocks slotted in among the factories. I noticed the occasional pot of geraniums on a window sill; the odd battered tricycle beside a doorway; a woman pushing a baby carriage – humanity carrying on regardless.

In the middle of all this, like a treasure in a Christmas cracker, stood Hunedoara Castle, blackened and resigned. It had withstood six hundred years of invasions, sieges and political upheaval, and seemed prepared to withstand the steel works. It was huge, its large scale offset by graceful pointed towers, Renaissance loggia and slender battlements, classic yet flamboyant. It was all that Bran Castle should have been.

It was still drizzling. Even the ticket office was deserted. We ran over the massive drawbridge and spent an hour exploring the empty rooms and corridors that all led back to the inner courtyard. There was no sign of life anywhere except outside, where one lone stall in the car-park was open and selling souvenirs. I knew they would have little business that day, so I went over and bought an embroidered blouse I knew I would never wear.

By the time we arrived back in Deva we were seriously hungry and drove immediately to the hotel that had told us to return in the evening, apparently the only place where two strangers in town could get food.

The lobby was dark and deserted but loud music was coming from the end of a corridor and we groped our way towards it. Behind a pair of heavy doors was the hotel dining-room and a large, noisy private party was in progress. The long tables were filled with people and covered with bottles of wine and platters of food. Everyone was drunk or in the process of getting drunk.

At one end, half-hidden by thick square columns that must have been supporting the building, a band played noisily, while a female singer belted out an unrecognizable song. A few couples danced a strange half-rock half-ethnic step, their arms circling each other's waists. Several men stood at the side, swaying back and forth as they sang, their arms linked as if to hold each other up. Little children chased each other around the tables.

We tried to stop a waiter as he scurried past but could not manage to do so. In desperation we sat down at the only two empty places we could find and hoped for the best.

Within minutes a waitress appeared and placed a plate of food in front of each of us as well as a bottle of wine, proudly labelled *Vin de Regione*, produced by *Agricola de Stat*. It was pure poison and undrinkable. The sip I took burned all the way down into my stomach. The food was worse. The French fries had been refried many times, and the chicken was just a slim wedge of meat and bone buried inside a batter fried coating that tasted rancid. We decided to leave. The *maitre d'* mysteriously materialized at the exit, a bright smile on his face. Clifford gave him one US dollar.

## Clifford

Wednesday, 30 May 1990
9.00 a.m.

It rained all night. We huddled in our nasty room like two hibernating moles and, in the pale morning light, we watched the people going to work, wading across the street like novice skiers. We had seen no plastic bags in Romania and now we knew why: the people of Deva horde them and wear them on their heads as hats and over their shoulders as capes.

We left without breakfast. There was still no food in the hotel. The woman at reception summoned up a vague and exhausting shrug. She had candle-white skin and the sagging appearance of a model in wax. We humped the bags out to the car. The Polish umbrella turned itself inside out in a mischievous gust of wind and we abandoned it. 'This weather,' Iris commented. Her voice sounded hollow. The wind had vanished and, like the stillness that follows a gun shot, it left a feeling of apprehension, a calm that froze the air and would seem, later that day, an odd counterpoint to the turbulence being generated deep below the earth's surface.

I drove slowly up the steep hill, skirting the crumbling citadel and, as the last house in Deva disappeared behind us, it stopped raining. We had crossed some invisible border and had entered another world, green and sunny below an almost blue sky. The Carpathians swing in a looping zig-zag across Transylvania and each successive valley scooped from the waves of rock offers an astonishing contrast: so ugly and pitiful you despair for mankind; so enchanting you have to pinch yourself to make sure it is not a dream. Horses trotted along the country lanes, rose stems woven in their manes. I saw flowers pouring over fences that concealed private gardens; secret supplies of vegetables. The lilac trees in one tiny dot of a village were so colourful I stopped to steal a bloom and, in imitation of the gypsy horses, I decorated the dashboard in the car. I could see sheep in the far distance, like blobs of paint on a billiard table. Small birds were flying in mad circles close above our heads, spiralling up and then swooping down at such speed it was a miracle none of them collided.

A ragged peasant wearing baggy trousers and no shoes approached us from the fields leading a goat that was clearly reluctant to be led. The animal, halting abruptly every few moments, balanced on its front legs in order to kick out with its hind legs, and screeched all the while with the stifled sound of a small

Japanese motorcycle. The man wanted us to take his photograph, which I did. '*Foto minuto?*' he then asked, pantomiming the magic of a Polaroid. It had been an oversight not to have brought one. There had been mothers who had never seen a picture of their babies; gypsy children who would have enjoyed a memento more lasting than a chocolate bar. Even at the wedding in Bulgaria, there had been no one except ourselves with a camera.

'We must bring a Polaroid next time,' said Iris.

The peasant grinned as if he understood and offered me a scarred and dirty hand that I shook. We watched him continue into the village dragging his stubborn goat behind him.

The lilac trees ended at the first bend. The road curved up between two dark hills and, as we plunged down into Lugoj, a dusty, featureless shanty town, I began to wonder if the entire country really had been planned on a cartographer's table in Bucharest: bucolic splendour, followed by gypsy slums, fruit trees in parallel lines, dormitory tenements, green fields that carpet meadows rising to meet the horizon, industrial wastelands spreading slowly like deserts, one of those endlessly overlapping five-year plans designed by megalomaniacs and, in the case of Nicolae Ceaușescu, not at all far-fetched. According to the former secret service boss, General Ion Pacepa, who defected in 1980, the dictator wanted a telephone linked to a recorder in every home in Romania and had begun, in 1978, by having devices installed in the apartments of his ministers and senior aides. The idea was to listen in on each family periodically, with suspect houses being monitored around the clock. 'We will be the only country on earth able to know what every single one of its citizens is thinking. A few years is all that separates us from a new, more scientific form of government,' Ceaușescu once told Pacepa, according to his 1988 book *Red Horizons*.

Elena Ceaușescu kept cassette tapes of ministers' wives in bed with their lovers. The despised son, Nicu, was constantly drunk and frequently assaulted women in public. He was being prepared to take over as president at his father's death. The dictator had been an old time king in Communist disguise and, having travelled across his blighted kingdom, the greatest surprise was that his subjects had been so patient.

We were heading for Timisoara, where the revolution had begun, and, for some reason, I was in a hurry to get there. I had turned off the country lanes on to the main route. We passed through Lugoj and, true to Communist logic, the road beyond narrowed and became busier, a procession of donkey carts, cyclists, farm-workers with razor-sharp scythes across their shoulders, Trabants, cement-mixers, army trucks. The surface was rutted as if turned by a steel plough and crushed by retreating tanks. Every family in every cottage possessed a pair of ducks and every pair of ducks was teaching its brood how to waddle across the highway. Children we ignored tried to wave us down. A drunken driver steering a serpentine course around a series of obstacles only he could see sent us swerving into a field, around two fighting geese and a naked child and back again. Trucks pulling trailers moved down the centre of the road, swinging around gypsy wagons with a virtuoso skill one had to admire. A white BMW with a West German licence plate sat on my rear fender for thirty seconds and then passed me like a shooting star. Then, quite suddenly, everything came to a standstill. A haystack, twice the size of the peasants' cottages, had claimed the entire thoroughfare, including the cinder track that ran along each side, and the two gallant steeds pulling it moved leisurely along as if to make a philosophical point for the serious traveller.

## Iris

Wednesday, 30 May
3.00 p.m.

Before we had even turned off the engine outside the hotel in Timisoara we were surrounded by the howling mob – children wanting chocolate bars, gypsies wailing for hard cash, a family of four who, like the woman in Bucharest, presented me with a folder containing letters and photographs. I had no idea what it was they needed or what they hoped I might do for them. Several men approached with the inevitable request to change money and then a younger man with a scholarly appearance implored us to mail a letter to France for him when we left the country. It was an application to a university, he explained.

'Is there a problem sending it from Romania?' I asked him.

'A letter from here will take three or four weeks – and maybe it will be stolen,' he replied. 'If you mail it from Germany, it will only take two days.' He had assumed we were German.

The letter seemed properly addressed, with his name and address on the back, and so I tucked it away in my green bag with the valuables.

Next in line was a 'professional photographer' from Bulgaria who needed a certain type of battery, which we did not have. The money-changers were outbidding each other on their rates. Then there was the village idiot, who just stuck out his hand and grinned and grinned.

I walked round to the back of the car and the mentally deranged man, still grinning, followed me, pulling at the leg of my jeans. He wanted them. 'No, no,' I said, making a face of exaggerated horror. I gave him 100 lei and he seemed pleased and went away.

I saw a new wave of gypsy children approaching us at high speed from the other side of the car-park and literally ran up the steps to the hotel carrying the small duffle-bag Clifford had brought to my suite at Claridge's a lifetime before.

The hotel was another bleak, Stalinesque high-rise, like so many we had seen in Eastern Europe. Even so, inside, the gaudy gilt mirrors and shredding mauve carpeting struck me as being especially garish.

## Clifford

Wednesday, 30 May
3.30 p.m.

I was looking for strong, resolute faces in Timisoara; set jaws, determined expressions. What I saw were small, anxious people, humbled, ground down and kept down. The first bullets of the Romanian Revolution were fired in this city of 200,000 because the people bent over lathes in unsafe factories and labouring with primitive tools in the fields could bear their fear and hunger and hardship no longer. The students rose up because they had to become members of the Communist Party before their degrees were ratified and their professors joined them because they hated themselves and their decades of hypocrisy. They were not brave men in Timisoara but repressed men; men small enough to make me at 5 feet and 8 inches feel tall; small because of the low protein diet and the lack of exercise. They lack so much that we in the Western world take for granted and, walking the broken, shoddy, grubby streets, they had no hope of acquiring it or of even obtaining knowledge of such a different existence.

We were in Unity Square studying the hotel's flimsy street map when Cristine came to our assistance. Her English was perfect. She was pushing a baby in an antiquated push-chair. Her name was Andrea, a sparkling little girl in clean, patched, hand-me-down clothes. Even the most smartly dressed citizens of Romania would look like street people in New York.

Cristine walked with us to Opera Square. She pointed out the spots where the battles between the people and the Securitate had occurred. There were bullet holes in the walls and windows. 'It will happen again, this year or next year,' she said. 'There have been no changes. Only promises. I still cannot get a job, even as a waitress.' I asked why. 'The Communist Party had eight million members and no believers,' she answered. 'I speak French and English, but I cannot work because I have no connections.'

'In the Communist Party?'

'The National Salvation Front.' She grinned. Cristine was pretty; her face was filled with life. I asked her why she did not join the Front.

She thought for a moment. 'Perhaps I will,' she said. 'Before, I had principles. Now, I have a baby. I am not so sure . . .'

We had reached the square. Picture book churches with pointed cupolas like spiked helmets competed to draw the eye with the opera house and the rococo buildings in blue and apple green, the façades as elaborate as opera sets. The paper seller was gathering in 5 lei coins as fast as he could systematically fold and hand out the afternoon periodical. An enormously fat woman like a circus performer was lodged in a small cubicle selling Lotto tickets. Two gypsy children, a boy and a girl with a burn scar on her face, joined our entourage. I gave the boy 25 lei and he gave it back to me. 'One dollar?' he demanded and so I gave him nothing. The girl was working on Iris. She had her hands pressed together in prayer and her scarred face was so full of grief she was quickly rewarded and the two of them scampered off.

'It is terrible. The gypsies . . .' Cristine remarked without enlarging on the subject.

I crossed the square to take some photographs. The day was very still. The pigeons had abandoned the cobbled footpaths and had taken to the trees. They were completely silent. I glanced back at Iris and Cristine. I had a feeling she was a woman alone, deserted, perhaps; or maybe her husband had shed his blood on the streets of Timisoara to help end the tyranny of Romanian Communism. There was no point in asking. There were so many bright young women with babies and what they needed was not what they had got: Ion Iliescu.

The quiet of the pigeons in Opera Square became more noticeable, uncanny and embracing. It seemed as if the entire earth had paused to draw breath.

## Iris

Wednesday, 30 May
3.55 p.m.

Andrea must have felt it first. Suddenly, she started to scream with terror. The very ground beneath our feet was moving. It felt as if I were standing in a small rowing boat in a choppy sea – I could not get my balance. Cristine and I reached out instinctively and gripped hands to steady ourselves. Clifford was on the other side of the square, taking pictures, and I saw him turn and hurry back towards us, running like a drunken man, lurching from side to side, in slow motion. There was a roar and rumble coming from all around, as buildings swayed and tiles and chimneys toppled. Nearby, an old woman fell to the ground with a terrible cry.

Earthquake. Steady now, I thought to myself. I knew it could not last

more than a minute, but it seemed to go on and on. Nothing made any
sense. If the very earth shakes under your feet, what can you believe in,
anyway? I wanted it to be over, to end, but it seemed we stood there
forever, Andrea rocking in her chair, screaming, her mother and I braced
against it, trying not to fall down. I was thankful we were out in the open. I
thought of the high-rise hotel we had left thirty minutes before, and our
room on the twelfth floor.

And then it stopped. Cristine dropped to her knees, took the baby in her
arms and started to sob. Clifford had crossed the square and we threw our
arms around each other. People had come pouring out of the buildings into the
streets and were crying, moaning or laughing the hollow laugh of people who
have had a fright. Everyone was dazed.

We sat down on the ground and braced ourselves for the after-shocks. They
were not long in coming, vibrating like ripples in the sea.

A car had run into a lamp post on the corner; the driver had a cut on his
forehead. A fruit vendor and his wife were scrambling to salvage what they
could from an overturned cart. The fat woman selling Lotto tickets was still
lodged in her cubicle, but tears were streaming down her face. The paper seller
had spilt his box of coins over the street and was shooing away the gypsy
children who were trying to pick them up. The square was filling up rapidly as
people fled in panic from the buildings.

When the worst seemed to be over, we got up to help Cristine and Andrea. I
felt a tremendous sense of anguish. Tomorrow, we would leave Timisoara,
probably forever. We would drive away, back to our own lives. I reached into
my handbag and took all the Romanian money I had, about £100 worth, and
pressed it into Cristine's hand.

'For the baby. I insist. Buy her something she needs. I'm leaving. I don't
need it. Please.'

She could see from my face that I meant it. I put the money in her pocket. It
was impossible to help everyone, but if you can help one person, it is a start.


## Clifford

The earthquake rocked much of Eastern Europe from the Baltic to the Black
Sea. More than three hundred people were injured; twenty died, mostly
around the epicentre at Vrancea in the Carpathians, 100 miles from Timisoara.
It measured between 6.5 and 7.5 on the Richter scale, the same as the
earthquake that struck Armenia in 1988 killing 20,000 people.

We had been lucky. Opera Square only trembled. The screams stopped. The
city quickly got back to normal.

In the early evening there was a service at the Orthodox Cathedral. We entered and watched for a few minutes. Women in black were weeping, giving thanks. The bearded priest was a tall man in a long golden robe. After twenty years of infamous collaboration with the Ceauşescu regime, it was business as usual in the Romanian churches.

We returned to the hotel and had some food sent to the room. The restaurant and lobby had been too noisy, too festive. The greater the poverty and suffering outside in the streets, the dimmer the lights, the cheaper the girls and the smokier the air in the hotel bars. We read. We picked at the food: cold soup and stale bread. There was a television with sound but no picture. Iris tried to call her sister but all lines out of Romania were temporarily unavailable. Before us we still had a long drive to the border and back across Europe but it was here that our journey reached its conclusion. From the Berlin Wall to Timisoara: from revolution to revolution. It was what we had set out to do and I had feelings of both satisfaction and a little sadness now that it was over.

There was a part of me that wanted to go back to the beginning and start all over again. History was still being made: the Union of Democratic Forces narrowly lost the general election in Bulgaria to the ex-Communist Socialist Party. At midnight on 2 October, East Germany ceased to exist; the two Germanys were united. Tourists from Czechoslovakia and Hungary began coach tours to the West, Venice being the most popular destination.

We had known the day we had arrived in Bucharest that it was only a matter of time before the National Salvation Front cleared University Square and that time came shortly after our return to London. On 14 June, coal miners armed with clubs were transported to the capital and it was they, not the police or army, who tore down the signs and sacked the city. Some of the *golans* returned the following day and the day after, but the miners stood guard and kept the square free of people demonstrating for democracy. They were deeply praised by Mr Iliescu.

Cristine had said there would be another revolution, this year or next year. If there is, our friend Stefan Cordescu will not be taking part. We telephoned the university where Sonia worked at least a dozen times before we managed to speak to her a week later on 21 June. 'I am sorry my English so bad,' she apologised, and then her voice choked with tears. 'Stefan, he dead now. In the square. They kill him . . .'

We were quiet for a long time. I listened to the static, a mournful hum with the occasional blip, blip, hollow in the background. 'Is there anything we can do?' I finally asked.

'No, no. There is nothing.' Sonia said something in Romanian I was unable to understand and then added, 'We must hope.'

Somebody once asked Vaclav Havel if he were an optimist or a pessimist. He said he was neither. 'I just carry hope in my heart. Hope is not a feeling of certainty, that everything ends well. Hope is just a feeling that life and work have a meaning.' Hope is Katya Cordescu.

# Further Reading

Fermor, Patrick Leigh, *A Time of Gifts*. Penguin, 1979.

Fermor, Patrick Leigh, *Between the Woods and the Water*. Penguin, 1979.

Gilbert, Martin, *Second World War*. Weidenfeld and Nicolson, 1989.

Groueff, Stephane, *Crown of Thorns*. Madison Books, 1987.

Harding, Georgina, *In Another Europe*. Hodder and Stoughton, 1990.

Havel, Václav, *Living in Truth*. Faber and Faber, 1990.

Havel, Václav, *Disturbing the Peace*. Faber and Faber, 1990.

Ionescu, Ghita, *The Politics of the European Communist States*. Redwood Press, 1967.

Kundera, Milan, *The Unbearable Lightness of Being*. Faber, 1984.

Lewis, Flora, *Europe – A Tapestry of Nations*. Unwin Hyman, 1988.

Manning, Olivia, *The Balkan Trilogy*. Mandarin, 1990.

Pacepa, Ion, *Red Horizons: The Extraordinary Memoirs of a Communist Spy Chief*. Hodder and Stoughton, 1988.

Simpson, John, *Dispatches from the Barricades*. Hutchinson, 1990.

Smith, Ken, *Berlin – Coming in from the Cold*. Hamish Hamilton, 1990.

Vonnegut Jr, Kurt, *Slaughterhouse 5*. Jonathan Cape, 1968.

Wyman, David S., *The Abandonment of the Jews, America and the Holocaust, 1941–1945*. Pantheon Books, 1984.

# *Index*